PARIS FASHION

The Great Designers
and their Creations

PARIS FASHION

The Great Designers and their Creations

Edited by Ruth Lynam

London
Michael Joseph

First published in Great Britain by Michael Joseph Ltd
52 Bedford Square, London WC1

1972

© November Books Limited 1972

7181 1033 1

Produced by November Books Limited, 23–9 Emerald Street, London WC1N 3QL.

Typesetting by Horsfall & Sons (Startype) Limited, Startype Foundry, Birstall, nr. Leeds, and Perfect Typesetters Ltd, 15 Appold Street, London EC2A 2AA.

Printed by the Redwood Press Limited, Trowbridge, Wiltshire.

Colour processing by Colourcraftsmen Limited, 67–9 Chancery Lane, London WC2.

Colour printed by C. J. Mason & Sons Limited, Bishopsworth, Bristol.

Bound by Dorstel Press, Templefields, Harlow, Essex.

Designer: Linda Hanley.
House editor: Frances Kennett.
Typographical preparation: John Leath.

CONTENTS

ACKNOWLEDGEMENTS

This book is an anthology dedicated to the history of Paris fashion and I should like to express my sincere gratitude to all those who have made it possible. To the designers past and present who have created fabulously beautiful clothes, sometimes under very difficult conditions, and to all those associated with them. In particular I should like to thank the following people from the world of Paris couture today: Astrid Lehaire at Balmain, Régine Cardin at Cardin, Marie Louis de Clermont-Tonnerre at Chanel, Jacques Rouët at Christian Dior, Arlette Thébauld at Givenchy, Hubert Vicente at Jean Patou, Gabrielle Buchaert at Yves Saint Laurent, and Victoria Capnist at Ungaro.

There are numerous organisations that enabled my colleagues to search through archives of photographs and documents and provided them with material hitherto unpublished in book form. Our combined thanks are expressed in particular to La Chambre Syndicale de la Couture Parisienne, and its press attaché, Denise Dubois; Union Française des Arts du Costume and its president, Paul Caldaguès; Centre d'Enseignement et de Documentation du Costume, especially Yvonne Deslandres and her staff; The International Wool Secretariat (London and Paris offices, and their press officers, Suzanne Chivers and Nesrin Hickmet); and the Victoria and Albert Museum, London.

To the many photographers who have contributed their work we extend warm thanks for their kindness and co-operation: Richard Dormer, Peter Kent, Gunnar Larsen, Jeanloup Sieff, Seeberger Frères, Monique Valentin and Giancarlo Botti; we should also like to offer a particular word of thanks to the artist Francis Marshall, for his sketches for the post-World War II collections, and to Mrs John French, who so very kindly helped us to choose photographs from her late husband's fine and invaluable collection. Geoffrey Large, picture librarian of the National Magazine Company, threw open his extensive archives of British *Harper's Bazaar* and gave my colleagues much valuable assistance, while both Martin Battersby and Madge Garland contributed rare old volumes and magazines which yielded a number of unique illustrations for the book. We thank all these people for their kind and thoughtful help.

To those private individuals who spared time to recall moments from the past or who loaned material from their personal souvenirs we offer a special word of thanks: Zika Ascher, the fabric manufacturer; Mrs Kathleen Lumley, the sister of Edward Molyneux; and Diana Massie, formerly house model at Balenciaga and Dior. Francis Finlay is to be remembered for the assistance he gave to our researches in Paris. Of those manufacturers who helped us, our thanks are particularly due to Sally Stevens of Wallis, London; the firm of Dorothée bis, in Paris; and the London store of Fortnum and Mason.

In conclusion, I should like to offer the combined gratitude of myself and my colleagues to a loyal group of friends in Paris and London. They have used their talents and powers of persistence selflessly in the making of this anthology and although some of them are contributors they will know why their names are here too. Marjorie Dunton, Madge Garland, Madeleine Ginsburg, Penelope Portrait, Thelma Sweetinburgh, André Ostier – I thank them all. A few names only are needed to complete the list: my colleagues who produced this book – Richard Bacon, who devised it; Linda Hanley, who designed it; Caroline Shaw, who searched diligently on both sides of the Channel for the beautiful illustrations, and who brought true enthusiasm and a very keen eye to a most difficult task; and Frances Kennett who guided us all through the tricky job of welding diverse talents and temperaments into a whole. Without her unwavering spirit, patience, and unrelenting eye for accuracy, it would have been impossible for this book to appear.

RUTH LYNAM

INTRODUCTION

Nancy White

Dear Reader, I am proud to write a personal introduction to this book – such an important and much-needed volume. My undying affection for French couture, and especially for those designers I have been privileged to know personally, has prompted me to share with you some of my earliest and most treasured memories of Paris.

In 1934, when I was just 17, I was fortunate enough to go to Paris with my aunt, the legendary Carmel Snow, one of the greatest authorities on fashion that the magazine world has known. This trip was my introduction to the glamorous world of haute couture, and I remember the joy of watching my aunt ordering hats from Reboux, or Agnes. I can still feel the excitement of the moment when I fell in love with a coat at Marcel Rochas, and Aunt Carmel approved my choice! I think it was because I was so protected and encouraged by Carmel Snow, and later by that remarkable character, Marie Louise Bousquet, Paris Editor of American *Harper's Bazaar*, to whom all Paris paid court, that although I approached the great names of Paris with awe and reverence, I instinctively felt an enthusiasm, an empathy and a growing affection.

My awe, in those early days, was rightly founded on respect for what I saw, because it was unique in the world. Although I knew virtually nothing about the people who produced these exquisite clothes, I understood the workmanship, the creative thought and dedication that went into every seam and every stitch. In later years, when I was myself Editor of *Harper's Bazaar*, my awe slowly diminished: my respect grew even greater, and my affection for Paris couture and for what it means in the world of fashion today, began to flower. This affection is still with me. The couturiers have become so much a part of my life that they are, and will always be, indelibly identified with my Paris. They became my friends.

I would like to give you an idea of what I mean. I shall always remember at the twice-yearly collections, the beautiful flowers from the great houses, especially the lovely basket which Robert Ricci would personally arrange, that made my hotel sitting room in Paris look like a wonderful garden;

7

the charming lunches with Marc Bohan; Pierre Cardin's evening parties in his magnificent Hotel Particulaire; Yves Saint Laurent, in his apartment after he had left Dior, and before he opened his own house, showing me his brilliant sketches for the ballet. So many happy memories crowd in: climbing the steep stairs to Mademoiselle Chanel's apartment, after her ravishing collections; the kindness of Jacques Rouet of the house of Dior on the night of my most unforgettable birthday in July; the classic beauty of Madame Grès with her elegant head forever swathed in a turban, a pincushion at her waist for last-minute emergencies; the house of Dior, with the lovely scent of muguet filling the air as one moves towards that elegant stairway; the warm friendliness of the Lanvin family, Bernard and his beautiful wife Maryll, especially during the excitement of remodelling and expanding their boutique in the 'sixties; finally, the image of Hubert de Givenchy, so tall and elegant, who would with such tenderness escort the miniscule figure of Marie Louise Bousquet down the steps, after his collection . . .

Then Balenciaga, the legend, the master, comes to mind. The expectation, the suppressed excitement, was always intense as we waited for the little Spanish leather lift before we presented our cards and entered the salon. I was fortunate enough to see the Balenciaga collection that showed the famous brown lace midi. It was hard to see then, but on reflection we can understand that it has everything to do with the sort of clothes we wear today. Here was the master, the law of taste, acknowledging the existence of a new order in the world. With that simple slip of lace, Balenciaga, who had always been famous for his formal ballgowns, made us realise that rigid rules of dress were a part of the past.

When Balenciaga closed his doors, one of my greatest regrets was that I had never had the opportunity to meet him. Then it happened. Due to a marvellous, unexpected set of circumstances, I was invited to Paris for a brief 24 hours, to visit Marie Louise Bousquet. As we were sitting, talking, enjoying a drink, suddenly, with no announcement, there was Balenciaga. He was so extraordinarily handsome, so very charming, and so much younger than I had imagined. Such encounters were the delight of Paris to me. On my last evenings there after the collections, I would dine at Maxime's with Raymond Barbas, and listen enraptured while he reminisced about Captain Patou and those early days of haute couture.

Many, many words and pictures in this book convey the beauty, the artistry, and the discipline, which have transformed the making of simple garments into the art of haute couture. The dedication of a vast number of craftsmen and creators is reflected in these pages. As the great Christian Dior wrote:

> 'Fashion is one of the last repositories of the marvellous. The maintenance of the tradition of fashion is in the nature of an act of faith; the outward sign of an ancient civilisation that intends to survive.'

1

THE CLASSICAL TRADITION

Inside Couture   Ginette Spanier

In spite of all the obituaries pronounced in its honour, haute couture is by no means dead.

Our numbers may have melted, but those of us who still carry on the tradition are very much alive. Our customers are those women, and there are a great number of them, who demand quality, to whom elegance is synonymous with simplicity of line (though this seeming simplicity is obtained by a complicated and difficult cut) and to whom, perhaps most important of all, perfect fittings are essential.

Woman is not a symmetrical animal. No woman, however beautiful, is identical both sides. Hips, bust, shoulders always slightly differ if only by a millimetre or two, and these discrepancies, even though sometimes imperceptible to the beholder, make ready-to-wear clothes displeasing and even uncomfortable to those who are in the habit of having their clothes made to order.

Therefore, as long as there are women rich enough to have both sides fitted, as long as there are women who love quality and who demand perfection in their clothes, *la Haute Couture* will continue to flourish. It is difficult to make some people, and especially the cheaper fashion press, believe how many of these women still exist. It is hard for them to accept the fact that there are many women, quite apart from the very rich who buy all their clothes as a matter of course in the big fashion houses, who prefer to make sacrifices and order one or two things per season from the haute couture, one or two things lovingly chosen, minutely fitted, rather than buy a quantity of less expensive, lower-grade outfits. These women accept wearing the same clothes time and time again, season after season, sometimes year after year. Classical styles do not change radically as cheaper clothes do. Real elegance does not alter its face every six months. There is an evolution in line which makes it logical that last spring's fashion should give birth to next autumn's, but the change is not brutal, it is gradual. So, women who dress in the haute couture can, if they wish, carry on their clothes from one season to another with only slight alterations, a little 'refurbishing' here and there, which we, in those supposedly grand, unapproachable fashion houses, do constantly for our regular customers. This we do, not only for the less affluent, but also for those customers who buy ten or twelve outfits every season. Once you are used to custom-made clothes, to perfect fittings, it is very difficult to settle for the second-rate.

I remember my first haute couture collection after the war. It was in the summer of 1947. The eighteen-year-old daughter of an English friend came to stay with us and, to make this her first visit to Paris memorable, the family asked me to order two dresses for her from the new wonder couturier, Pierre Balmain, the man about whom Gertrude Stein had written an article in *Vogue*, the one about whom everyone was talking. I had not seen a collection since before World War II; luxury was a half forgotten shadow at the back of my mind.

The show started: to say that I was dazzled, or amazed, is an under-

One of Mme Grès' magnificent draped dresses, in fine jersey, with delicate petal decoration round the bustline. (1960.)

statement. This was something completely different from anything I remembered – ever. The perfection of every detail. Such discreet but overwhelming luxury. The way the girls showed the clothes on the runway – fast, without a smile, dramatic, dragging their coats behind them. I remember gr ys in different shades, in different textures. I remember the shoes: bronze kid with ankle straps from 'Peruggia' in the rue de la Paix. And the hair-styles. And the hats. Even evening hats. It took my breath away. The glamour, the simplicity, after what seemed a lifetime of drabness, of ugliness, of making-do.

By pure chance, that first visit led to an opportunity of working for

A photographic page from *Harper's Bazaar* after Marc Bohan took over at the house of Dior.

Pierre Balmain. I eagerly accepted, and have been a part of the strange, tough world of haute couture ever since. Haute couture has something of the madhouse, something of the factory, something of the artisan's workshop, something of the theatre. Its standards, its atmosphere, its way of life, were things undreamt of in my experience.

I found myself in a world where what I had considered to be the normal rules of behaviour did not exist. I do not speak so much of the customers – customers are very much the same all over, whether they are buying a tube of tooth paste or a thousand-pound dress – I am speaking of those with whom I found myself backstage, of those whom, a short time later, I had to control when Pierre Balmain made me his *Directrice*, of those with whom I have been working for a quarter of a century.

I found myself in a world ruled by hysteria, a world of ugly, sneaking disloyalties, a world of heart-given conscientious work 'beyond the call of duty', a world shaken by wild storms which erupt for no logical reason, a

13

world of calm endeavour, a world of no fixed hours, a world where nerves are raw to the point of cracking, where grown-up men and women scream and shout without an attempt at self-control, but a world where one thing is law, respected, unquestioned – *Perfection*. Its unrelenting demands are accepted blindly by everyone, from the smallest apprentice to the top director. To achieve it, no amount of work is too hard, no detail too infinitesimal, no state of exhaustion considered exaggerated. I have known dresses delivered at 1 o'clock in the morning, I have seen the lining of a dress started over five times because the dart at the bust was not at the perfect angle even though the lining did not show through the dress. Of such stuff is the haute couture made.

When I started work at Pierre Balmain's it took me some time to get acclimatised to the standard of perfection taken for granted by everyone in the place. My eye wasn't 'in'. I had to learn not only to accept the constant tension and hysteria, but to see, to note, to be horrified by, the tenth-of-an-inch of difference in the right and left side of a decolleté, in the evenness of a hem, by a seam not quite up to standard.

Now, as I walk along the street my eyes are drawn to details as if they were lit up with neon lights. The bodice which is a fraction too short due to economy of material, the skirt made of cheap stuff which crinkles, and bulges at the seat, the seam at the waist which shows above the belt, the pleat which opens too wide because of too little material left inside, the metal zipper as if made of tin blatantly obvious down the middle of the back, the woman who is constantly pulling at one side of her dress because of those two shoulders which are not identical, and a hundred other details too small to list.

In the cutting of a ready-to-wear dress, both sides have necessarily to be the same, half-an-inch of material inside a seam is of vital importance, pence extra per yard on the price is a tragedy. In couture the most expensive materials are carved into with royal disdain. The finished garment, impeccable in every detail, is the only, the ultimate, aim. The exact shade of a piping, the blending of the colours of an embroidery, the amount of fur inside the hem of a coat, are matters of life and death.

Twice a year, when the couturier produces a collection, he does so regardless of expense. When he is designing, the price of materials, of furs, of embroidery, of belts, of buttons, is not even asked; the hours of work that go into a dress do not count: 70–90 for a morning dress, 200–300 for an embroidered evening dress. Whilst the collection is being made, there is poetry in the air. Only when the collection has 'opened' – as a play 'opens', meaning, 'is shown in front of the public' – does the commercial side come in and create a business out of an artistic vision. Then and then only do we, the selling side of the organisation, try to cut down on the hours of work (because nowadays it is the hours of work which are the most expensive item in the making of a dress), try to curb the excesses, and attempt to make a certain measure of financial sense out of unrealistic chaos.

An afternoon outfit in black wool and dotted crêpe by Pierre Balmain, dated 1946. The post-war severity of cut is beginning to ease a little.

Pierre Balmain's *redingote* in red wool, with a muff and collar in panther fur, and a hat trimmed with a pheasant's feather. Autumn 1951.

A superb example of Givenchy's impeccable workmanship, from the autumn collection, 1971: a cape and culotte outfit in grey wool with toning sweater and stockings in brown wool. The circular sweep of the cape, and the fit of the culottes, are marks of the perfection in detail which the couture can accomplish.

The pricing of the clothes is a Chinese puzzle and one of my most arduous jobs. It is hard to believe that the mark-up on couture clothes is not as high as on cheaper clothes. Profits are far lower in haute couture than on manufactured clothes sold by the dozen or the gross. Hence the perfume, the scarves, the etceteras on which profits are high. But, for the

Hubert de Givenchy photographed in his workrooms.

real couturier and for those of us who work with him, haute couture, with all its extravagances, its disordered schedules, its madness, is a way of life which we would be loath to exchange for something more normal.

I am always being asked: 'Why so many hours of work in the making of a dress?'

It must be understood that every outfit ordered in a *Maison de Haute Couture* is made to the requirements of each individual customer. After having chosen the model she wants, sometimes changing the colour and even the material from that of the prototype which she saw on the runway, after having had her measurements taken, the client comes back for at least three fittings, sometimes more, until the garment fits like the proverbial glove.

Between each fitting, back in the workroom, the garment is *mis à plat* – laid flat on the table – taken to pieces and put together again according to the alterations shown to have been necessary at the last fitting. This all adds up to a great many hours of specialised work.

Each workroom is ruled with a hand of iron by one of the great fitters, bulwarks of a *maison de couture* and the equal of whom does not exist outside of Paris. This is an undisputed fact. These men and women have to remain in Paris, in the atmosphere of the haute couture to retain their chic, their skill, their artistry. Fitters have opened places of their own, some have moved to the provinces or to another capital city, but their exaggeratedly high standards, have wilted like a hot-house flower bedded out in the open air.

A typical model of the 'fifties, with the pencil-slim skirt and impeccable pockets, buttons and belt: Balmain, 1954.

In a *maison de couture*, each fitter has her own particular group of clients whom she 'dresses'. She knows and understands them, their bodies, their foibles, their weaknesses, their tastes, their idiosyncrasies.

In the workroom, each garment is made by a pair of seamstresses, a *première main qualifiée* aided by one on a less exalted level of efficiency, a *Deuxième main qualifiée*. The run-of-the-mill, simpler work is done by less expert hands. On the lowest rung of the ladder the apprentice or *arpette* is an integral part of the French couture. She often starts in the workroom at the age of fourteen, getting all her training there; she runs all the messages and is therefore one of the members of the workroom who has the most intimate contact with the salon. The intelligent ones often rise quite high in the hierarchy of the couture.

Everything that takes place in the *atelier* goes on under the eagle eye and guidance of the *fitter*, second only after God in her particular domain. At the fitting downstairs on the salon floor, the *première main* who has that particular dress 'in hand' is called down into the fitting room and the fitter explains to her what has to be done, what is right, what is wrong – in our parlance 'the language of the pins'.

Late the other evening, almost everyone having gone home, I was wandering through the empty firm and I happened to look into a deserted workroom. I was struck by the romance of it. All the lights were on, bright, low over the tables, long electric cords hanging from the ceiling. One actually felt the presence of generations of little *'ouvrières'*, stitching away, surrounded by priceless materials, sewing, sewing, chattering, a buzzing hive producing exquisite work unbettered anywhere in the world. High up on the shelves, were rows of solid wooden mannequins padded out to all shapes and sizes, bulges in strange places, headless, legless replicas of the clients of the workroom, the only witnesses of the silent scene.

As well as her own particular fitter, the customer has her own particular saleswoman who is responsible for the whole operation of the order. The *vendeuse* – or saleswoman – looks after the client from the moment she walks up the stairs to the moment the order is delivered, greeting her as she arrives, reserving a seat for her in the salon to see the collection, keeping a fitting room for her in which to choose her dresses after the show, helping her over the choice of the models, the choice of the materials, humouring her through the traumatic ordeal of the fittings and dealing with the sudden tragedies which occur during the course of the exercise. It is the *vendeuse* who discusses all with the stock-room, with the embroiderer, with the furrier, and who sees that the dresses are delivered on time after having carefully inspected them as they come down finished from the workroom. In all of this the *vendeuse* is seconded by a young assistant, *la seconde vendeuse*, who is constantly screamed at and spends a great deal of her time rushing up and down the stairs to the different departments of the firm.

There often grows up between *vendeuse* and client a real relationship, an intimate understanding. Over the years, second only to the hairdresser, a *vendeuse* gets to know almost everything about her client's life: private, public and financial. She is desperately possessive of her clients, ready to go to almost any length to retain them, but it does occasionally

Skilled hands at work on a piece of exquisite lace, photographed in the atelier at the house of Balmain, which is famous for its beautiful evening and bridal gowns.

Pierre Balmain with Alice B. Toklas, the lifelong companion of Gertrude Stein, who was befriended by him after the latter's death.

occur that a client wishes to be divorced from her *vendeuse* or fitter, that for some reason she takes a dislike to one of them and wishes to change. It is one of my more disagreeable duties to break this to the fitter or *vendeuse* and to try to make them understand that the customer is under the illusion that she is ordering her clothes from Monsieur Pierre Balmain and not from Madame Monique or Mademoiselle Lucie.

The *vendeuses*, the *secondes vendeuses*, the clients, the orders and the problems which stem from all of these are my particular responsibility. Mine is the authority in that particular area, assisted and upheld by the two commercial directors. Although it may seem unbelievable to outsiders, with very few exceptions – I repeat, with very few exceptions – customers bargain. They almost all try to get a bit off the price and no day is too long and no trouble too great for them to achieve their object. One of my most constant, toughest and most exhausting jobs is to see that they do not get away with it.

As far as foreign customers are concerned, the jet aeroplane has greatly added to the complications of our lives in haute couture. In the old days, rich ladies came to Paris and would stay two or three months, their large cabin trunks royally lined up in the corridors of the big hotels. They would go and see the collections, fittings would be arranged at decent intervals to suit their convenience and that of the workrooms; there would be time for 'retouches' (those last-minute alterations after the dress has been delivered and tried on quietly at home); all this in plenty of time for delivery on the required date, thus allowing the workrooms to plan their work rationally.

Nowadays, every delivery is a juggling feat. The customer flies in; chooses; dashes off to some far-away place; pops back exhausted, and enervated, for the fittings which have to be arranged to slot in with her travel dates, the whole operation in an atmosphere of rush and hysteria. To organise the work of the ateliers is a mathematical problem: five customers fly in the same week, all dressed by the same atelier which already happens to be overcrowded with work whilst another workroom is temporarily empty of orders. But, there is no alternative: the dresses have to be made, fitted and got out on time, even if it means borrowing seamstresses from another workroom (a tricky thing psychologically: the girls dislike it, even if it means overtime), and dresses finally delivered in the middle of the night. The leisurely atmosphere associated with couture is a thing of the past. At Balmain's, I insist if it is humanly or even almost inhumanly possible, that an order should never be turned down. The daily, the monthly, the yearly figures are my especial duty, and the firm in all its echelons, is geared through much practice to these wild bouts of overwork. This is something that Balenciaga never accepted. The rules in that house were rigid and, unless adequate time was allowed for the making of the clothes, the order was turned down. Balenciaga was as unbending, as uncompromising, with his customers as he was with his staff. But his ideal was higher than what is generally considered to be perfection, almost exaggeratedly so.

So far, I have spoken of private customers. But they form only part of the business of haute couture. There are also the buyers – manufacturers and retailers who come to the couture collections to buy models and inspiration. Twice a year, in January and July, for the couture openings, buyers and press from all over the world flock to Paris, the proof that Paris is still the fountainhead of fashion whatever proclamations to the contrary are made periodically. In some houses, the more eccentric ones, the buyers constitute the most important part of the turnover. In classical houses, the private customers form the bulk of the business, although that provided by the wholesale trade is very important as well.

The buyers write ahead and reserve their seats. During the first two weeks of the collections, they pour in at three o'clock in the afternoon to see the show, completely changing the atmosphere of the house, which suddenly becomes a changing house rather than the usual soft-voiced,

A forward-looking model from Pierre Balmain in 1959, made of white satin.

luxurious establishment of the rest of the season. To protect itself as best it can from the pirating of their models, couture houses charge an entrance fee to the wholesale and retail firms coming in to see the collections. This fee is scaled according to the number of people coming in from each individual firm; more details about this aspect of couture organisation are described in the chapter on the Chambre Syndicale. Some of the firms come in only to get an idea of the 'line' and forego the entrance fee. In this case, they are of course not allowed to reproduce any of the models they have seen. They have bought the right to inspiration.

But most buyers come to buy and the entrance fee goes towards the payment of their order. They buy either: a model, made up exactly as seen in the collection. (The price the buyers pay for this is higher than that paid by private customers.) Second, and less expensive, is a *toile*, which is the model made up in *toile de coton*, unlined, but with the details sketched in. A sketch and a pattern of the original material is attached. Third, and less expensive still, they may choose to buy a paper pattern of the model, also with sketch and pattern of the material attached. Once the model is bought in any of these three ways, the buyer has the right to reproduce it and to mention the name of the house from which it comes.

The buyers, having seen the collection, return next day in the morning to choose their models. Buyers must be divided into two categories: the aristocrats and *hoi polloi*. The aristocrats such as Sir Charles Abrahams of Aquascutum, Ethel Frankau of Bergdorf Goodman, New York (in the old days), and some shops and manufacturers coming from many countries, are treated as Roger of 'Maxim's' treats his special guests. They are received with ceremony as they arrive, they do not even sign, they have the best seats in the salon, they have a special secluded fitting room when they come in to choose, and usually two mannequins are set aside specially for them so that they do not have to wait between dresses as they make their decision.

With the rest of the buyers, the choosing operation is a riot. As they enter, they are again severely filtered at the door, so that anyone who has not seen the collection should not sneak in for the choosing, with a view to getting a look at the models free of charge. They give the list of the models they want to see to their *vendeuse*. These models are not necessarily the ones they want to buy. The ones they want to buy are among them, but the ones to which they give the most attention, the ones they pull to bits, are the ones they have no intention of buying, but about which they want to glean the most information possible so as to remember them.

The *vendeuse* brings back the dresses from the *cabine* (the little room where the girls change and the dresses are hung) in a great pile over her arm, and drops them on the chair next to her clients – our lovely new dresses which, only two days before, were treated with reverence, tissue paper sewn round their hems.

During the first two weeks of the collection, in the mornings there are up to a hundred people in the salon, pushing, scrabbling, grabbing,

From the sketch to the reality: a comparison of a suit in black wool, trimmed with a white satin, over-stitched collar, from Pierre Balmain's autumn 1971 collection.

turning the dresses inside out (until we take them out of their hands), and writing, writing, writing, because writing is allowed – sketching forbidden.

The mannequins, who work almost twelve hours a day at that time, are on call to put on and show again the dresses asked for by the buyers; they push their way among the crush as, from all corners of the salon, there are cries of 'Mademoiselle! Mademoiselle!' from the customers wanting to take a look at a dress yet once again. The scene is one of a fairground, of the market-place, not to be believed by anyone who has not witnessed it. As can be imagined, it is during this time that most of the stealing of ideas, the copying of models, goes on, which is also described, with all its fascinating and highly devious trickeries, in the following chapter on the role of the Chambre Syndicale.

Twice a year, during the two or three weeks of the buyer period, by dint of detective-like suspicion and hawk-like vigilance, we try to sniff out the copyists and bar them from entering our doors or throw them out if we catch them 'in the act'. It becomes almost a sport. We have no illusions, we cannot stop it altogether, all we can do is try to limit the mischief. It goes on season after season on an enormous scale. One English buyer with a sense of humour and a certain knowledge of her Shakespeare said to me once: 'This is the cruellest cut of all. Impossible to copy this season.'

Some buyers try to get in under the guise of private customers so as to avoid paying the entrance fee. Others try the dodge of two firms coming in as one, thus saving one entrance fee. However, I must insist on the fact that not all buyers are thieves. The majority of them ply their trade with complete honesty, we trust them absolutely and we have nothing but gratitude for their loyalty to us. Often a feeling of friendship grows up between us over the years.

Many wholesale buyers are very influenced by the fashion press. Not so private customers who, when they buy a spring dress in March or April do not remember or care about what they have read in the newspapers at the time of the openings in January. Private customers shop around looking at various collections and listen to what their girl-friends have to say. Some there are who never see more than one collection, going straight to the house whose style they like and whom they feel knows them and understands them. With wholesalers it is different. In the old days, the press followed the buyers, going to the more important ones to find out what they had chosen and then writing up and photographing these

Bettina models a design by Hubert de Givenchy, in the spring 1965 collection, and the artist Francis Marshall makes an on-the-spot record of the dress.

23

models. Now, it is the contrary: many of the buyers seem terrified of missing 'something new' and do not appear to have confidence in their own judgment.

The press, especially what is called the cheaper press, wanting a 'story' at all costs, obviously concentrate their reporting on the houses which produce gimmicky clothes. I understand that the buyers who cater exclusively to the young should follow these guidelines, but for those who have an older clientèle – and by older I mean 23 and upwards – I am surprised that they do not take more note of what the 'classical' houses are doing.

For the last twelve years I have lectured all over England and the United States and, everywhere I go, I am asked why it is that in the shops there is such a small choice of models and of sizes for those who do not want eccentric clothes. I am amazed by the fact that this outcry is so general. The women in my audiences also complain that they do not read about or see enough pictures of what they call 'normal' clothes. I know that classical clothes do not make an exciting picture, but I firmly believe that many readers of the woman's page, as well as enjoying the 'dolly birds', want to see what the really elegant woman is wearing so as to get a little inspiration for herself.

It is not only the older generation who appreciate the classic beauty which the best-established couture houses can provide. It seems difficult to believe that in these days of 'Women's Liberation' and the youth cult we still dress a surprising number of big, white, splashy weddings, bridesmaids and pages included. Accompanied by her mother, the prospective bride usually comes in to see us dressed in corduroy trousers, boots, a

How a couturier modifies his techniques to suit different fashions: striped detail as trimming is used with equal success by Pierre Balmain for a model in the spring 1956 collection, and for the autumn collection, in 1969.

heavy leather belt around her hips and a big buckle on her tummy. She peels off all this to try on our wedding dresses, forgetting that she will be wearing delicate shoes on the occasion and that a wedding dress does not look its best worn with boots!

From one stage to another, the dress is chosen, the head-dress decided upon, the veil measured, the train embroidered, the fittings gone through, until the final pre-wedding photograph session takes place in our show-room. This is an anachronism, so old-fashioned it is hard to believe it. A real, old-time photographer, the great specialist of chic, Paris weddings, Jean Leclerc still works with a large camera on a tripod and plates, and I have the feeling he must say 'Look at the little birdie!' The session takes hours. The family stand around damp-eyed, pulling a pleat into place here, a fold in the veil there: one can imagine the photograph in a silver frame on the piano of a rich bourgeois home. When it is all over, the bride discards her dress, her veil, her shoes, her gloves, her prayer book and, her Alexandre hair-do monumental on the top of her head, she gets back into her trousers and her boots.

Another important side of couture of which the general public is not

An example, made of white silk organdie, appliquéd with pink roses, of Pierre Balmain's glamorous extravagance in this evening gown designs: from the 'Jolie Madame de Paris' spring collection, 1958.

generally aware is the dressing of shows for the theatre and the cinema. Internationally, the house of Balmain is the most renowned for this kind of work. The shows on both sides of the Atlantic, on both sides of the Channel, which have been dressed by Balmain are countless.

Yves Saint Laurent also is very stage-minded, but his work is generally confined to France. What he enjoys best are big, feathery, musical extravaganzas, and he has dressed Zizi Jeanmaire on and off the stage for years. Another of his theatrical customers, who always wears his clothes, but more serious as a type than Zizi, is the great French actress Madeleine Renaud.

Dressing shows for the stage and for the screen is very specialised work. It is a branch of his profession which appeals very strongly to Pierre Balmain. After he has launched his haute couture and ready-to-wear collections, it is a breath of fresh air to him to be able to give free reign to his inspiration in a way so completely different from the usual discipline of his everyday work. Some producers approach Balmain direct, but so many of my friends being in show business, it mostly happens that an actress, a director, a producer, come to me with the plan for the dressing of a play or a film. The procedure is that I read the script and we discuss preliminary ideas for how many dresses, outfits, hats, jewels, accessories, will be required. Then I speak to Pierre Balmain, explaining the story, the character, the period and approximately the number of things they have in mind.

If the project in question appeals to Balmain, an appointment is arranged. The actress arrives at rue François Premier, usually accompanied by her director and they are taken up to Pierre Balmain's office, where the big session takes place. Balmain can sketch as quickly as he thinks, and he thinks very quickly. His brain teems with ideas. As each outfit is discussed, with its place and importance in the story, its psychological implications, the mood of the scene, the accessories required, Balmain sketches, discusses, throws away a sketch, does another, sends downstairs for a dress, sends for a roll of material, calls for a sample of embroidery, drapes things on the actress until, after hours of concentrated effort and high excitement all around, the sketches are finally decided upon.

Decisions are not easily reached. Actresses have very definite ideas about what they can and cannot wear and these are sometimes in direct opposition to those of the director and couturier. There are actresses with obsessions about what they think does and especially does not suit them, and, in their minds, the suitability of a dress in the context of the story comes second to what they think makes them look their best.

In one play that Balmain dressed I saw a producer slap the face of an actress who refused to wear a costume designed by him (in conjunction with Oliver Messel, who was doing the sets) which had been accepted with enthusiasm by the director, and previously approved of by the actress herself. The costume was made and delivered and, at rehearsal, the actress arrived having altered it completely. (Noel Coward has said to me that the only really big rows in the theatre are over clothes.)

Pierre Balmain's success with designs for films is typified by this glamorous model for Cyd Charisse, in 'Two Weeks in Another Town' (1962). The house added this description to their press photograph of the dress: 'What is even more interesting, the sleeves come off and fold up, like a fan. This is what Balmain means by travel-minded.'

The task of fixing the price for the clothes for a show once the designs have been agreed upon usually falls to me. This is a tricky hurdle to cross. Producers argue about prices in a most monstrous way. It always amazes me how much money is carelessly wasted, especially in the making of a film, and how avaricious producers suddenly become when it comes to paying for the clothes. Then and only then do they seem to dig their toes in. 'A page in the programme', 'Your name among the film credits', 'Think of the publicity', they exclaim. Obviously the publicity is precious to us, but there is a limit as to how many financial concessions can be made. No amount of publicity can pay for the exorbitant expense of materials, furs, embroideries and the hours and hours of labour involved. When a customer buys a dress from the collection in the ordinary way, the models, the patterns, are already established and have only to be reproduced to her measurements; but for special models, such as those made for the stage and the screen, every detail has to be worked out from scratch. This is a long and difficult task.

Once Balmain has signed a contract for a show, he spares nothing to make the job a success. When he dressed *Tender Is The Night* Pierre Balmain and his assistant, Erik Mortensen, went to Hollywood for the whole job: designing the many outfits over there, overseeing the fittings of the clothes which were made at the studio, the choosing of all the accessories on the spot and that even included the gloves. He gets so carried away that, in the course of fittings, he often discards a dress and starts it over again adding expensive details to the model. All this costs a fortune. The person made responsible for the carrying out of our theatrical work, after having assisted at the first session during which decisions are arrived at, then takes over, Balmain giving an occasional look at the fittings and keeping his eye on the evolution of the order. Mlle. Madeleine Kohler finds all the materials and so on, and translates Balmain's sketches and ideas to the fitter who specialises in this kind of work. Then come the fittings – hours and hours of them – and the usual hysteria and drama inherent to this operation.

The approach to making clothes for films and for the stage is very different (unless, of course, it is 'costume', when the period rules everything). For the theatre, the materials and the cut are enhanced by the footlights, which give illusion. For a modern story, in the theatre, ideas that are slightly exaggerated can be used to the full. The play is usually produced in the near future, so that clothes do not have time to go out of fashion. If the play runs for a long time, it has been known for the producer to order new clothes to bring them up to date. Hugh Beaumont did this for Dame Edith Evans in *Waters of the Moon* and, in Paris, Balmain remade the clothes several times for Grédy and Barillet's *Ami-Ami* which ran on and on.

For the cinema, the problem is much more complicated. Between the ordering of the clothes and the film coming out, months elapse. If clothes are made which are too exaggeratedly up to the minute, they are already

Audrey Hepburn as the star of 'Breakfast at Tiffany's' (1961), was dressed by her favourite couturier, Hubert de Givenchy.

The incredibly glamorous Marlene Dietrich, in white mink from the house of Balmain.

out of fashion when the film comes to the screen. Also, a film, if it is successful, can run for years all over the world and be revived twenty or thirty years later. Nothing looks more ridiculous than fashionable clothes that are fashionable no longer. (The chapter on Mademoiselle Chanel provides many examples of this.) They can ruin the story and make people laugh when they ought to be crying. Clothes must never look fancy dress – of which the 'twenties are a catastrophic example. When dressing a play of this period, the clothes must be 'interpreted' and not an exact replica of the clothes worn at that time, just what Pierre Balmain achieved when he dressed Jennifer Jones and Joan Fontaine in *Tender Is The Night*,

29

and as Donald Brooks did for *Star*. So, for the cinema, clothes have to be classical, although of course imaginative. The hemline must be very carefully studied, neither exaggeratedly long nor exaggeratedly short. Shoulders too are a terrible give-away, not to mention hats, which are the worst of all.

As for the fittings of the clothes for the cinema, it was Marlene Dietrich who pointed out to me the big difference between fittings for the stage and the screen. 'In films', she said, 'with the screen getting bigger and bigger every year, with close-ups twenty, fifty times life-size, every ruckle (which she pronounced "wuckle") looks like the Rocky Mountains.' As we do not want our film stars to have the Rocky Mountains criss-crossing their busts, we took note of Marlene's practical wisdom and have acted in accordance ever since.

It would be tedious to enumerate all the actresses, all the shows, which have been dressed by Pierre Balmain. If I were asked to give a Number One amongst them all, I would say Bernard Shaw's *The Millionairess*, which was dressed as a play for Katharine Hepburn and as a film for Sophia Loren. Those two actresses playing the richest, most elegant, woman in the world – a couturier's dream! As for the others, they go from the Comédie Française to revue. I remember we made the first 'pantajupe' – half trousers, half skirt – considered terribly daring at the time for Arletty, who was appearing at the Etoile Music Hall.

A typically hectic collection scene, at the house of Dior, spring 1950.

Perhaps now the reader will have a clearer picture of the world of haute couture as it seems today to one who has worked in one of the great houses for a quarter-of-a-century. To me, the tradition of haute couture rests in those classical houses, of which Balenciaga was king, and whose tradition is carried on nowadays by only three couturiers: Balmain, Givenchy and Grès. Other chapters in this book will describe the history of couture, and the new revolutionary developments which are breaking away from this great tradition. But before that, what of the three men who since the war have been the most important protagonists of the classical style – Balenciaga, Givenchy, and Pierre Balmain?

Balenciaga was one of the few Spaniards to rise to the top of French couture. He was born in 1895, at Guetaria, a tiny fishing village near San Sebastian; very little is known about his early life. When he was still a boy it is said that he saw the ageing Marquesa de Casas Torres on her way from church and as she passed he murmured, 'How elegant'. She heard him; he asked to be allowed to copy the Drécoll outfit she was wearing. He did, desperately nervous in case he should spoil the silk she gave him for the task.

As this story has now become one of the many legends which surround Balenciaga, it follows naturally, that he copied it beautifully. That he made a dress for the Marquesa at an early age is a fact; but it gives an idea of how little anyone ever knew about Balenciaga, even at the height of his fame, that no two versions of the story are ever the same: no one can agree on how old the precocious boy was, or from which Paris house the original dress came. The most reliable sources defer to Drécoll.

By the time he was 20, he had opened his own dressmaking establishment in San Sebastian, learning every stitch of his craft by choosing the cloth, cutting, sewing, and fitting the clothes himself. He became well known to smart Spanish señoras, but it was not enough for his ambition and his talents. In 1937, when he was 42, he came to Paris and opened the doors of his salon at 10 avenue George V.

Carmel Snow, the editor of US *Harper's Bazaar*, was the first to recognise his genius. She published page after page of his evening and afternoon dresses, and marvellous suits. 'Effortlessly classical' is how she herself described them. His clothes appeared in magazines far more often than has been possible since. Balenciaga did not care for publicity. After the war he showed his collection to the press a month after the rest of Paris, which was both maddening and expensive for the press who had to trail back a second time to see his collection. By that time he was too important to ignore and so back they came. The reason, he said, was to protect his important American clients – the buyers, who were already paying more to see his collection than any other couturier dared to charge. Not even Carmel Snow was exempt.

His manner was as uncomprising as his clothes. He was a perfectionist in the true meaning of the word. He made absolutely no concessions, whether it was a question of his work-rooms or his clients. His success was

Balenciaga, in a rare photographic study by Sir Cecil Beaton.

built almost entirely on private clients. One of the best known, and most beautiful must surely be Mexican dancer Gloria Rubio who was to become Mrs Loel Guinness. With her thick black hair, classical good looks, and perfect figure, she was his ideal.

People who have worked with Balenciaga have said that the height of professional enjoyment was to be privileged to see him with a piece of material in his hands, explaining what he wanted done with it. If the word genius can be applied to a contributor to what is essentially one of the minor arts, Balenciaga would certainly have been the only one to deserve it. It is true that to many, many women, the name of Dior holds the magic of Paris; his New Look was more epoch-making than revolutionary in that it gave women back their femininity after seven years of dreary utility. But it was Balenciaga alone who revolutionised the way women were to dress during the 'fifties and 'sixties.

Writing in British *Vogue* in 1962, as the preface to an unprecedented splash of Balenciaga models selected by Harrods in London, who were selling line-for-line copies in the original fabrics, Ailsa Garland, then the editor, wrote: 'There is one brief, pithy Spanish word, *cursi*, that Balenciaga uses to describe what he hates most in fashion: vulgarity and bad taste. Of these he has never, ever, been guilty. Almost since the first day he launched his salon he has been acclaimed as the great leader in fashion: what Balenciaga does today, other designers will do tomorrow or next

top left
Mme Juan Larivière, who epitomised the elegant chic of Paris for many years, dressed by Balenciaga.
top right
Balenciaga's clients were some of the most elegant women in the world. Here Mme Arturo Lopez-Wilshaw (far left) in a characteristic ball gown.
bottom left
Mrs Loel Guinness, 1947.
bottom right
Rapt attention at a collection: Mme Arturo Lopez-Wilshaw, wearing a Balenciaga hat.

A softer Balenciaga model from about 1950.

year, by which time he will have moved on again, out in the forefront of true elegance and chic. Because of his obsessive shyness, a kind of mystique has built up around him. His colours are black, accentuated with white, brilliant reds, turquoise, yellow, warm cinnamon brown.

'He has destroyed the time element in fashion. What Balenciaga designed in 1938 looks uncannily right today. He has a complete and utter disregard for public opinion, caring not a fig whether press or customers like his collection, and because he follows no ideas or trends but his own, everybody follows him . . . practically every woman is now wearing something that has been influenced by him.

'Implicit believer in the golden rule of fashion, that the essence of chic is elimination; therefore it follows that he has the most elegant clientèle in the world.'

Harrods had chosen well for their country customers. There were pebbly tweeds, worn with what *Vogue* described as 'transcendental wellingtons'. Indeed they were. If you had a pair of those soft, calf, knee-high boots today, they would still be smart. They were loose, cut like a wellington boot, with an almond-shaped toe and low block heel. It was Balenciaga being first again, this time with boots, which are still,

33

ten years later, an important fashion accessory.

His innovations were so subtle that you had to look twice or three times and then go back again to be sure you had seen exactly what had happened. It was often only in retrospect and at other collections that you realised that it was Balenciaga who had been that way before. The sack, which changed every woman's wardrobe and which he introduced in 1957, was directly evolved from his loose tunic tops, which he showed for the first time worn over long slim skirts, in 1954. He also eased the shape of suits, fitting the front, curving the back, and gradually letting out all the seams until there was nothing of the mannish *tailleur* – or tailor-made – left. He shortened sleeves to a pretty three-quarter length to balance exactly with the edge of the loose jacket, and opened the neckline, setting on it a soft rounded collar which made an elegant and feminine frame for the face. His coats were cut with generous sloping sleeves, almost kimono-like. All these ideas of an easy elegance were widely copied. But his evening dresses were inimitable. They were a miracle of intricately-cut simplicity; wildly extravagant and hideously expensive, and at their most sumptuous

Three sketches by Francis Marshall which trace the development of the 'sack', one of Balenciaga's innovations.

34

in yards and yards of Abraham's silk 'Gazar'.

Mr Zika Ascher the London fabric manufacturer who introduced so many new prints and weaves to Paris during the time when Balenciaga was The Master, recalls showing his soft, whispery silk 'Gizelle' to Balenciaga. 'It is beautiful', he said, 'but I do not know how to use it.' It was true. Balenciaga only ever worked with firm materials with plenty of body, treating them as a sculptor would a lump of clay or block of marble, and setting his inspiration in them. On another occasion, when Ascher, first took his fluffy bouclé mohair tweeds to Paris, Balenciaga was delighted. But before he sampled one, he wanted to see exactly how this brand-new fabric would behave. He asked for a piece and then and

A sketch of a Balenciaga ball gown from the late 'forties, by Francis Marshall, who sketched for *Vogue* and later, the London *Daily Mail* during the 'fifties. His women epitomised the cool, elegant chic so admired at the time.

there he made a buttonhole. Later that same week, Ascher took the fabric to a second couturier. He looked at it, loved it, but pronounced it impossible to work. When Ascher produced the piece with the buttonhole, the designer was stunned. 'It is so perfect you should frame it', was all he could say. And he ordered it too. This was in 1958 and mohair tweeds became such a rage that Ascher was flying it to the USA by the plane-load. Apparently none of the designers was really interested in what fabrics anyone else had chosen, except those that were favoured by Balenciaga. He was the first with chenille tweeds, and later, with cotton lace.

Ask any chic Parisienne which of Balenciaga's clothes she coveted most, and she would probably reply, an evening dress and a black suit. When Sir Cecil Beaton came to look for a classical black Balenciaga suit for his fashion charivari at the Victoria and Albert Museum in London at the end of 1971, he had a problem. Although their owners were among the richest women in the world, these suits were so ahead and yet of their time, and such a joy to wear, that the women had literally worn them out. It was only with the greatest difficulty that one was found.

Balenciaga's whole life was couture. During the last years of his 'reign' the difficulties inherent to modern couture depressed him, and the 1968 revolution was the last straw. On a sudden impulse, disgusted, he closed down his firm, the staff hearing on the radio that the house of Balenciaga was no more. In one of his rare interviews, given to Prudence Glynn, fashion editor of *The Times*, just a few months before he died in Valencia in March 1972, he said: 'The life which supported couture is finished. Real couture is a luxury which is just impossible to do anymore.'

In Balenciaga, the influence of post-war couture had its beginning and its end. It is worth remembering that unlike any other designer working in Paris during the 1950s and '60s, only he never served an apprenticeship with another couturier. He came straight from Spain, with long hard years of practical dressmaking and designing experience behind him; and his mind made up. Paris could not touch his personality. Can it be coincidence that the one couturier who had something entirely new to say in the '60s, André Courrèges, was trained by Balenciaga? Look at the coat from his early collections (on page 196), still under the Spaniard's spell. Then suddenly, in 1964, Courrèges broke through with the beautiful young coats and suits which had a world-wide impact on fashion. Ironically, Courrèges' young fashion also appealed to a new, younger generation who could not care less where it had come from.

Balenciaga's disciple and friend was Hubert Taffin de Givenchy, born in the town of Beavais on 20 February 1927. Givenchy went to the École des Beaux Arts and to the Faculté de Droit – the Paris arts university, as well as to the law school. But couture was Givenchy's real vocation and he worked for Lelong between 1945 and 1946, for Piguet (1946–8), for Jacques Fath (1948–9), and from 1949 to 1951 he became Schiaparelli's designer. In 1952 he created his own firm.

Givenchy, like Balenciaga, lives for couture. He has no social life out-

A Balenciaga full-skirted day dress, summer 1954 collection.

side of it and is never seen at the café society parties where the Paris couturiers are made so much of. Work is Givenchy's obsession. People say that he starts his new collection the day the previous one is shown. He arrives at work at 8 o'clock in the morning. When he is fitting the clothes on the mannequins, he cannot stop improving a detail here, a detail there. He goes on and on exaggeratedly: there is a limit to how much one can finick a fitting of a dress especially on the mannequins who change constantly. This obsession with work necessarily makes him difficult to work for. But he has beautiful manners, and he is tall and good looking.

Givenchy was the only couturier Balenciaga trusted, going so far as to show him his collections – unheard of with anybody else. Balenciaga considered Givenchy his heir and, when Balenciaga closed, Givenchy took over many of his work-people.

Pierre Balmain comes from the Savoy mountains. He was born on 18 May 1914 in the village of Saint-Jean-de-Maurienne. In the way of character he is the opposite of Balenciaga and Givenchy, for he is an extrovert. He loves social life, parties and his vitality is boundless. He is seen everywhere. He is ready to go to the other side of the world at 24 hours notice if the chance arises. He loves the prizes couture has to offer to those who serve her. He has a passion for houses. He has an apartment in Paris, a big house on the island of Elba, a house in Marrakesh and one in Normandy. As soon as a house is finished, the last detail in place, he gets tired of it and longs to get on to the next one.

Casual chic in white jersey: Givenchy, spring 1972.

Balmain, like Hubert de Givenchy, went to the École des Beaux Arts where he studied architecture; however, with him as with the others, couture was his true love and a devouring ambition; he managed when still quite young to get Molyneux to accept him as junior designer – Molyneux, one of the greats of the classical couturiers.

In 1939, Pierre Balmain went to Lelong's. During the war he was mobilised in Savoy and helped his mother run her dress business in Aix-les-Bains. In 1941, Lelong reopened his house and called Balmain back to Paris where he shared a desk with another young designer called Christian Dior. They envisaged opening a business together but decided against the idea, and each opened his own house: Pierre Balmain in 1946, Dior in 1947.

Balmain's method of working in no way resembles that of Balenciaga and Givenchy. He is inclined to leave things to the latest possible moment, loving to work in a rush of high-voltaged excitement. His approach to creation is not mathematical as is Balenciaga's and Givenchy's. He relies much more on improvisation and on the inspiration of the moment. The atmosphere of the house is therefore much less sedate than Givenchy's and Balenciaga's. Customers remark on it being more like an exclusive club than an aloof maison de couture.

There will always in couture be new names who, at intervals, rise like fireworks in the sky and burst with *éclat* on the world. The press will rave,

the women will flock, the new fads will be adulated, written up, talked about. And, quietly, through it all, as they have done time and time again, the classical houses will carry on, the headlights of publicity turned away from them, continuing the high standard of their work, and dressing hundreds of the most elegant women in the world.

Givenchy's simple elegance, in silk Gazar, for the spring 1972 collection.

right
The Duchess of Windsor, dressed by Dior, and the Vicomtesse de Bouchamp, dressed by Balenciaga, December 1965.

left
The styling of this dress and jacket by Givenchy (spring 1972), with its easy simplicity of line and soft collar detail, amply justifies his place as Balenciaga's successor.

Every newcomer interested in French high fashion eventually poses the salient question, 'What precisely is the Chambre Syndicale de la Couture Parisienne?' It is reasonably safe to say that there is nothing comparable in any other country. This powerful couture organisation in Paris could be described as half union and half guild, incorporating many of the best features of both.

The Syndicale is simultaneously a judicial and legislative body intended, in the words of Monsieur Daniel Gorin, the late President, to represent, advise, and defend its members, who include the vast majority of great names in the French couture. Since World War II, the social sector dealing with the hundred-and-one details of labour relations in the couture houses has become more important than ever. It concerns itself with social security, pensions, salaries, paid holidays, maternity benefits, housing, labour disputes, unemployment – in other words, all relations between labour and management in the high fashion industry.

In addition, this multi-faceted organisation copes with style piracy, operates its separate departments to handle foreign relations and the bi-annual influx of professional buyers and press who migrate to Paris for the openings; and run the couture school, founded in 1929, to train young hopefuls in every phase of dressmaking.

Another vital function is to arrange calendar dates for the couture openings each season so that major houses do not conflict or overlap; seemingly not a monumental task until one considers the famed individualism of the French. For instance, one designer may decide to switch to another's traditional date; one will not show on any day or hour which includes some specific digit due to long standing superstition, and so on. The Syndicale steps in with the aplomb of a veteran diplomat, soothes ruffled feelings, and smoothes the way.

The origins of the Chambre Syndicale de la Couture Parisienne date back to 1868, when France already had a number of trade unions protecting workers in varied industries, from bricklaying to dressmaking. Monsieur Despaigne was the first President presiding over the women's tailoring industry and ready-to-wear, as well as the couture. Following Monsieur Despaigne was the first President presiding over the women's tailoring Monsieur Dreyfus from 1878 to 1884. In 1885, Monsieur Gaston Worth, son of Charles Frederick, English-born founder of the Worth dynasty, held the presidency for three years.

According to a biography on the house of Worth by the Brooklyn Museum: 'In the late 'eighties Charles Frederick Worth retired more and more to his over-stuffed mansion at Suresnes. But the couture house he had established was to flourish many more years under the prosperous and practical leadership of his sons, Gaston and Jean Phillipe.

'Times had changed, and the sons were faced with competition from the important couture houses of Doucet, Raudnitz, Rouff, Callot Soeurs, and others. To prevent cut-throat rivalry in the flourishing haute couture, Gaston Worth, moving with great diplomatic caution, organised the

LA CHAMBRE SYNDICALE

Marjorie Dunton

top left
Raymond Barbas, president and general manager of Jean Patou, who was president of the Chambre from 1950–57, since when he has been the honorary president.

top right
Lucien Lelong, president of the Chambre Syndicale from 1937–45, when he became honorary president.

bottom left
Jacques Heim, president of the Chambre from 1958–62.

bottom right
Daniel Gorin, the first non-couture president of the Chambre Syndicale, and a Chevalier of the Legion of Honour. M. Gorin held many posts within the Chambre throughout his distinguished career, beginning in 1937 as general secretary.

40

industry into the Chambre Syndicale de la Couture Française. More than sixty years later we see this directorate has grown and still controls its economically important trade.'

From 1885–1911, the association was quietly carried on by eight succeeding presidents. In 1911, the Couture Parisienne formally organised its own Chambre Syndicale, which was headed by leading names in the dressmaking profession during the next half century. Madame Paquin, 1917–19, was the only woman ever to be elected President. Charles Frederick Worth's grandson, Jacques, was President from 1927–30, and held the office again from 1933–5.

The year 1936 marks an important date in the history of the couture for it was this year, doubtless influenced by the disturbed social climate, that a general reorganisation of policy and administration took place in the Chambre Syndicale. The two men largely responsible for these changes were Lucien Lelong, who was named president in 1937, and Daniel Gorin, who became General Secretary. They were the promoters of the first effort to regroup the Paris couturiers around one dominant purpose, that of professional unity. This basic policy began to take direction in 1937. Even the most individualistic members understood that apart from the special interest of each house, large or small, there existed a 'common good' to be defended by one strong professional organisation.

During the German occupation of France in World War II, when Hitler visualised transporting the Paris couture, lock, stock, and talent, to Berlin or Vienna, the late Lucien Lelong, president during those crucial years until 1945, and Daniel Gorin, succeeded in persuading the Germans that the French couture would be totally unable to operate, let alone create, on alien soil.

The couture kept its doors open during the four years of the occupation and, with typical ingenuity, managed to turn out new collections twice a year. Fabric was strictly rationed, in minimum quantities, and of poor quality. Also, unusual materials were employed, such as wood shavings, to concoct some of the craziest hats on record. The Syndicate played a major role in avoiding the deportation of skilled workers; the school continued to function, and many apprentice designers who are at the top of the ladder today received their initial training during those difficult years. Germans still evoke the same admiration for French creation, and, for some time, West Germany has spent more money in the Paris couture than any other country post-war.

After the liberation, the Chambre Syndicale rallied all its forces to prove that the couture had come through with flying colours and to re-establish its prestige as the world's fashion centre. Leading designers banded together to create the 'Théâtre de la Mode': a collection of dolls dressed in the latest silhouettes. They were sent on tour of major capitals throughout Europe and eventually across the USA from New York to San Francisco. These dolls, veritable ambassadresses of French fashion, became naturalised Americans and are still on display in the Maison de la Légion

Souvenir
du Théâtre de la Mode

Londres
Sept. 45

A quick sketch from inside the cover of the souvenir catalogue of the *Théâtre de la Mode* by the artist Christian Bérard, from a copy found in a London bookshop.

d'Honneur in San Francisco.

At the end of World War II, with Monsieur Lelong's resignation, Monsieur Gaumont Lanvin, nephew of Madame Jeanne Lanvin, became President from 1945–50, followed by Monsieur Raymond Barbas, brother-in-law of the late Jean Patou and head of the house of Patou. Monsieur Barbas, 1950–7, in turn was succeeded by Monsieur Jacques Heim, 1958–62, and then by Monsieur Robert Ricci, son of Nina Ricci. Monsieur Ricci, who held office for one year, 1962–3, was the last of

43

the couture presidents, who numbered twenty-five in all, elected by the members of the Chambre Syndicale. At this period, the couturiers decided that the unpaid honour of the president's chair was taking too much time from their personal business, and it was agreed to name the most competent man (and one no longer affiliated with any couture house) to the office of President. Monsieur Daniel Gorin and his assistant, Monsieur Jean Manusardi, were unanimously nominated President and President-Delegate, the latter from 1963–4. M. Gorin died on 24 April 1972, causing the greatest sadness and sense of loss among all those people who had been his friends and working colleagues. The Chambre Syndicale was deeply indebted to him for his brilliant direction and tireless devotion.

Madame Madeleine Godeau, who has been affiliated with the Chambre Syndicale for the past 38 years, was administrative secretary from 1933–50, and is now both General Secretary and manager of the Syndicate schools which operate under the supervision of the French Ministry of Education.

In the present, the Chambre Syndicale has a multitude of responsibilities to perform, and perhaps the most visible to the outside world is its activity on behalf of the couturiers at that most important time, the bi-annual showing of the collections. One of the tasks of the Chambre Syndicale is the issue of the press cards to the world's journalists.

To obtain a 'couture press card', it is necessary that the editor responsible for the magazine or newspaper in question request in writing that the fashion correspondent for his publication be accredited with the Chambre Syndicale, and then the board of directors examines the case of each applicant. Couture press cards have to be renewed each season, and those receiving cards are required to pay a small fee for services and mailing.

The selected journalists appear on the official press list together with the name of their publication and Paris address. This information is then sent to the press department of each member couturier who, in turn, issues personal invitations. Without the precious invitation, the chances of attending the openings are about as slim as breaking the bank at Monte Carlo. In addition, the Chambre Syndicale press card usually assures that the journalist is invited to all gala parties held during the openings and literally opens all doors in the couture world.

The couture press card is as personal as a passport, carrying the bearer's photograph, together with the rules and regulations imposed by the couturiers of the Chambre Syndicale. The regulations include that the correspondent will not misuse fashion information, that no sketches be made during the fashion showings without express authorisation of the couturier, and that the release date of photographs, as set by the Chambre Syndicale, be respected. Both editor and correspondent give their signature to these formalities. This procedure also applies to editors wishing accreditation for photographers or sketchers. Approximately 800 journalists attend the spring and summer openings held in January, and approximately 1,000, attend the autumn and winter presentations, held in July.

To obtain a 'carte d'acheteur' (buyer's card), the applicant is required to state the name, address, and character of the firm he or she represents and include two passport-type photographs. The request may be made directly to the Chambre Syndicale or through a resident commissioner. The buyer's card defines certain rights reserved by the couturier, and his general conditions of sale. The principal condition is a deposit covering the cost of one or two models depending upon the individual house. This is known as a 'caution', and is deductible from purchases. Those holding buyer's cards are also eligible for certain services of the Chambre Syndicale. For instance, the Syndicale provides a special, free, calendar for buyers' showings only, giving the names of the houses and the dates and hours of showings.

below
Gaumont Lanvin, nephew of Mme Lanvin and president of the Chambre from 1945–50, with the late Countess de Polignac, Mme Lanvin's daughter.

below right
Robert Ricci, vice-president and president of the Chambre from 1962–63, since when he has been honorary president, with his mother, the late Mme Nina Ricci, founder of the couture house of that name.

These regulations may seem elaborate to the outsider, but there are several weighty reasons for their existence. Not the least of these is plagiarism. Style piracy has been a problem in France as far back as the 18th century. At that time, courtesans tried to bribe Rose Bertin, Marie Antoinette's dressmaker, to reveal details of the Queen's latest gown before she appeared wearing it for the first time at some gala function. During the 1950s, thefts of original models almost put the real gangsters to shame.

The first clear-cut law protecting fashion creation was passed by the French Tribunal in 1920, and couture designs registered with the Chambre Syndicale are accorded the same legal protection as literature, cinema, and patented inventions. Every model created by every member of the Syndicale is registered in his files, with an exact sketch, photograph, and swatch of the fabric, before the official showings, to buyers and press.

French courts prosecute the high fashion 'mafia' as severely as perpetrators of false paintings and counterfeit money.

Nonetheless, the question of plagiarism is often hard to define. It suffices occasionally for the black marketeer to alter the original collar, substitute other buttons or trimmings, replace a pocket, and sell the design to a mass produced or retail outlet as his own.

In spite of careful screening of buyers, press, and private clients who attend the openings, there are four major sources of fashion leaks, often resulting in the loss of thousands of francs for the victimised couturier. In fact, the illicit profiteers often make infinitely more money from the stolen designs than the creator.

Although most seamstresses are completely loyal to their house and take immense pride in feeling they have contributed in a small way to a successful collection, it needs only one dishonest worker to steal the pattern she has been cutting all day, slipping it in her pocket, to return it unobtrusively the next morning. Or, if she is skilful enough, she might reproduce it at home without the original, and send it off to some copyist, either in the provinces or abroad. If the culprit is eventually caught, the result is instant dismissal and legal prosecution resulting in a heavy fine or even a jail sentence. However, these are rare happenings.

While 99% of the professional buyers are as honest as Abraham Lincoln, fork up their deposit money with a smile, and are pleased that both the house and the firm they represent are going to earn money on their selections, there is always an occasional buyer who is dishonest, has a perfect photographic memory, and can accurately sketch many of the models he has seen paraded during the showing as soon as he returns to his hotel room.

The press and bevy of socialites (the latter often make a full-time occupation of attending the couture collections each season) have also been known to 'sell Paris down the Seine'. Accredited journalists are allowed to sketch and photograph in the days immediately following the openings, in time to publish on the official release date established by the Chambre Syndicale three to four weeks later. Unfortunately, over the years, an occasional sketch has found its way into the wrong hands and photos have passed under a xerox machine. The late Christian Dior once personally evicted a so-called client who was quietly photographing his models during the presentation with a miniature camera hidden in the trimming of her hat. Christian Dior slipped on a pair of white gloves and coolly showed the lady the door.

Before World War II, piracy had really been perfected to a fine art, with teams of two or three specialists working separately on specific portions of the silhouette. One was a neckline expert, while another concentrated on skirt treatments, so that it was an easy job to assemble the total look in some cloistered corner, right after the show. Thanks to the non-stop efforts of the Chambre Syndicale, style piracy is on the wane. However, this cancer in the haute couture will probably continue to exist as long as Paris seduces the fashion world and keeps her creative lead in the market.

To turn to more praiseworthy talents, the Chambre Syndicale takes particular care to encourage new designers, keeping couture vital and self-renewing. The Chambre Syndicale Schools, directed by Madame Madeleine Godeau, comprise two separate departments under the same roof at 45 Rue Saint Roch, Paris 1e.

One division is for French students; the second, shorter, course, condensed into two years, is primarily designed for foreigners. The French school, founded in 1930 under the auspices of Monsieur Jacques Worth, President of the Chambre Syndicale at that time, is a continual source of skilled labour and fresh talent for the couture houses, assuring the formation and improvement of the needle trades and their allied arts, for which

France is world renowned. This section comprises three stages of training: apprenticeship, finishing courses, and, finally, superior school of the couture.

The superior course is also open to foreign students. The classes are in French, so that it is advisable that the student has a working knowledge of the language beforehand. However, a practical course in conversation and technical vocabulary is offered. The school year is divided into three terms, from October to the end of June. Tuition includes fashion design, and sketching from live models and figurines. During the year, each student must execute an album of original sketches on a given theme.

Fifteen hours are reserved each week for cutting, and nine for design; the patterns are cut in muslin on dummies, stressing the study of proportions, the perfection of balance, adapting the garment to the body in movement, and exploiting the value of personality.

One section of an atelier at the Chambre Syndicale's school, where the international, two-year course is taught.

Permanent contact with Paris fashion and its evolution is assured by conferences given by famous designers and invitations to see their collections. The students can make visits to textile designers, museums and exhibitions. There is also a conference course in French history and civilisation in relation to the Paris haute couture. Following World War II, many GIs enrolled at the Chambre Syndicale School, being eligible under the GI Bill of Rights.

One of the most famous graduates of the French division is Yves Saint Laurent who won a design award given by the International Wool Office. One of the judges was the late Christian Dior, who offered the young man a position in his house working under his personal direction in the design studio. The rest of the story is fashion history, and Paris couture will certainly continue to flourish as long as each generation produces its quota of talented creators.

The schools and the Chambre Syndicale de la Haute Couture have both taken an apt quotation from Germaine Beaumont as their motto:

> Quand tout sur la terre nous parviendra rapidement et passera par l'anonymat des machines, quand tout leur devra une perfection sans âme, il nous restera encore l'ultime aristocratie du travail à la main, du travail dont on dit avec tant de grâce, qu'il est 'perlé'. Et ce travail manuel, dérobé aux influences, aux variations des mœurs, sera la sauvegarde et la noblesse de l'art dans l'avenir.
>
> GERMAINE BEAUMONT, poet

PRESIDENTS OF THE SYNDICALE SINCE 1868

Despaigne	1868–1869
Bernard Salle	1870–1877
Dreyfus	1878–1884
Worth, G.	1885–1888
Marcade	1889–1890
Brynlinski	1890–1892
Felix	1893–1895
Perdoux	1896–1900
Bonhomme	1901–1902
Pichot	1903–1904
Storch	1905–1907
Reverdot	1908–1911
Doeuillet	1912–
Aine	1913–1916
Paquin, Mme.	1917–1919
Clement	1920–1927
Worth, J.	1927–1930
Gerber, P.	1930–1933
Worth, J.	1933–1935
Gerber, P.	1935–1937
Lelong, L.	1937–1945
Gaumont Lanvin	1945–1950
Barbas, R.	1950–1957
Jacques Heim	1958–1962
Robert Ricci	1962–1963
end of couturiers serving as president	
Jean Manusardi	1963–1964
President Delegate	
Daniel Gorin	1964–1972
President	

2 THE BIRTH OF COUTURE

1900-1910

Alison Settle

Where does the history of haute couture begin? Strangely enough, a minor art which has been dominated by the French ever since owes its birth to the achievements of an Englishman, Charles Frederick Worth. It was due to his efforts that the haute couture found itself, at the beginning of this century, at the heights of its power and influence, symbolised by the tremendous interest which it brought to the great *Exposition Universelle* held in Paris in 1900.

Charles Frederick Worth was born on 13 October 1825, in the small town of Bourne, Lincolnshire. He made an early entry into the world of commerce, because his father, a lawyer, had a disastrous propensity for

below
Charles Frederick Worth, founder of the house of Worth, and the father of French couture.

above right
Charles Worth's wife, Marie Vernet, who worked closely with her husband throughout her life, and was the first mannequin.

gambling, and quickly brought financial ruin on his family, his wife and three children. It seems that Mrs Worth had married beneath her, and the only help which her relatives felt prepared to offer was to provide support for her alone, while the children had to fend for themselves. But with Mrs Worth's humiliating pleading, the relatives softened a little in their attitude, and Charles Frederick acquired a suitable position in London. He found himself, therefore, at the tender age of twelve, apprenticed to the drapery trade, in that famous London store of Swan and Edgar.

Then followed eight years of hard, conscientious labour, during which Charles had the opportunity to observe the *beau monde* of all Europe,

51

parading in nearby Piccadilly. This was an age in which men led the field of fashion, in beautifully cut frock coats, satin waistcoats, and frilled shirts. Women were mere shadows in comparison with their partners. These years provided Charles Frederick with a firm foundation for his later career: he learnt about current tastes from the gentry of London; he developed a flair for salesmanship which proved invaluable in later years; he absorbed a great deal of experience about fabrics, trimmings, shawls, and bonnets; and he became versed in all the rules of book-keeping. He spent his free hours visiting the newly-opened art galleries of London, where his eager, artistic eye absorbed the beauties of old masters, Titian, or Vandyck, and revealed to him those eras when women dressed far more flamboyantly than the subdued citizens of Victorian London.

It was during his years of apprenticeship that Worth formed the plan of moving to Paris, for he must have become aware that all the newest ideas of fashion emanated from the dressmakers and milliners of that city – from such creators as Leroy, and Rose Bertin. At the age of twenty, speaking not one word of the French language, Charles Worth set out for the capital. Once more, he was financed by a small sum which his mother had begged from her relatives.

How hard it must have been for the young Englishman to find himself all alone in the bustling capital of the Second Empire. Yet, with the courage which never failed him throughout his life, Worth determined with a firm will to find employment. As luck would have it, he found a job in a small draper's shop, where he had to work a tiring twelve-hour day, sweeping the floor, dusting the shelves, and serving customers, in an immaculate dark suit. It is not quite certain where his first position was taken, but his son, J. P. Worth, believes that it was at *La Ville de Paris*. After a year or so, he managed to secure a position at one of the most fashionable Parisian shops – Gagelin and Opigez, 93 rue de Richelieu. He was to bring changes of fortune to that establishment which could hardly be imagined from this humble beginning.

At this time, haute couture did not exist, as it is known today; a bevy of female dressmakers such as Madame Camille, provided ladies at court, and the city's socialites, with their fine gowns, but they did not, as a rule, create designs or suggest new styles to their customers. They merely executed their orders, with perhaps minor alterations. It was just this aspect of couture which Worth revolutionised.

Charles Worth had met and married a young lady *vendeuse*, or sales assistant, at Gagelin's – Marie Vernet – in the early 1850s. She had an innate elegance and style which throughout her marriage was of great assistance to Worth's career. He made her a few simple dresses which she wore to work, evoking the admiration and curiosity of her colleagues and customers. Worth used the same technique throughout his life – sometimes against the wishes of his wife, who would have been quite happy to be just a little more conservative in her dress, instead of launching a succession of Worth's newest creations. Madame Worth was thus the first 'mannequin' which the haute couture world knew. Charles Worth went to his employers at the Maison Gagelin, and explained how interested customers had become in his wife's dresses. Could he set up a small dressmaking department, where he could produce the clothes which Marie so successfully modelled? After initial reactions of horror at so radical a suggestion, the proprietors agreed. They did not have cause to regret their decision, and for the next decade the designs of Charles Worth increased the fortunes of the store dramatically. In 1851, the Maison Gagelin took their goods to the Great Exhibition in London, and won the only Gold Medal awarded to France. Their shawls and smart dresses earned 350,000 francs in that same year.

This was the age of the crinoline, a style which Worth is said to have invented. Even if he did not, he certainly established it as the only accept-

Typical Worth crinolines, sketched by Worth *c.* 1865. The figures' faces are reminiscent of the Empress Eugènie's features.

able mode of the Second Empire. Silk, gauze, lace, trimmings of flowers and ribbons, spread in vast swathes over the cage-like hoop which supported the structure. Worth, in his years at Gagelin's, designed hundreds of these exquisite creations, which are perhaps best remembered from that famous portrait by Winterhalter of the Empress Eugènie, surrounded by her ladies-in-waiting. Tradition holds that the dress which Her Majesty wore was a Worth design, ordered for her from the Maison Gagelin, although at the time, the Empress would not have known its creator.

Indeed, this posed a problem for Worth. His designs were bringing the store new success, and although he was made a partner in the firm, he did not receive much direct profit from the relationship. He worked hard and long hours for his employers, and his wife and growing family (he now had two small sons) were an additional responsibility. So, in 1858, Charles Worth decided to leave Gagelin and Opigez, and open a business of his own. His new enterprise was financed by a Swede, Otto Gustave Bobergh, who had also been trained in the drapery trade. Together, they opened their little shop at 7 rue de la Paix. Worth was most fortunate in his choice, for although at the time there were few other couture establishments in the quiet street (Doucet's lingerie shop was the nearest, at number 17), in that same year, the Emperor Napoleon decreed that a new opera house should be erected nearby, and very soon, the rue de la Paix found itself at the hub of a smart, fashionable area, growing up around the now-famous *Place de L'Opera*.

Although Worth was not one to miss or fail in taking the initiative in a business enterprise, it was his devoted wife, Marie, who took the step that led to his established prosperity. In 1860, she decided to approach a newly-arrived (and rather badly-dressed) socialite to Paris, the Princess Pauline de Metternich, wife of the Austrian Ambassador. Considering the political power of the Austrian Empire at the time, the Princess was destined to hold a most important position in Parisian society, and the Worths thought she would be a most excellent patron, if only she accepted the role. Marie took an album of Worth's prettiest designs, and presented herself at the Austrian ambassadorial residence. She requested the honour of a commission for her husband's new business, and the Princess, who was delighted with Worth's sketches, ordered two crinolines, one for day, and one for evening wear.

The Princess was the instrument of good fortune for Charles Worth: the following week she wore her new ball gown to the royal Palace of the Tuileries, where she so impressed the Empress Eugènie with the simplicity and elegance of her attire that she was asked for its creator. The Empress, hearing the name of Worth, ordered that he should attend her, at 10 a.m. the following morning. From that day forward, Worth was patronised by the most powerful and prosperous clientèle of the Second Empire, so much so that it is often referred to as 'the age of Worth'. At the age of 35, success was assuredly his, and he began his career as the first *grand couturier*, the first arbiter of fashion. Worth dressed all those women who had any influence in any walk of life: the court, from the Empress herself to her ladies-in-waiting; the foreign aristocracy, including the Czarina of Russia, and the Grand Duchess Marie, the Queen of Italy, Margaret, the Austrian Empress Elisabeth, and (although the dresses were ordered through dressmakers, and not direct) Queen Victoria. One of his most faithful customers from the ranks of high society was Madame Charles Moulton, the most elegant American in Paris. From the world of the arts, Worth received the patronage of Madame Octave Feuillet, wife of the famous novelist and playwright, although his son, Jean Pierre, later developed this aspect of couture much more.

At the court, Worth maintained a studious politeness and distance from his clientèle. The one phenomenon which never came to Worth in his lifetime, by his own choice, was social acceptance in the high society of France. Unlike his descendants – Dior, for example – he never mixed on equal footing with the *beau monde* of his day. He considered himself always

Imaginative detailing appliquéd onto a jacket of blue wool exemplifies the styling which made the house of Worth famous. (1901.)

A Worth model of 1905 from the house archives, now in the Victoria and Albert Museum, London. The couturier's skill with trimmings and sleeve details is apparent.

Another of the Worth models from the house archives: an evening wrap decorated with the tassel, which remained in fashion for more than twenty years. (1905–6.)

as a 'tradesman', rather than a socially accepted artist, although he came to live in regal splendour at a country house he had built outside Paris, at Suresnes, and both he and his wife Marie, developed warm and intimate friendships in a private way with their best customers. This was a development in the status of the couturier which emerged with the social changes of World War I. But on his own territory, inside his salon in the rue de la Paix, Worth was as majestic as any of his clientèle. He would create and re-create models in a flamboyant and dictatorial fashion, ignoring his customers' pleas of 'Enough! enough! It is splendid as it is!' and ripping near-finished dresses apart, to start again. His mastery with sleeves with novel and tasteful decorations on the skirts and bodices of the everlasting crinoline, seemed endless in its originality. But the crinoline was not his only success: he caused the demise of the deep-brimmed bonnet, or *bavolet*, which had hidden women's faces for so long; he created ankle-length walking dresses, which were a sensation when they appeared in the summer of 1860. After many futile attempts to dislodge it from favour, Worth was the only couturier with influence enough to do away with the crinoline, introducing narrow skirts with trains as early as 1866.

Like Dior, Worth had great links with the French textile industry, particularly the silk manufacturers of Lyons, who found their industry expanding rapidly with the demand for luxurious fabrics to fill out the crinoline, and later, the bustle and train. This made it all the harder to banish the crinolines, and Worth had to effect the change he so desired, gradually. In 1866 he introduced a modified version, the princess dress, flat at the front, and gathered into a long drape at the back, and the *fourreau*, or sheath dress. By 1868–9, customers had become adjusted to a new, slimmer silhouette, and the crinoline disappeared altogether. The bustle, with its S-curving line to the figure, became the predominant mode.

By this time, Charles' two sons, Jean Philippe and Gaston, had entered the business. There was never any question that they would pursue other careers; although Jean Pierre had inherited his father's love of the art of painting, and would perhaps have followed this as a métier. (He studied for a time under Corot.) Gaston inherited his father's shrewd business sense, and thus the two brothers were compatibly equipped to carry on their father's enterprise. Worth's partner Bobergh, handsomely satisfied with the development of his investment, retired in 1870, and four years later, the two sons took up their official posts in the company. As we have seen in the preceding chapter, Gaston Worth formed the Chambre Syndicale de la Couture, and gradually their father retired from direct control of the business.

Worth suffered a vividly painful setback during the revolution and bloodshed of the Franco-Prussian War, during which time Paris was besieged, and the citizens set up the Commune of 1871. The safe, secure world of the Second Empire was burst, like a bright balloon. Charles Worth converted 7 rue de la Paix (now an expanded edifice housing 1200 workers), into a temporary hospital for the wounded. He found himself facing a very different world, at the conclusion of hostilities, one to which he never fully adjusted. All those people to whom he owed gratitude and affection had been swept away by the new Third Republic. The Empress Eugènie was living in exile, and the Princess de Metternich lived in Austria, although she continued to visit Paris as a private traveller, and never failed to order her clothes from her loyal friend, Charles Frederick. The imposing Palace of the Tuileries, to which she had brought Worth, and changed his fortunes, was now razed to the ground. Charles, out of his love for the past Empire, bought as much of the ruins as he could, and incorporated the relics in his grandiose villa at Suresnes. His home was as legendary as a palace in the *Arabian Nights*, with mirrors, chandeliers, tasselled cushions, ornate brocades and rich carpets.

But even the new Republicans, it seemed, were prepared to spend vast sums on their dress, and the house of Worth continued to prosper. Of his new customers, it is recorded in Edith Saunders' excellent and definitive biography, *The Age of Worth*, that Worth preferred the Americans, for they had 'faith, figures and francs'. By the 1890s the cosmopolitan world of Paris was once again as extravagantly elegant as it had been under Napoleon's rule. It is best typified by the tastes of Eleanora Duse, one of Jean Philippe Worth's best clients, and the lavish costumes of Sarah Bernhardt. Stage costume began to exert a great influence on couture, presaging the success of the second *grand couturier*, Paul Poiret.

Charles Frederick Worth died in 1895 on 10 March – a date for which he had always held a superstitious fear, ever since the death, on that date, of the Duc de Morny, one of the most powerful and influential statesmen of the Second Empire. Five years after his death the haute couture which Charles Worth had brought to its height of success, was perched on a new century, and a new era. How sad it is, that the *grand couturier* did not survive long enough to see that great exhibition at the *Exposition Universelle*, where the French haute couture, under its new umbrella of the Chambre Syndicale confidently and expectantly displayed its finest creations to a new world. For it was virtually a living testament to all that he had achieved. Other names were rising to join the house of Worth, but none gained the unique supremacy which Worth had enjoyed for five decades.

The turn of the century leads those who live through it to expect marvellous happenings, almost magical advances. Parisians seemed to have realised this expectation in the great 1900 *Exposition Universelle*, dominated by its splendid *Palais de l'Electricité*, drawing, it was reckoned, a million visitors to the French capital to explore a show which was called 'the corridor of the world'. In that 'corridor', exhibiting the newest advances in everything from science to art, the Paris haute couture for the first time presented a united display to show what high couture stood for.

In the *Palais des Fils, Tissus et Vêtements* was set aside a section named

A model by Doucet, one of the first couturiers, from a book entitled *Les Rois de la Mode*, 1901.

A model by Paquin. The dress shows the typical 'S-line' of the decade.

right
The pictures of Paul Poiret's designs are taken from a volume entitled *Les Choses de Poiret*, 1911. '*Celles de Demain*'. These designs by Poiret were added to the end of *Les Choses*, as suggestions for the future. They are among the earliest and prettiest couture designs for women's trousered outfits.

56

Georges Lepape

right
Mme Paquin founded her couture house in 1892 on the rue de la Paix, and was the only woman to be elected president of the Chambre, holding office from 1917–1919.

left top
'La Robe Rose' Toilette de Garden Party de Doucet from *Gazette du Bon Ton,* May 1913.

left bottom
A sketch for an afternoon dress from *Les Choses* captures many of Poiret's favourite motifs: close-fitting hats, silky flowing fabrics free from restriction, and luxurious textures. The designs for the cushion covers pre-figure fabric patterns of the 'twenties and 'thirties.

near left
A turbaned head, a typical Poiret look, from *Les Choses,* which was inspired by a visit the couturier made to the Victoria and Albert Museum, London. Here, Poiret became fascinated by the collection of costumes and fabrics, which added to his enthusiasm for eastern styles.

over page
Paul Poiret interpreted in the Cubist mood by the artist Lepape, from *Gazette du Bon Ton,* June 1914. The artist has evoked one of the first suggestions of the cloche, which swept fashion in the 'twenties.

Toilettes de la Collectivitée de la Couture. So, for the first time the million or so visitors who could never otherwise have been able to see, publicly, what was worn by the *haut monde,* were enabled to know what couture stood for. It would be fascinating to be able to read the minutes of the group of couturiers and hear the heated, even furious arguments as to whether this was not lowering the whole tone of couture, taking part with exhibits in other sections aimed at the generality, and, if co-operation was decided upon, then what form the exhibit should take. Marie, wife of the famous Worth, was certainly the first woman to model clothes on the human form, but to follow this up at a mass exhibition would never do. The models, it was finally agreed by the exhibiting houses, should be made in wax. Worth's sons, Jean and Gaston, excelled by showing, in the *Salon Lumineux,* their exhibit against a finely furnished drawing-room, just such a one as would be familiar to the distinguished clients of the house.

It was a revelation to the international crowd attending. The exhibiting houses included Paquin, Rouff, Cheruit, Callot Soeurs, with Redfern also, the English tailor who had introduced ladies' suits (walking costumes was the current phrase) from his London to his Paris salon. Drécoll was probably the best known couturier, first of the *Fin de Siècle* period, then of the opening twentieth century, now known as *La Belle Époque*, and was responsible for the founding of other houses. A Belgian by birth, he had as head designer a Viennese, Mme de Wagner, whose daughter was Mme Maggy Rouff. She in turn trained Mme Paquin, who became the dominant partner in a famous husband-and-wife couture house.

The exhibit by the couture must have startled their distinguished moneyed customers. The desire to be *à la mode* was dominant in their lives of total leisure, ones in which they expected also total privacy. In a world where no lady could bear the thought of her toilette being duplicated (just think of two *élégantes* passing one another on the grand stairway of the Opera, one dressed just like the other) most couturiers had to declare, hand on heart, that the design chosen was entirely exclusive. All the same, the idea of Paris couture as 'an ideas factory', as it is often described in recent years, grew from the time when the great Worth designed intensely romantic clothes for the Empress Eugénie, clothes which every woman dreamt of possessing. Then, once the court ladies and other élégantes had had delivery of the orders, foreign buyers would appear, far more welcome than the provincial ones seeking admission, because of that problem of 'exclusivity'. But Charles Frederick Worth had never forgotten the frightening years of the mid-century when foreigners and tourists deserted the capital, and everyone economised until it seemed that there could be no future for French fashion. With the advent of foreign buyers there would be prosperity also for the great textile trade of France which had supported him, and to which he in turn had magnificently responded, a partnership which, at least until the rise of ready-to-wear clothes, has endured to the profit of both the couture and the textile world.

The bourgeoisie, even the *bourgeoisie aisée*, the really well-off, did not aspire to being dressed by top couturiers but were able to find 'little women' to make up for them, some of whom, in Paris, had daughters among the shockingly underpaid seamstresses in the great workrooms. As we have seen in the previous chapter, these girls could, undetected, bring out the toile of a model as they left work late in the evening, returning it, unseen, the next morning.

Times were indeed changing. Monsieur Paquin (no first names were ever used in the house), one of those taking part in the *Exposition Universelle* exhibit of 1900, was around that date none too happy at the way some of his clients were behaving. Ladies of fashion, dressed in the enticing richness of fabric and silhouette (that of the so-called S-bend, 'Silhouette Serpentine', or in English preferably called 'the Swan-bend', emphasising the backward curve of the behind – although it would have been considered indelicate to mention the *derrière*, however much emphasised – and the forward curve of the bosom). The waist was minimised

A particularly fine photographic study of the *salon de vente* at the house of Paquin, reproduced in a book entitled *Les Créateurs de la Mode* in 1910.

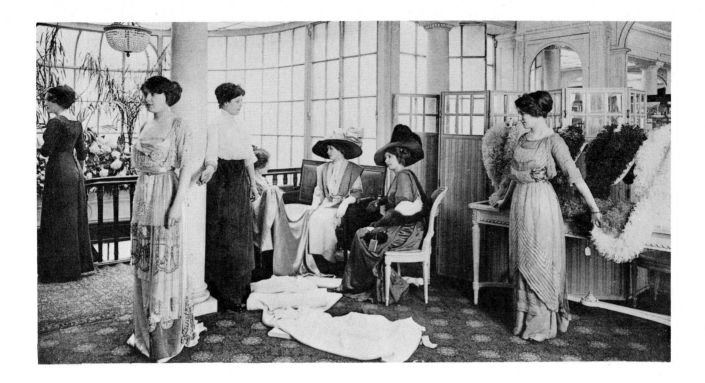

Another study from *Les Créateurs de la Mode,* showing a group of house mannequins. The girl's figure on the far right is classic of the era, with her graceful neck and full chested, curving figure.

by the fiercely boned corsetry. These static figures Monsieur Paquin knew and appreciated, their trained, flounced skirts trailing on the ground or held by a gloved hand to show the elaborate dust ruffles, a parasol or giant muff in the other hand, stiff net and lace collars supporting a high-held chin: 'Bright fowls about to take wing' he might quote about them, although the weight of fabric and corsetry would surely have made that

impossible. But, he stated bitterly, now his clients turned into *ces femmes sportives*, tennis playing, skating, addicted to that menace, automobilism. How, he asked, was he to dress such strange creatures when birds of fashion they were not?

He was not alone in noting change. With the first Metro line, horse carriages gave way to the *promenade en automobile* for which his clients dressed (could you believe it?) in dustcoats, flat caps and veilings. But the Paris crowds still waited on the pavements just to catch a glimpse, as they passed from restaurant doorway to carriage, of famous, superlatively dressed courtesans, squired by dandies, also highly regarded customers of the couturiers although now being somewhat ousted by noted actresses and dancers. La Belle Otero and Cleo de Merode bridged the transition, Cleo de Merode, indeed, dancing at the *Exposition*. The Avenue de Bois now held plenty of high and squarely built automobiles, open in front, the driver sitting high, pedestrians running to avoid them as they had run before the clatter-clatter of horses hooves a little while back.

One other who saw how things were changing was Gaston Worth, younger son of the great couturier. He was at odds with his elder brother, Jean, who wished the house of Worth to remain as it had been in his father's day, serving great ladies, even if they had got past wearing new fashions, and some of them could no longer pay their bills. Regarding this as an outdated attitude to be combated, Gaston engaged a young designer, one Paul Poiret, who had worked for Doucet. He was briefed by Gaston, as Edith Saunders describes in her already mentioned book. Things are, he pointed out, changing; ceremonial dress was less and less worn. 'Indeed, princesses occasionally take the bus when they go out, and they walk on foot in the streets, like the rest of us.' So what Gaston required of

Afternoon frocks designed by the house of Worth in 1914: an early fashion-plate from *Gazette du Bon Ton,* which was amongst the first and finest of the women's magazines.

Jacques Worth, son of Gaston, Charles Worth's elder son, in turn became president of the Chambre Syndicale from 1927–30, and founded the Chambre's schools in 1930.

'*Quatre à Sept ou Une Heure de Musique*': A fashion-plate by Pierre Brissard dated 1913, from *Bon Ton*.

Poiret were designs 'for ordinary women, simple and practical', and, if necessary he would devise a '*rayon de pommes de terre frites*' in which to sell them, or, as we would say, a fish-and-chips boutique. Poiret, much as he admired Gaston's taste (and the ceremonial clothes he made innumerable English peeresses for the Coronation of Edward VII were magnificent) could not stand between two warring brothers, and left. Only a very few years were to pass before he opened his own establishment and soon revolutionised fashion.

While the ladies were still corseted to the great danger of health, while the amount of underpinnings, boned, stitched, shaped to hold the unnatural form that was fashionable, continued past the middle of the first decade of the new century, there was one sign of a softening. That was the *peignoir*, the *déshabillé* (the teagown in English) into which fashionables changed in the hour or two before they started on their long and elaborate ritual of dressing for dinner. Among the exhibits at that same 1900 exhibition in Paris, the largest crowds gathered to see, in the Palais des Vêtements, deliciously light and seductive negligées which, it was reported, 'fired the imagination', delicate in silk-crêpe or fine satin, much embroidered: in our current phraseology they would be called sexy. And, strange in that period, they even announced in the exhibition the names of aristocratic ladies who had ordered them.

Among the loveliest examples made between 1900 and 1906 were those of that marvellous couturière-to-be, Mme Madeleine Vionnet, whose history is related in the following chapter. I have seen a sketch of one of her 1901 models 'from Mme Vionnet's Lingerie Collection', with deep vee-drapery down the back, leaving nape and neck bare, which must have been a marvellous relief after all-day wear of a high-boned collar, and fiercely boned corset. Here was what was to become the greatest of all the Paris couturières (Mme Paquin, Mlle Chanel, and Mme Jeanne Lanvin not excepted) she who, in the 'twenties, made dresses on the bias of the soft fabrics, joining seams, yokes or what was necessary with faggoting (*à jour*) work, for even greater flexibility. Célia Bertin, that admirable reporter, in her book *Paris à la Mode* saw her rapt attention when she attended a Jacques Griffe collection in Paris in 1954, Mme Vionnet being then 79 (she had her 97th birthday in 1972), and asked to interview her. 'Remember', she told Célia Bertin, 'it was I who got rid of corsets; in 1907, while I was at Doucet, I discarded corsets,' and she induced the mannequins to show with bare feet and sandals, 'and in their own skins'. She started for herself around 1912 in the rue de Rivoli but the 1914 war ended her venture. It was after the war that Galeries Lafayette offered her the lease of a mansion in the avenue Montaigne, a house which she made famous.

Modernity might be coming on apace (Isadora Duncan's dancing aided the bare feet and show-of-body movement) but the patrons of the couturiers still expected an almost unbelievable amount of the finest handwork in all that they wore, work painfully trying to the eyes of the

The workrooms at the house of Charles Worth, in the late 'twenties.

workroom hands so ill paid (there had been the first workroom strike in 1901, but it seemed to accomplish nothing). 'One of the smartest garments of the *belle époque*', says Doris Langley-Moore, 'was the blouse', a triumph of patient eyesight-destroying labour in the workrooms, pintucking, piecing together, inserting lace and ribbons, faggoting, all forms of 'niggling intricacies'. The privileges of wealth were taken for granted. As said Osbert Sitwell, knowing Paris almost as well as London, 'they lived then as if this world would last for ever . . . enormous social changes were hidden by the still shadowy outline of the new century'.

It was again Osbert Sitwell, in *The Scarlet Tree*, who said that the corsetière rather than 'the costume designer' was the fashion dictator of that time, and you have only to see women represented on the racecourse, in the ballroom, at a soirée or in their internal combustion engines, 'steaming and vibrating' on fashionable streets, to realise that those impossibly narrow waistlines, as it would appear, are due to the corsets which they wear. One time in 1959 when I, as fashion editor for the London newspaper *The Observer*, was accompanying Jane Bown, our talented photographer, looking for a suitable outdoor background in Montmartre,

The staff kitchens at the same establishment.

accompanied by two lovely models, it began to rain. From an upstairs window a delightful old lady called to us to come up to her husband's studio, to take shelter (he was a member of the *Académie*, it appeared). Whose clothes were the girls modelling? she asked, and was enchanted to hear that two of the outfits were from Lanvin. Why, think of it, she herself had been a mannequin at Lanvin in 1906 and 1907. Then, all day, the mannequins had to wear straight-fronted corsets boned to hold in the waist and to tilt the figure into the 'kangaroo form', as Lanvin's American clients called the S-form, puffing out the bosom and the derrière while keeping the front rigidly flat. Such corsets, she said, started high under the breasts and went down to the knees, so that it was not possible for the girls to sit, only to lean when fatigued. Such 'contraptions' had to be kept on until the last client left the rue du Faubourg St-Honoré (the same that the house of Lanvin still occupies, run by the same Lanvin family); only when that last customer disappeared, at however late an hour, could they relax, she told us.

Artists in France have always taken the Parisian art of couture seriously. In the early days of the first decade Renoir even helped his dressmaker friends to 'colour up' their ranges of fabrics, advising on what went with what. Pablo Picasso's *Aux Courses* perfectly mirrored the *mannequins de ville* with their vast feathered hats, puffed-out coiffures and silhouettes, as, earlier, Claude Monet and Degas had shown their knowledge of dress movements and trends. Yet I cannot trace any movement of protest against such unnatural figures, covered up until evening from chin to feet. But did anybody, discussing *Les Fauves*, the 'wild ones' leading a movement of liberation in painting, brilliant, enthusiastic, generally denounced, realise that Rouault, Matisse, Derain, Vlaminck, Utrillo and Van Dongen (although he was also a painter of ladies *à la mode*) were leading a whole new way of thinking and acting which would sweep away the static female silhouette of the first half of this early decade, leading on to an appreciation of brilliant colours, to a new form of illustrating fashion? It was all leading, in fact, to 1907, the year when all that had been admired was overthrown in favour of a new interpretation of what was praiseworthy.

Already between 1903 and 1904, when Poiret was preparing the opening of his own house in the rue Auber, with some 5000 francs in capital and eight employees, he who was later to say 'I freed the bosom, shackled the legs, but gave liberty to the body', that same Poiret was planning, even that early, a collection based on the loosening of the line. The couturiers did not know what they would, within a few years, have to contend with. Drécoll certainly, by 1905, showed a more upright silhouette, as in afternoon dresses with the high collar but deep vee-shaped net yokes, outlined with lace frillings, foreshadowing the vee-neckline to come. Such a dress, perhaps in striped surah, was worn for summer with an outsized hat piled high with ostrich feathers. There were pear-shaped pearls in the ears; hands and wrists were gloved in white kid (never worn more than once)

Paul Poiret (second from left in the top row) surrounded by his mannequins on the feast-day of the couturiers – the fête of Ste Catherine. A young unmarried girl of 25 covers her hair with a hat and takes on the persona of the saint herself for the day, on behalf of all the girls working in the atelier. (See centre of top row.) The girls were called the '*Catherinettes*'.

lightly holding a parasol. Nor was noted couturier Doeuillet aware of changes to come, nor yet the milliners (Reboux was the most famous) providing hats lavish with ospreys, aigrettes or whole birds, although the writer Colette was to make a spirited protest against the intense cruelty involved in obtaining these 'ornaments'. If there was a revolution afoot, the ladies, who were just beginning to learn to drive a fashionable motor car (perhaps a De Dion Bouton), felt that this act was revolution enough, even if 'afoot' was not the *mot juste*.

Even the young women felt the strong influence of Mme Sarah Bernhardt, never thinking that soon she would be considered demodée. She was dressed by Worth and by the English Monsieur Fred, and wore the enormous feather-laden hats of the 1906–8 period, with caped mantles ('*de type Carrick*' for summer), producing a general effect of bulk soon to be considered clumsy in silhouette, although she sometimes wore a collar which stood up behind the head, in the Medici style, which had yet to be adopted. They went to her dietician, Dr Caissarato, and foreswore, like her, sweets, tea, coffee, took baths of rosemary and milk (hyssop and bran if so much milk was not available), and coated their faces with alum, ground almonds and rosewater, which her doctor said would prevent wrinkles. And if it was not Bernhardt whom they were imitating it was Duse or Réjane. Yet just one thing made a connecting link with the cycle

to come: Sarah Bernhardt was one of the first to appreciate Art Nouveau, shown at the 1900 *Exposition* but there making only a slight impact. It was 1908 when it swept into popularity, when everything that was straight appeared curved, but well before that Mme Bernhardt was wearing snake bracelets, snakes whose large, flat heads decorated the back of the hand, delicate chains forming finger rings to keep the design in place. Today such a piece of jewellery, set with gleaming stones, would be considered avant-garde.

Vionnet or Poiret – which was the initial innovator who rejected those tight-laced corsets and the high-boned collars by 1907? It was certainly Poiret's campaign against corsets which disturbed financial interests to the greater extent, the Paris Chamber of Commerce sending a deputation asking him to reverse this trend. Trade would be greatly hit, they said, and, when he appeared indifferent to this thought, they added that, anyhow, the trend 'was immoral'. Certainly he must have been blessed by the younger *élégantes* when, without all the under-boning, underpinnings and stiffening previously considered essential, the weight of a dress was reduced from 8 lb to as little as 2 lb.

That there was a revolution in taste became apparent through the birth in 1908 of a new magazine, the *Gazette Du Bon Ton*, appearing quarterly, its declared purpose 'to mirror a different climate of taste'. It was edited by M. Lucien Vogel, with his wife Cosette and her brother, Michel de Brunhoff, the men each in turn later on to become editors of the French edition of *Vogue* magazine. The fashion reporting of *Bon Ton* was as accurate as it was elegant; its team of artists drew in a delightful way which had never been seen before, their black and white pages delicately coloured by hand under their directions. The team included Georges Lepape, Bernard Boutet de Monvel, both Jacques and Pierre Brissaud, Georges Barbier, André Marty and Charles Martin. They reported what the fashion writers and they themselves approved at Cheruit, Doucet, Paquin, Vionnet, above all at Paul Poiret, forming a marvellously talented team visually reflecting the movements of Paris couture in a way that was as delicate as it was informative. Poiret gave a grand garden party in their honour, and it was only war in 1914 which closed the issues of the paper, although it was briefly revived when that war ended, and continued its influence in the 1920s.

More or less simultaneously, photography received a new lease of life. Hitherto it had been singularly uninspiring as fashion reporting, with the one outstanding exception, through this first decade and on, of the work of the Baron de Meyer; Sir Cecil Beaton describes him (and as a writer-artist-photographer he should know) as 'the first of the editor-photographers'. Only photographing what suited his conception of the photographer's art, he chose clothes with fine form, lit them to perfection, and photographed them with a soft focus camera in a way hitherto unknown to fashion magazines. Around 1910 he was followed by the American Edward Steichen, associated through his life with *Vogue*, again using soft focus and diffused lighting, but obtaining sharper, clearer reports.

That was the craft side of the revolution in fashion. The true basis for an explosion of changed taste, which went off like a mine, was the arrival in Paris in 1909 of the Diaghilev Ballet. In advance it had been very coolly welcomed, largely on the grounds that it contained male dancers: traditionally the ballet was for girl dancers. Accordingly, the company could only obtain the comparatively small Théâtre du Châtelet, but when the virile, spectacular Polovtsian Dances set in Borodin's opera, *Prince Igor* (with Chaliapin singing the principal part) burst upon the eyes and ears of the audience, they went wild with excitement. The applause seemed

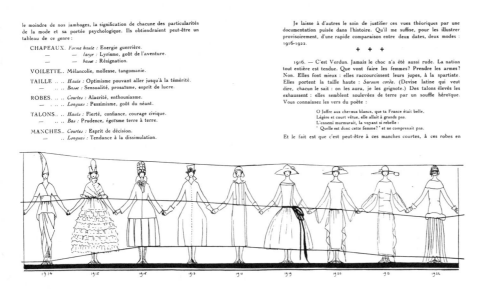

le moindre de nos jambages, la signification de chacune des particularités de la mode et sa portée psychologique. Ils obtiendraient peut-être un tableau de ce genre :

CHAPEAUX. *Forme haute* : Energie guerrière.
— — *large* : Lyrisme, goût de l'aventure.
— — *basse* : Résignation.

VOILETTE.. Mélancolie, mollesse, tangomanie.

TAILLE .. .. *Haute* : Optimisme pouvant aller jusqu'à la témérité.
— .. .. *Basse* : Sensualité, prosaïsme, esprit de lucre.

ROBES. .. .. *Courtes* : Alacrité, enthousiasme.
— . .. .. *Longues* : Pessimisme, goût du néant.

TALONS.. .. *Hauts* : Fierté, confiance, courage civique.
— .. .. *Bas* : Prudence, égoïsme terre à terre.

MANCHES.. *Courtes* : Esprit de décision.
— .. *Longues* : Tendance à la dissimulation.

Je laisse à d'autres le soin de justifier ces vues théoriques par une documentation puisée dans l'histoire. Qu'il me suffise, pour les illustrer provisoirement, d'une rapide comparaison entre deux dates, deux modes : 1916-1922.

✦ ✦ ✦

1916. — C'est Verdun. Jamais le choc n'a été aussi rude. La nation tout entière est tendue. Que vont faire les femmes? Prendre les armes? Non. Elles font mieux : elles raccourcissent leurs jupes, à la spartiate. Elles portent la taille haute : *Sursum corda*. (Devise latine qui veut dire, chacun le sait : on les aura, je les grignote.) Des talons élevés les exhaussent : elles semblent soulevées de terre par un souffle héroïque. Vous connaissez les vers du poète :

O Joffre aux cheveux blancs, que ta France était belle,
Légère et court vêtue, elle allait à grands pas.
L'ennemi murmurait, la voyant si rebelle :
' Quelle est donc cette femme?' et ne comprenait pas.

Et le fait est que c'est peut-être à ces manches courtes, à ces robes en

The development of the hemline up to the early 'twenties, illustrated in *Gazette du Bon Ton* in 1923.

never to stop, for it was not only the troop of spectacularly leaping warriors whom they saw dancing but, in an introductory single act, Nijinsky, never yet seen outside Russia, performing his marvellous *élévations*, teamed up with Karsavina, forming a combination of talent such as Paris had not witnessed.

The ballet was the talk of Paris. Wherever the dandies congregated, as at the Jockey Club, or the mondaines in the salons at soirées, or at Armenonville after the races, there was but one subject – Have you seen the Russian dancers? They might refer to Melba's voice, to the writings of Gide, Daudet, Maupassant, but the ballet was the current subject for discussion. What changed couture, later house decoration also, was not the music nor yet the sensational *élévations* of an unknown dancer, but the colour which Bakst put into the background of those ballets to which he contributed décor, above all in *Schéhérezade*, that fantastic choreographic drama, sexier by far than anything now produced on the stage, which, with Nijinsky as the black slave, was seen in Paris in June 1910, followed by the hardly less sensationally splendid *Thamar* with décor and libretto by Bakst.

No wonder that fashion emerged from the Victorianism (as the English called it) of the Belle Époque. Poiret always declared that he owed nothing to Bakst, having created his own brilliant and colourful new style before he ever saw the Diaghilev ballet, and certainly he ordered the richest colours, reds dominating, for the fêtes which he gave in his gardens, to which he invited clients. The younger ones came, their curiosity winning the day (well, the night), even though among themselves they said that he was 'acting out of his class'. But would he have had such quick success if his colour sense had not coincided with that of Bakst and others working with the ballet? He always declared that he had already advocated colours 'like a blow in the face' – brilliant reds in many tones, violet, gold, greens and blues, and dismissed the then fashionable 'swooning, washed-out blues', the 'suppressed pinks', 'morbid mauves'. And when after 1910, the English court circle was recovering from a year of black, mourning the death of Edward VII (even Ascot had been black), the stuffiness of first-decade corseted fashions had disappeared, and the well-dressed were wearing supple soft fabrics, such as charmeuse, crêpe georgette, or chiffon, to form a slender silhouette, often with an equally slender overskirt slashed and draped. It was inspired mainly by the lovely Lily Elsie's stage dresses, made for her by Lucile, Lady Duff-Gordon, London's leading couturière.

One of Paul Poiret's mannequins, Spineky, in a dress designed for her trip to the USA in 1920.

Poiret, following the example of Rose Bertin in her far-off days (though she with doll models and he with living mannequins) toured from capital to capital to show the new lines and colourings, taking orders and measurements from the Russian and Austrian courts in particular: such wealthy ladies, Americans included, as could not get to Europe at any particular season had sketches sent from which they could order. In his fashion tours he took with him eight mannequins, all beautiful, and, to prevent gentlemen in the various capitals from abducting his young Parisiennes, he dressed them alike in blue serge uniforms complete with belts, buckles, and epaulettes, even though they were skirted. This I know from personal experience, although of many years later, well after World War I, because my first fashion assignment after joining the *Daily Mirror* (London) reporting staff was to get an appointment with the famous M. Poiret, briefly in London en route for a round of other capitals, in order to get his views on fashion. I really knew very little about the movements of fashion. I had only sketchy schoolgirl French and he not a word of English.

He invited me to lunch with him in the restaurant of the Carlton Hotel, even more chic than the Ritz, and when I joined him in the lounge he and I marched in to a prominent table, at the head of four mannequins, by this era in uniforms of green and gold complete with peaked caps. While he studied the menu I turned to speak to the girl next to me. He put a hand on my arm, warningly: 'No, mademoiselle', he said, 'do not speak to the girls; they are not there.' Quite definitely, they were, but not socially, he was indicating. So I never forgot his model girls. And the fashion report? I suddenly remembered he was not only a fashion king but the president of *Le Cent*, the hundred best eaters of France. So I asked his advice about an inexpensive tour my husband and I proposed to make to the Midi, and got invaluable advice on where to eat and drink. 'If you see a host of bicycles piled up outside what may seem a rather miserable wayside café, go there: they will belong to workmen and nobody cares more about good food than the French working man.' So what I wrote was a column on 'Paul Poiret adores Food', and my news editor infinitely preferred it to a fashion report.

By that time, with a war and its aftermath lying between, few remembered with what abhorrence M. Poiret had been, earlier, regarded in England, second only to public condemnation of Mrs Asquith, wife of the British Prime Minister. Mrs Asquith, visiting both the Diaghilev ballet at its opening season in Paris (it did not come to London until 1911) and the Paris couture, went to see Poiret's collection. This proved a visit which passed not only into fashion but into political history. Enthusiastic about the new colour trend in particular, she invited the designer to come over with his collection not merely to London, but to show it in the British Prime Minister's official residence, 10 Downing Street, henceforward, not surprisingly, to be renamed 'Gowning Street' by the press. The Prime Minister looked in on the party, and was reported as 'looking grave', as well he might. It was a time of trade crisis for the British textile and dress trades. Tariff reform was under debate. It is on record that 160 newspapers and magazines expressed outraged anger at Mrs Asquith's ill-timed, ill-regarded fashion parade. Bleriot's cross-channel flight of 1909 had been said to link the two countries: Mrs Asquith's passion for Poiret's fashion designs made a rift between them.

When the excitement over Poiret's lines and colour schemes (considered most chic when worn in a black-painted room) had somewhat died down, fashion was, in fact, left with slender women in place of the more than opulently curved silhouettes of the recently past years. Once again, to quote Osbert Sitwell, that observant eye on the social scene, 'the thin woman had hardly aspired to be *femme fatale* until Leon Bakst introduced her as a paragon into Western Europe'.

It was not just Bakst and Poiret preferring a slender silhouette, topped by a now even wider and ever wider hat, to prevent the silhouette being too much like an exclamation mark: there was also more open-air life. It was a peak year for 'the lady motorist', her hair, high-piled on her horsehair padding, covered for the road, in the open cars of the day, with a large, flat cap that was wrapped in a long-ended scarf (and here we remember the manner of Isadora Duncan's death along the Riviera coast road, due to just such a floating scarf). By 1909 or 1910 there were, too, the fashionable flying machines. There was not only at that time a flowering of the arts but also the beginning of an urge towards sport such as had been familiar to the English for some decades past, but that had not greatly appealed to the type of Parisienne preoccupied with the choosing of couture clothes, their accessories, hats and shoes, an occupation that, until now, left her singularly little time in daylight to think about, far less to take part in,

Valentine Gross, an artist more famous for her scenes from the ballet, including rare sketches of the Russian Nijinsky in Paris, also worked for the *Gazette du Bon Ton,* and continued their development of depicting fashion in realistic settings. This plate, entitled *'Il Pleut Encore'* showed suits made by Paquin, Lanvin, Doeuillet, and a topcoat by Paquin.

'*Rugby*' – a model by Redfern, 1914.

Georges Barbier was one of the many artistic talents who lent their skills to fashion work. The designs were printed in the *Bon Ton* between 1913 and 1915.

'*Le Cyprès et La Rose*' designed by Doeuillet.

sport. One recalls the 'fabulous' Mrs Philip Lydig, marrying her second husband in 1902, travelling between New York and Paris in the first fourteen years of the century and leaving to the Museum of Costume Art, in New York, her hundred coats of hand-cut velvet, damask and lace, her hundred-and-fifty pairs of shoes, each made for her by the curator of the historical shoe collection at the Cluny Museum; her fifty lace and hand embroidered blouses; also the Russian leather trunks, lined with white velvet, in which her clothes travelled, the shoes compartmented in three such trunks.

We can, even if we only enjoy looking at clothes of the past, sympathise with Marcel Proust, when, writing his great work, *À la recherche du temps perdu*, he sought from his older women friends details about what his Princesse de Guermantes, and other characters, would have worn at a certain date and for certain occasions, only to find that women neither kept old models, nor recollected details about them. He reproached them, because he wanted to touch the actual texture of the fabrics, to see the exact colours, details also of their make. Did they not even keep hats of, say, a dozen years back? To his deep disappointment, no, they did not. Photographs he had collected in great numbers, but they did not provide exactitudes, and Proust was nothing if he was not accurate.

In 1951 I visited, as always with pleasure, the Galerie Charpentier in the rue du Faubourg St-Honoré, to view their current exhibition, *Deux Siècles d'Élégances: 1715–1915*, a collection of clothes which aimed at 'making the past the present', as wrote Louise de Vilmorin in a foreword to the catalogue. The exhibition was on behalf of the *Union Française des Arts du Costume*, founded two years earlier to include the *Société de l'Histoire du Costume*, and aiming to found a permanent Museum of French Dress, essential to Paris, capital city of elegance. Tomorrow, said the Galerie, this dream must become a fact, although they were not to know just when 'tomorrow' would come.

Led by Mme E. de Galea, who lent her wonderfully rich collection, dating from the 18th century onwards, and supported by the Vicomtesse de Bonneval, whose ancient family had for a very long time kept examples of outstanding interest, the *Union* could start with at least a thousand items on show, although, obviously, all could not be shown in the Galerie at one time. There were contributions from the couture and from artists working in the fashion field. Mme Madeleine Vionnet contributed models. So did M. Barbas, of Patou; M. Drian, the artist; members of the family of the famous painter, Boudin, and also most of the *Gazette du Bon Ton*'s team of artists. Mme Paul Poiret added her share, and the collection was backed by the heads of the State Library, the State archives, and the Musée Carnavalet.

Worth was represented by a 1900 model: another of that date was by Valentin. Maggy Rouff, Paquin and Marcaine Lacroix had 1905 models on show; Paul Poiret 1908 and 1911; Callot Soeurs a 1914 dress, Jacques Doucet one of 1915, together with a teagown in pleated chiffon created for Mme Sarah Bernhardt. Hats shown included one (by Esther Meyer) made for Cleo de Merode. As well we saw the original Paul Iribe *Album: Robes de Paul Poiret*, dated 1908, together with invitations to two of Poiret's collections, held at 37 rue Pasquier, as well as one to view his designs for children's clothes, in the same year. (By 1912 invitations from the Maison Poiret were issued from 26 avenue d'Antin.) But what was shown represented far more the Belle Epoque than the Poiret–Bakst–Diaghilev outburst of colour and orientalism, and to my best recollection, totally ignored the 'simple young girl' silhouette which replaced both in the years which took viewers up to the date which the exhibition had set as the last with which they dealt – 1915, and then onwards. This was to be the silhouette of women who were discarding the static life of the century's opening years, even the dramatic picture inspired by the Russian ballet, and were year by year becoming livelier, more active and certainly slimmer. The nearest that I can remember was a Doucet highwaisted, hobble-skirted satin dress of 1915.

Poiret, who unfortunately for him lived to be old and very poor, in writing about his epoch, bitterly regretted 'the lost world of gallantry', by which he meant the apotheosis of the famous cocottes whom he had dressed, as also that of the professional beauties, although mainly his thought rested with the splendid courtesans: 'They were the goddesses of fashion – and what have you now? Why, *the movies*.' You can imagine the scorn in his words. He attributed what was to him the sad decline in luxurious fashion to two causes, the first income tax, the second dieting. It was that 'thin woman' noted by Osbert Sitwell around the end of the first decade of whom Poiret thought, and she had more the look of a girl than of a woman, whereas nobody in the world of couture had yet bothered about girls, what they wished to wear, or how they looked. The couturiers dismissed them until they should have developed their bosoms and acquired some sense of attitude. Now, in the last peaceful years of the century's opening, bosoms were unimportant. The princess form dress that had appeared around 1909–10 young women considered 'old hat' because, although beltless, it emphasised the hips in a manner which their mothers and aunts admired but which they did not. But already Doucet, never one to be slow to see what was in the air, had produced slender dance dresses with lifted waistlines, merely tied by ribbon under the bosom. Chiffon was the accepted fabric with the bodice softly crossing over. Here was something typifying youth and simplicity. The 'Dorothy bag' now became an essential, forerunner of all the handbags to come, dangling from finger or wrist, because the narrowness of skirts did not allow of the pockets that had always been so hidden. In winter the Dorothy bag vanished, when hands were hidden in huge, flat muffs into whose linings purse-like pockets could be built.

Girls very soon became young marrieds with incomes to spend and it would be unwise for couture to ignore them for long. The girls' mothers, and their elders generally, became envious of the admired look of youth,

'Le Jeu des Graces', an afternoon frock by Paquin.

A fashion drawing by Sem, one of the earliest artists in the field, executed in sepia ink and wash. The tight skirt and the pillow muff are characteristic of the period. (1913.)

hence the dieting which Poiret, in retrospect, so greatly deplored. The couturiers' collections began to dovetail the continuation of what 'adults' were used to expecting with softly designed models for youth. What triggered off the great popularity of the 'thin woman' outline was a passion for a new form of dancing. Girls had always attended dancing classes to learn the waltz, polka, lancers and quadrilles, recently also the cakewalk, a negro dance imported from America. None led up to a new type of dance, the tango, which, from 1911 well into the war years dominated the dance floors, started up nightclubs, made restaurants and hotels put on *thés dansants*, to enlarge the dancing hours well beyond dinner and supper dancing. With the tango, of which the steps and postures had to be carefully learnt to produce a pseudo-South American effect, there was also the maxixe, less popular, more difficult to learn, but of which dance floor addicts were expected to have a good knowledge. Then, seemingly in no time at all, there followed (without displacing the tango) dances from America. Syncopation was there, in the shape of the Bunny Hug, the Turkey Trot, to the tune of Alexander's Ragtime Band, to be followed in due course, although not until war years, by the foxtrot. Where sultry-eyed, Argentinian 'tango lizards' had dominated dance floors, now smart young Americans were the sought-after partners, and dancers aimed to look as like as possible to the trans-Atlantic married couple, Mr and Mrs Vernon Castle, whose performance on the ballroom floors was enthusiastically applauded.

For these ballroom floors the girls wore dresses of charmeuse, chiffon and crêpe satin, with narrow, lightly draped skirts below brief, side-wrapped bodices (fur edged in winter), their feet moving to the rhythm in silk stockings, wearing what were, even in syncopation days, called 'tango-laced' shoes. Narrow skirts they certainly were, for by 1911 the hobble skirt was all the rage. 'Every woman', wrote James Laver, 'was determined to look like a slave in an oriental harem', thanks to the excitement over the ballet *Schéhérezade*. Indeed, even harem skirts had been worn in the open by some avant-garde fashion followers, who, however, found themselves being shouted at for their 'immodesty', and chased off the streets. Although Drécoll's harem-skirted dance dress was accepted as definitely chic, yet the harem mode did not generally catch on, although it was revived in 1914. The hobble skirt, on the contrary, gained general acceptance, impractical as it was (in London even suffragettes fighting the police wore it), narrowing down to the feet so that walking was difficult, stepping upstairs a problem, to dance the tango in one impossible: nevertheless it succeeded. In a short time it was modified, the front partially slit up, the skirt lightly draped so that more of the 'tango-laced' legs showed than had so far been considered proper.

In 1912, Poiret designed the costume, in Paris, for performances of *Le Minaret*, using the draped-open version of the hobble skirt but, over it, Persian tunics from waist to knees, including tiers of pleated tunics. With such skirts went some bolero-style jackets of which the neckline opened in a small vee over the bare neck, the collar rising, rather like a Medici style, only at the back of the head. Immediately two things followed. Tunics over hobble (or at least very narrowly-cut) underskirts became the rage, a very quick fashion reaction. In addition there appeared the first of the vee necklines, tentative initially because they caused an outcry that sounds out of all proportion to the change, which so much better suited the simpler, more slender silhouette, the general effect of lines adopted, not excluding the widening over-tunics. 'Outrageous', 'immodest', were some of the epithets thrown at wearers who so greatly preferred the slightly open neckline to the high-boned collars that had ruled for so long.

It seems odd that when evening dresses for decades had been worn so low that they might well have been declared immodest, this slight vee opening should meet an opposition that lasted, among older people, for very many years. Some seven years later I can remember visiting my grandmother in a simple vee-necked navy serge dress and being met by her horrified cry, 'My dear child, surely you do not go out *naked* like that?', at which she fetched a large white silk square and draped it over the offending vee, called in Paris *la decolletée du jour*.

The result of the new neckline cut was that all but the young stood in need of beauty treatment for the neck, closely covered as it had been with stiffly boned collars; even the low-cut bodices so long approved for evening had not left the neck free, the 'dogcollar' necklace that was fashionable acting on the skin in the same way as did the boned collars for day. Advice columns in women's magazines now pointed out how ruinous to contour and texture of the neck had been those tight, high-confining collars. Women were urged to 'scrub the neck with hot water and best Castille soap, then use iced water to tone and tighten the skin. Next, after patting in skinfood, bandage it with cotton gauze soaked in lavender cologne overnight'.

The minaret tunics set over tremendously narrow underskirts were not the only tunic form seen. By 1913, there were egg-shaped and also ballooning forms, some dropping down and out from sloping shoulders a line that in itself formed a complete fashion innovation. Others ballooned out from a narrow waistline. Lepape drew such for the *Gazette du Bon Ton*, including even a fur coat in egg shape, sleeves set in very low down, the skirt below exceedingly narrow, decorated with buttons down the front. This curiously egg-shaped figure had discarded the big hats (they were going out, anyway), in favour of a head-hugging cap, and held both hands in a huge, egg-shaped fur muff. By the summer of 1913 the egg-shaped tunic or coat turned into a silk jacket, no less ovoid: the ladies said that there seemed to be anarchy about.

It was, of course, war that was in the air, though the young, while their tangoing, roller skating and other forms of fun went on (plus hard and long daily work for the mass of the population), discounted all the fears of war and the tensions that occupied more serious minds. It was noticeable how heads of state went from country to country, exchanging formal visits, all calling, in particular, on the French President at the Elysée Palace. But this, surely, was to ensure peace, not to discuss war, although everyone admitted that one could not wholly trust the peaceful intentions of the Kaiser. Street and student demonstrations in the cause of peace took place in Paris with banner bearings and shoutings of slogans (times have not much changed in half a century and more), but were dismissed as 'more of their troublemaking, if not for one cause, then for another'. The causes which provoked street demonstrations were two: poverty, allied to shocking housing conditions, for one, the fear of war for the other. It is interesting to note a curious connection between dress in this still Poiret-dominated period and the war to come. Artists, it has been noted, regarded dress designing at its best as an art instead of the industry that it was, so much later on, to become. The artist Erté, whose name is in fact Romain de Tirtoff, a Russian from St Petersburg, was one of Paul Poiret's designing team: in 1971 he was still designing, his lines carried out by Loris Azzaro in Paris, and still exhibiting in many capitals, as at the Grosvenor Gallery in Mayfair, London. But in 1913, Erté, on behalf of the house of Poiret, designed costumes for Mata Hari, one of their customers, a name soon to become notorious in the long history of war and spying.

In the dress world the news was that the chemise frock introduced by Mme Lanvin was 'sweeping the board'. The chemise was a simple, unfitted dress (frock was the current word for dress) that hung straight from

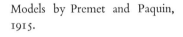

Models by Premet and Paquin, 1915.

the shoulders. Although some of the couturiers scornfully dismissed it as 'just like a pillowslip', it made Lanvin even more famous and was eagerly accepted for daily wear by girls who were now leading highly active lives, and were not, like their more clothes-conscious elders, prepared to spend long and tiring hours in a couture fitting room. Instead, they immediately accepted the simplicity of the chemise frock, chosen often in navy blue serge, easy little dresses in which it was considered quite correct to go to *thés dansants*. This simplicity by no means ousted the 'tailor-made girl', wearing skirts under pleated tunics, topped by short, rather angular jackets, heads covered in 'flippant', high-rising toques. The kiss curl on either cheek by the opening of 1914 marked the chic of both the chemise wearer and the tailored girl (the same girl at different hours), as also the same wearer when, at night, she wore her minaret or lampshade tunic wired out over her hobble or harem skirt. Skirts, in the opening months of 1914, were still down to the instep, still narrow, and the tunic, whether pliable or in lampshade form, was high favourite.

So it came to the high summer of 1914, and it was war. The little navy serge chemise dresses were still worn, but to hospitals, there to be exchanged for V.A.D. (Voluntary Aid Detachment) nurses' uniforms until released in time for a late *thé dansant*, or the girls worked during the day at rolling and packing bandages, or in one of the many crèches opened to allow young mothers to work in the munition factories. The tunic dresses still moved to syncopated music 'just to keep the boys on leave happy'.

It was a strange divided world of war work and pleasure, the girls quickly becoming women as the ghastly lists of dead and missing grew daily longer, men on the dance floors rarer.

'La Saison des Prunes Mirabelles' created by Redfern, *Bon Ton* 1914.

74

THE TWENTIES

3

Sport & Art

Madge Garland

In 1920, two years after the Armistice, women's skirts dipped unevenly around their ankles, and at the end of the decade uneven hem-lines, though in a different manner, again accentuated the legs. During the intervening ten years, for the first time in history since the days of the Spartan maidens and Diana's classical tunic, skirts were worn to just below knee level.

The dipping hem-lines of 1920 were weighted down by tassels similar to those which decorated the cushions and lampshades of that epoch, an accessory much favoured by Paul Poiret, whose extraordinary talent had made him able to impose his taste as much on the interiors of rooms as on the exterior garments of their inhabitants. Not only in dress but in the design of furniture, wall-paper, textiles and millinery, Poiret reigned supreme.

But in 1920, it was already afternoon in Poiret's triumphant day: he was still world-famous but he and all he stood for, an ideal of sophisticated luxury attainable only by those few who were idle, rich and beauty-loving, was not attractive to the post-war generation. During the war some women had taken part in the struggle, even if only in rare cases and in un-important roles. It was true that when they went to the Front they wore specially-made garments tailored in suitable shades of grey and were transported in their own chauffeur-driven cars, yet some had gone; and if society women did none of the unpleasant tasks in the hospitals which private funds and enterprise set up on the northern shores of France, still they had worn nurses' uniform.

Poiret's shock tactics of introducing violent colours instead of the pale flower-shades beloved of the pre-war generation had pointed the way to Jacques Doucet's exit from the fashion scene. The soft gentle clothes in which that great couturier, to whom Paris owes an exquisite museum and a magnificent library, became out-moded when the brilliant scarlets, pinks and apple-greens of Poiret, inspired by the Ballet Russe, took the stage. Now, although the corsets which Poiret had forbidden his manne-quins to wear were being discarded by all and sundry, when the petticoats he had not permitted beneath his straight skirts were no longer worn, when the turbans he had launched were now an accepted mode, when the long ropes of jewels he preferred to the hard brilliance of diamond neck-laces were current wear, now, almost unnoticed, the sun was setting on his career. A new type of woman, the very antithesis of his elegant wife Denise, entered the scene.

She came, not from a politically enfranchised section of society, or from the fashion world, but from the hitherto ignored area of sport. Suzanne Lenglen dashed onto the tennis court wearing what a spectator in 1921 described as 'a white silk dress that barely flutters below the knees, white silk stockings and white shoes'. With a brilliant orange bandeau holding her black hair tightly to her head she summed up the incoming craze for plain, light colours and practical clothes which permitted freedom of movement. Oriental splendour withdrew from daily life and found refuge in Hollywood, and sport, which had had a decisive influence on menswear during the past century, became a dominating power on women's clothes. From now on, 'P' in the fashion world did not necessarily stand for Poiret; it might be for Patou, for it was Jean Patou who had the prestige of dressing this new star, a plain, brown girl, very unlike the blonde beauties then in fashion, but who presaged the trend towards an open-air way of life, and the end of the boudoir and its lace-trimmed tea-gowns.

Patou was preparing his first collection when the war broke out and it was not until after the Armistice that he began his career as a couturier. He was an immediate success and in 1922 took over the huge and elegant

hotel in the rue St Florentin which once had been the home of Madame de Souza and her famous son the Duc de Morny.

So large did Patou's collection become, and so important did he consider the sports section, that it was shown in two sections, the morning devoted solely to sports clothes, both active and spectator, beach pyjamas, wraps and so forth, and in the afternoon formal day and evening clothes were paraded. He was an immediate success: he did not want to dress women in complicated trailing chiffons, tassels and barbaric embroideries, but to present a new type of emancipated girl, and though it was two years before Suzanne's short, pleated skirt and simple tunic became obligatory wear for all women, all day, all over the world, the suggestion had been made and when the change came it was total.

Jean Patou, a tall dark man described by Elsa Maxwell as 'that Hercules' was as attractive to women as he was attracted by their beauty, and the fascination of creating their clothes. (It is worth noting that the first great couturiers, Worth, Doucet, Poiret, were all devoted to the opposite sex, and many had long, happy marriages.) High fashion was firmly entrenched in Paris and was the work of passionate woman-lovers in the best sense of the words. It was not until later, beginning in the 'thirties, that it became international and ruled by a masculine style that was more effete than masterful. Patou also showed that he could dress superbly a very different type of emancipated woman, and when the lovely ballroom dancer Leonora Hughes appeared at the night club, '*Jardin de ma Soeur*', her full-skirted dresses, drifts of pale chiffon, often held at the low waistline by a flower, were all the creations of Jean Patou.

The 'twenties was a dancing decade: it was customary to dance most evenings either in the smart restaurants on the Champs Elysées, at the '*Boeuf sur le Toit*' where Jean Cocteau and his friends gathered, in the Montmartre *boites*, or in the disreputable rue de Lappe, with its myriad *bals musettes*. One of the most popular rendezvous was the *Bal Nègre*, and if the white clients tended to remain spectators it was because the negroes danced with such abandon that they were a delight to watch, not because of any colour consciousness. When Josephine Baker, popular star of the music hall, and famous for her outrageous costumes, was painted by Van Dongen in the nude, it was the splendour of her body which was commented on, not its colour.

Jeanne Lanvin began as a simple seamstress, then became a milliner, but because many people admired the dresses she made for her little daughter, she started to design children's clothes. Her first success with the chemise frock was described in the preceding chapter, before the war. Subsequently, she set up in a small salon in the Faubourg St-Honoré, where her huge house now stands, and her business flourished until she had couture salons, special departments for children, sports clothes and menswear. She had exquisite natural taste and made a remarkable collection of Impressionist paintings, including some particularly fine Renoirs, all of which reflected her intensely personal, feminine preferences. She invented

LE BOEUF SUR LE TOIT

The Princesse de Polignac, daughter of Jeanne Lanvin, sitting in front of a portrait of her mother by the artist Vuillard, which now hangs in the Musée D'Art Moderne in Paris.

An imaginative representation of *Le Boeuf sur le Toit* where *tout Paris* gathered in the early 'twenties. The sketch, by Jean Cocteau, captures the feeling of the time: the *monsieur en habit*, the lady in décolletage, and the negro playing billiards, were familiar figures of night-life in Paris.

the romantic 'picture' dress as an adornment for her beloved daughter Blanche, later the Comtesse de Polignac, at a time when clothes were sophisticated and anything but girlish, and continued to make them all through the 'twenties when they were the antithesis of the 'garçonne' mode. Somehow she managed to make them acceptable. Yvonne Printemps was one of Mme Lanvin's favourite clients who looked equally lovely in spreading picture gowns of pale taffeta, or in the luxurious furs for which the house was famed, or in the trim outfits of navy and white which she wore by day. Jeanne's colour sense became legendary; the famous 'Lanvin blue' was derived from the heavenly blue of medieval church glass. She imported luxurious materials from the east and liked to make evening wraps lined with brightly coloured velvets or satins. She herself often wore a short quilted coat of some such fine material and

A pretty watercolour by Pierre Brissard depicts a true-life scene: Jeanne Lanvin launched herself in fashion by making dresses for her little daughter, which were so admired by the ladies of Paris that she soon built up a business on their orders. Brissard's sketch includes two of Mme Lanvin's children's designs for 1914. (*Bon Ton*.)

liked a plethora of exotic jewellery in which turquoises and corals predominated.

Madeleine Vionnet, one of the most original designers ever known, was the child of a tax-collector in the Jura. She was married when she was eighteen, had a child who died, was divorced and went to London where (luckier or unluckier than Balenciaga who ten years later failed to find a job in London), she began her career in a tailoring workroom with Kate Reilly of Bond Street. After a while she returned to Paris and worked for Callot Soeurs, and then Doucet where she, like Poiret before her, insisted on the mannequins discarding their hideous corsets, but her ideas, like his, were not a success with Doucet's elderly clientèle. Eventually, she opened a small house of her own but she was thirty before she was able to make her own models. In 1923 she moved into splendid premises in the avenue

Matignon, then far out from the accepted fashion centre, and in large, beige, empty salons, showed clothes of revolutionary cut. They were untrimmed and uncopiable. Vionnet was never the mecca of the buyers because her clothes could not be repeated except by superlative cut and careful handwork, yet she could never be ignored because there was no one else like her. Jacques Worth, grandson of the first great Worth, considered her the finest technician in the whole fashion world. She was the first to make all her first *toiles* on quarter scale figurines, thus assuring the model-in-the-round essential to her predominantly asymmetrical cut.

Gabrielle Chanel, perhaps the most widely-known of the women couturiers who emerged in the 'twenties, is described at length in another chapter of this book, but some of her favourite fabrics and techniques are mentioned here to show how influential on the period her tastes became. Chanel had special fabrics, jerseys, woven exclusively to her requirements, smoothly surfaced, sometimes patterned but more often plain, and made into suits with their jackets lined with splendid silks to match the blouse or jumper beneath. She would add fine braids and fabulous buttons worthy of a Mogul's tunic. She visited England and Scotland in an effort to make the textile manufacturers more fashion conscious, but in a market based on menswear in which durability and a desire to be inconspicuous were predominant characteristics, she had only a limited success. Nevertheless, she did launch wool for formal wear and women who previously changed after luncheon into silk tea-dresses now appeared in the afternoon in little wool suits. An alternative to ordinary wool, called kasha, was produced by

One of the first model gowns to move away from the *garçonne* silhouette, featured in *Gazette du Bon Ton,* in 1920, was designed by Jeanne Lanvin.

A rare photograph of Madeleine Vionnet, creating a model on a little dummy.

right
Sketches for sportswear in the early 'thirties from the house of Patou.

80

left
Original sketches from Elsa Schiaparelli: the dress in butterfly-motif fabric was shown in February 1937 for the summer collection, and the musical notes dress was shown in May 1939 for the mid-season collection.

Mrs J. Scudamore was one of Jean Patou's most elegant clients, a well-known *mannequin de ville*, and typified the refined good looks which were admired in the 'twenties, with her elegantly shaped head and fine figure. The gems she wears were designed by Boucheron, one of Paris' finest jewellers.

Monsieur Rodier, woven from the hair of special sheep bred on the slopes of the Himalayas, which was light in weight, smoothly surfaced, and best in beige, but also seen in bois-de-rose and shades of dim green.

Chanel was also the first to launch costume jewellery, and her exquisite lapel-pins were an essential for every suit. Hitherto, artificial jewellery was considered extremely vulgar, and no one with any pretensions to good taste would dream of wearing it. A row of graduated pearls was the correct ornament for young girls, with strings of amber or jade for day wear, sometimes weighted down with a carved pendant and long earrings to match. Diamonds were for married women, and for most girls engagement rings were their first glittering jewels. Chanel changed all this; her clothes might have been deceptively simple, but her jewellery was frankly ostentatious. Huge emeralds and rubies, rajah's jewels, were her favourite stones and were set in exquisite designs, for many of which the elegant Comte Etienne de Beaumont was responsible.

Bracelets were immensely important, including the newcomer which clanked with myriad charms. To collect these was a popular pastime and the gift of a charm was often a would-be suitor's first offering. Among real jewellery, flexible ribbons of diamonds, some wide, some narrow, were first favourites, and when several were worn they were known as 'service stripes'.

Not only did women admit false jewels among their ornaments, they also went off the gold standard and most real jewellery was set in the silvery sheen of platinum. Even wedding rings were made of this white metal, although many considered the vows hardly binding when cemented by such a novelty. A series of 'eternity' rings (narrow circles entirely surrounded with small diamonds, sapphires or rubies) sometimes replaced the conventional large-stoned engagement ring, or were worn on the adjacent little finger.

'Le sport' became such an important influence on women's clothes that some houses opened special sports lines, though the clothes presented were more suited to 'spectator sports' than to real outdoor exercises. Other, smaller, houses appeared which dealt solely in this type of clothing, among which Vera Borea was outstanding. Her simple, relatively inexpensive models were suitable for the new whim of 'les weekends', for the Midi and for winter sports. Above all beach wear became important, bathing suits were no longer merely utilitarian but attractive, and such beach assessories as wraps and bags began to be included in holiday wardrobes, as well as beach pyjamas, and so on.

But most lingerie disappeared and chemises, drawers, corset-bodices, petticoats, under-petticoats, lace frills and ribbon-threaded broderie-anglaise all shrank into one short slip and brief drawers, or cami-knickers. As skirts grew shorter in 1925, the more modest took to hideous knickers of silk jersey gathered in just above the knees.

In spite of their unprecedented display, stockings were undecorated except for the obligatory 'clock' on the outer side of each ankle, were uniformly flesh-coloured, and of silk for evening or lisle thread for every-day wear. Shoes also, though now on view as never before, remained dull and conservative in style with brown lace-up Oxfords for the country, black for town and satin dyed-to-match for evening, all with a single strap across the instep. A fourth possibility was the tan court shoe with white uppers considered so 'fast' that they were known as 'co-respondants', but worn by most smart women at Deauville and Le Touquet.

Legs might be exposed but foreheads were not: deep crowned hats had to accommodate a chignon and cover the forehead, and later, when hair was shingled, the 'cloche' reached the eyebrows. Indeed, so low was the hat level that in a snapshot of Suzanne Lenglen, wearing her habitual head-band, talking to the blonde and pretty Ranee of Pudakota, the latter can hardly be seen because her cloche rests on the bridge of her nose. Strange as it may seem in view of this, great emphasis was laid on the eyes, rimmed with kohl, and on the novelty of lips painted a brilliant red, which necessitated a new accessory, the lip-stick, which was never, never used in public.

Hats were made to measure and fitted as carefully as any dress. Once the colour and fabric had been chosen, felt for winter and ballibuntal or bangkok straw for summer, the crown was made the size of the head and pulled well down, when the meagre brim was arranged at the required angle by an expert. Although Caroline Reboux had begun her career in the previous century, her house was still considered the top in Paris, and a cloche by Reboux a sure sign of success, though Gloria Swanson re-turned to America in 1924 with a selection of hats from the rival firm of Marthe Regnier.

Designs by Lucien Lelong, from *Art, Goût, Beauté* June 1925, are typical of the flattened shapes of the 'twenties.

The close-fitting helmets and turbans so successfully draped by Agnès were equally forehead-concealing, but suited this milliner particularly well since she was the fortunate owner of magnificent dark eyes and regular features. In summer, broad brims, which often jutted out wider in front than at the back, superseded the cloche, but still the hat line was not far above the brow line. To be highbrow might be a compliment in intellectual circles but was disastrous in the fashionable world.

Poiret and Vionnet had waged war against corsets for over a decade; now the battle was won, and those manufacturers who survived had to alter the whole mechanism of their production. Whalebone, busks and brocade became anachronisms, and the new 'corselette' was a straight piece of milanese silk, held up by shoulder straps, not bones, and which flattened the bust, ignored the waist and encircled the buttocks. Those unfortunate women endowed by nature with curves were much pitied, but by some extraordinary redistribution of the genes, a remarkable num-ber of big-bosomed 'stunners' painted by Boldini and admired by Edward VII had given birth to daughters whose figures were hardly distinguishable from their brothers.

It was not only their brothers' figures that the females of the 'twenties emulated but also their heads, and most smart women wore their hair cut

82

as short as any man's. The centre-parting of the early years of the decade gave place to the 'Eton' crop of the mid-'twenties, with its revolutionary side parting, at first considered very daring. With this cropped hair ear-rings were essential but the long dangling stones at first popular were later superseded by screw-on, single pearl studs.

The leading figure among hairdressers was Antoine, a Pole, whose premises in the rue Cambon consisted of one vast, mirrored salon, not, as hitherto, a series of small cubicles in which women could in privacy take off their switches, false fringes and the 'rats' which supported their up-swept puffs of hair. Now the wretched clients were not only nearly bald but were exposed to the gaze of all the others. Antoine's method of razor-cutting the hair when it was wet was as painful as it was efficient, and a shingle set by this master could be relied on to keep its shape, with every hair lying flat to the shape of the head.

As always it was luck which decreed who would be the beauty of the moment: many a girl with a bad back to her head but with fine shoulders and bust, who would have been considered a glory to her sex in an earlier generation, was now an object of pity, while some skinny flapper with a well-shaped head who would have been ignored, was now greatly admired.

Jane Renouardt, one of the best actresses of her day, shortened the Marcel-waved coiffure, in which she was painted by Vuillard, to reveal the shape of her head, but covered her forehead with a fringe. Her pose reveals yet another step on the road to nudity, for her short, bead-embroidered shift reached barely to her non-bosom and exposed the naked upper and under-arm, a totally new, and not altogether fortuitous, disclosure.

This casual way of dressing required quite a different type of manne-quin to those trained to display languorous tea-gowns and elaborate evening wear. Poiret had often complained about the stupidity of his models and took great pains to train them, but the role of mannequin then carried no social cachet and the girls who undertook the job had no first-hand knowledge of the world they understudied, and certainly no experience of 'le sport'.

Jean Patou on a visit to the USA had been struck by the zest, good carriage and free movements of the American girls, and he arranged for six American lovelies to come to Paris as his mannequins. All had high social rating: the pretty red-head became Mrs 'Foxey' Gwynne, friend of the Duchess of Windsor, the lovely blonde, Mrs Leo d'Erlanger, and between them they carried Patou's clothes into every ball-room and important social occasion in France. So began the story of the mannequin's rise to fame and status, a far cry from Marie Worth's first tentative efforts.

Among the anonymous mannequins in some Paris houses at that time were two or three of a noticeably different breed, Russian princesses, penniless and pale, who walked through the white and gold salons in a manner which separated them from their surroundings, while their male equivalents, if young and handsome, danced in night clubs dressed as 'Cossacks', or, if plain and inelegant, drove taxis.

There also existed a now-forgotten race known as 'mannequins de ville', a title which applied to smart women of social significance who were dressed free by a maison de couture, provided that her husband (or lover) was able to supply all the requisite accessories, not only the shoes, hats, gloves, and so on, but also splendid furs and jewellery. The usual arrangement was for some twenty to thirty outfits each season at the end of which the clothes were returned and disposed of *en solde*. It was part of the understanding that the lady would never appear in public in clothes from another house, and a matter for much gossip when one couturier lured a particularly chic client from a rival house.

This apparently carefree gift of an expensive wardrobe meant real hard-work for the recipient, who was obliged to spend two to three weeks twice a year in Paris assembling it, to stand long hours being fitted, and to attend to the innumerable extras of shoes and hats to be made to match the selected garments. Success could be attained only by a combination of informed good taste, of excellent health, great energy, self-discipline, and a concentration on detail which, used in another cause, might have led to a useful career. Perhaps her descendants are the fashion editors of today?

A fourth, and also extinct, type of mannequin was the child-model, who attended race-meetings and garden-parties attired in elaborate organdie dresses and flower-trimmed hats, often hand in hand with an adult somewhat similarly dressed.

The openings of the bi-annual collections were events of great social importance which *tout Paris* attended, the women sumptuously dressed

Two *mannequins de ville* photographed by Seeberger at the races at Longchamps, in 1927, and dressed by the house of Worth.

At Patou, husbands could wait in most pleasant surroundings at a little bar inside the house, while their wives tried on their models and paraded for approval. A sketch by the artist, Sem, dated 1925.

One of Lelong's models featured in *Art, Goût, Beauté*, in February 1929 shows the development of the 'situation' fashion drawing, now slightly stylised.

and bejewelled, accompanied by lovers or husbands. A mere gathering of professional women with a sprinkling of business-men was unthinkable, and only a chosen few of the most important journalists or representatives of famous firms were invited to the first nights. The rank-and-file attended during the following two or three days, with a protocol of importance as strict as that of any royal court.

Jean Patou seated his guests at a series of small tables throughout the *enfilade* of salons with a vendeuse at each doorway to announce the name and number of the incoming model, and waiters circulated incessantly with champagne. Chez Lanvin, Madame Jeanne would sit at a small table near the gilded lift which brought the guests up from the ground floor, and to be placed in this first room was a sign of favour and a clear statement of social and/or financial importance.

Louiseboulanger and Augustabernard, the former known for her exquisite colouring and the latter for her inimitable cut, arranged matters less pompously, and their openings were more like a gathering of friends. Both houses deserve to be remembered as outstanding examples of the understatement so typical of this decade and it was personal circumstances, not lack of success, which forced these firms, each entirely dependent on the personality of the designers, to close their doors.

The 'garçonne' fashion reflected not only woman's increasing personal and political freedom, but also a levelling of class, for these simple models were eminently capable of being adapted to mass-production. The USA already had an extensive market of ready-to-wear clothes and was proficient in the highly technical procedure of translating a model, made by hand in the round, into one which could be cut simultaneously in several dozen layers in the flat, and made up by machine. In Europe, ready-made clothes were only for the *petit bourgeoisie* and the lower classes; no woman with any pretensions to dressing well would buy ready-made garments. If she could not afford the couturiers or the court dressmakers she relied on 'little women' who copied the styles from drawings in the fashion magazines, and most smart women had their (kept very secret) 'little' dressmakers who copied their original models in other materials or colours.

The international buyers who came to Paris to buy and to copy (sometimes to copy without buying) became increasingly numerous and important, until the buyers, rather than the private clientèle, became the background of the big houses. The selection made by the buyers and the press became more and more the criterion of success and this, together with the rise of ready-to-wear in the social scale, resulted in a swift worldwide distribution of fashion and the end of local deviations.

The organisation behind the scenes was complex: all buyers did, and do, use the services of a 'commissionaire' who acts as a scout, spy and counsellor to the overseas buyers, keeping them in touch with developments in the market, of the rise of new figures of importance, and of the decline in popularity of some houses. Once the buyer had made her choice all arrangements were made by the commissionaire who was charged with the delivery and expedition of the models at certain dates in order to coincide with the sailings of the big trans-Atlantic liners which took the models to New York or Buenos Aires. The press was not permitted to reproduce illustrations until a given date, some six or eight weeks later, and it was generally agreed that a new Paris fashion took as long as two years before it became universally accepted overseas. When Vionnet introduced the bias cut in 1926, it was thought this new method would not be copiable but, although more difficult than when seams were on the straight, in no time at all the manufacturers adjusted their plants and workers to meet these new demands. Skirts were shorter than they had ever been before, but they fluttered in petal-points and flowed out in flares and panels. Godets were everywhere.

A design by Raoul Dufy for the fabric manufacturers, Bianchini, was featured in *Gazette du Bon Ton* in 1920, and captures the dominant influences of the decade – sport and art.

It was not until 1929 that a few of the haute couture houses opened ready-made departments, forerunners of the boutiques of today, with Patou, Chanel and Lelong in the forefront of this development. Later, it became usual for a small selection of models to be made up in 'average' size and for the purchase price to include one alteration in order to make the garment fit the client. There was no agreed system of sizing and the best that could be hoped for was 'small', 'average' and 'large' – though there never were any of the last.

Tube dresses made definite demands on the material selected, for the fashion for veiling and for over-dresses of chiffon, tulle or lace, so typical of the first two decades of the twentieth century, now entirely vanished. Quality and surface interest became all-important and the great success of the mid-'twenties was the chiffon slip, heavily beaded from the knee to bateau neckline. Several new crêpes made their appearance, among them de Chine, marocain, and georgette, of which only the first has continued into contemporary use. Ducharne was among the first fabric houses to develop new techniques for printing these silks, and Bianchini continued to foster that close alliance between artist and manufacturer which has been one of the prime reasons for France's position as the centre of fashion. No less an artist than Raoul Dufy produced several hundreds of designs in the 'twenties, both for dress fabrics and furnishing materials. One of the latter, inspired by the new vogue for sport, called 'Le Tennis', showed the nets as cobweb-like links between the figures of the players. Another great personality in this field was the Russian Sonia Delaunay, whose brilliant colours enriched many of the long patterned scarves, then an essential accessory to the uniform of pleated skirt, tunic and cloche hat.

Afternoon frocks by Captain Molyneux, one of the few successful English couturiers in Paris.

The invasion of foreign talent into the French fashion market was nothing new: Worth had been an Englishman, and was followed by the two successful English Houses of Redfern and Charles Creed. Now a fourth Englishman appeared in the elegant person of Edward Molyneux, known as 'the Captain', a title he had won with distinction in World War I. He had made his début in London with Lucille, in private life the Canadian-born Lady Duff-Gordon, but her work reflected the aftermath

86

of the Edwardian era and was not to his taste nor to that of the new generation. Molyneux created clothes which were the despair of the journalists, who could find nothing obvious to report, but were the delight of his customers, because they were absolutely right for whatever the occasion. In Molyneux's clothes one was never over- or under-dressed, a great advantage at a time when social modes were changing rapidly. The printed silk suit, still current wear, was one of his most successful innovations.

On suits and coats, flower buttonholes, either real or artificial, were obligatory. Carnations or gardenias were worn by day and on evening gowns poppies, dahlias and roses were placed on one hip to accentuate the low waistline. It was still usual for men to send a girl an orchid for her to pin, to its detriment, on her evening cloak or the shoulder-strap of her gown. Both day and evening coats had high, upstanding collars of fox, probably in the reddish tone of 'cross' during the day, and white for evening.

The couturier Captain Edward Molyneux.

Button manufacturers were having a slim time, and the only buttons to be seen were on a few double breasted, longish jackets destined for morning or country wear. There were many capes, both long and three-quarter length, and all coats were of the wrap-over style which had to be held by one hand. Handbags also were of the clutch variety, flat in shape and known as 'pochettes', and it had not yet entered anyone's head that a lady would carry a parcel or require a large useful bag. When Hermès made a small bag of Russian leather which stood upright on its narrow base, was fastened by a new-fangled 'zip' and had two handles, it was considered very eccentric and caused much comment.

During the 'twenties the influence of art was second only to that of sport, and at no time in history since David designed the costumes for Napoleon's coronation was the current vernacular of the art world so familiar in fashionable circles. The abstract patterns of the Cubists were seen on the new woollen jumpers, on the turbans designed by Agnès and on many printed silks.

The combined influences of sport and art were responsible for two theatrical productions which were a synthesis of the current mode. The Ballet Russe still had an immense influence, but it was no longer synonymous with the exotic magnificence of Bakst; Diaghilev produced two ballets which reflected the gay and casual approach both to fashion and life typical of the 'twenties. 'Le Train Bleu', with sets by Derain, and 'Les Matelots', with sets and costumes by Pruna, dealt with the new vogue for the Riviera (hitherto a winter playground for the elderly) as a summer resort for the young, and the increased importance of beach and casual wear. Sailor pants, striped blue and white cotton vests and navy-blue berets were worn by both sexes, and beach pyjamas made their first appearance. To add to many borrowings from the lower ranks of nautical life was added the navy-blue double-breasted jacket fastened with brass buttons, its cuffs turned back to show a flash of scarlet lining – a whim of

Jean Cocteau's adapted by Chanel with tremendous success for her female clients.

The 'twenties conversion to simplicity found its definitive statement at the famous 1925 international exhibition in Paris, always referred to as the Expo. Deco. Rarely has a decade stated its aims and preferences more clearly, and rarely have these desires received more complete public acclaim.

It is against backgrounds by Louis Sue, André Mar, Rhulman and Djo Bourgeois that the clothes of this period must be recalled. Boutet de Monvel, asked in 1925 what his ideal home would be like, replied it would be exclusively modern and as austere as possible, yet these modern interiors, though severe in line, were luxurious in execution, with built-in cupboards and divans composed of fine woods, and heavy but comfortable chairs. The French tradition of fine workmanship, plus the profession of *artiste-decorateur* continued without a break. Réné Lalique experimented with new techniques in glass, Puirforcat produced superb silver, and the lacquer screens of Jean Dunand equalled in quality those of ancient Japan – indeed the French version of simplicity was every whit as luxurious as the most sumptuous décor imagined by Poiret, and the antithesis of those theories which inspired the Bauhaus. Curtains of hand-woven silk, walls

All the plastic arts developed side by side during the 'twenties, and were designed quite often by a group of people who passed in and out of the various artistic milieux with facility. The paintings in this interior were by Charles Martin, and show fashion styles current at the time; the furniture was by Groult, whose wife Nicole was Paul Poiret's youngest sister.

A most important innovation from the house of Patou, in the winter 1922 collection, was the deep-set sleeve, which brought a new easy line to women's coats.

covered with the finest matting; or hand-printed wall-papers designed by Marie Laurencin; armchairs of the softest hide; André Groult's elegant furniture covered in shagreen; hand-knotted rugs all in white or shades of beige – composed interiors which were as subtle as they were novel. One of the first shops to deal in such treasures was in the Faubourg St-Honoré, called Jean Desart, a pseudonym which hid the identities of two English-women, Eileen Grey and Evelyn Wyld. The latter's rugs designed in abstract patterns carried out in natural coloured wools, hand-knotted by the peasants near Grasse (when they were not working in the jasmine fields), and the former's lacquer furniture, were of a surprising originality. One of the chief practitioners of this new style was Jean-Michel Franck, who liked to add a single piece of African sculpture, or one picture by Picasso, to his neutral coloured rooms, and commissioned Giacommetti to design his lamps.

In the fashion magazines, drawn illustrations were still all important and their prime exponents a group of talented young men originally recruited by Lucien Vogel, who was, as we have seen in the previous chapter, the brilliant founder and editor of *La Gazette Du Bon Ton*. The drawings of Lepape, Marty, Martin, Benito and Brissaud are without equal in evoking the atmosphere of their era, but a few practitioners behind the photographer's velvet cloth were beginning to reveal the magic potential of the camera. Genthe's simple statement of Greta Garbo's beauty, Man Ray's portrait of Nancy Cunard with her kohl-rimmed eyes and arms heavy with African ivory bangles, revealed new possibilities.

Towards the end of the decade, fashions became more feminine. Hair was still short but allowed to wave softly over the ears, and foreheads, no longer hidden by cloches, were partly revealed by hats. Some of the prettiest were by Rose Descart who rose in the millinery scales by having her advertisements drawn by Marie Laurencin, whose reveries in tender colours now superseded the brilliant cubist designs. Her backgrounds and costumes for the ballet 'Les Biches', all pale greens, grays and pinks, with the dancers twirling their long ropes of pearls, revealed the soft centre in the apparently hard core of the young jazz set, just as Colette's wryly romantic stories struck a cord of deeply imbedded sentiment.

The silhouette became more varied, some hems remained knee-high in front but dipped at the back to the ground, while the handkerchief or petal-pointed skirts reached the ankles – much as they had done ten years ago. Women were about to look as feminine as they had at the beginning of the decade, but with what a difference in mood: in ten short years they had achieved not only political franchise but also gained their bodily freedom. No corsets, no hairpins or false hair, but all the pleasure of exercise, sun-bathing, the easy comfort of sailor pants, beach and house pyjamas and short skirts.

Atonal music was already in the air, Brecht's bitter satires shattering, '*Le Chien Andalou*' and other fantasies of the surrealists were familiar

Another of Patou's distinguished customers was the Princess Mdivani, known to the world as the actress Pola Negri. Her casual outfit is a classic of the 'twenties, and shows how Patou earned the reputation for launching the sportive look.

backgrounds now to daily life.

As the garçonne was about to grow up and appear in a more womanly guise, the fashion world was shaken in 1929 by the collapse of the New York stock market. Its repercussions were widespread. American buyers became fewer and less spendthrift, the monolithic Gertrude Stein remained, but there was an exodus of the American expatriots who had played so vivid a role in Paris during the 'twenties. It was true that, as Hemingway promised, '*The Sun Also Rises*', but in the 'thirties it rose on a very different scene.

THE THIRTIES

4 Artistry & Fantasy   Madeleine Ginsburg

"ART - GOUT - BEAUTÉ"

A sketch from *Art, Goût, Beauté* in September 1930 captures the atmosphere and style of evening entertainment in Paris. Those furs were miraculously sewn onto the sheerest and most delicate fabrics, and the dresses beneath had a deceptive simplicity, achieved with couture skill.

One of the most elegant trouser suits of the 'thirties was designed by Lucien Lelong, in spring 1930.

The Depression and World War II form the incongruous boundaries to a period in which couture was at its most diverse and imaginative. Despite financial depression and international unrest, the designers of the 'twenties continued their work, and a new group with enough vitality to flourish into the post-war period started their careers. More than a generation ago, they created clothes that to us are still good fashion, in an immediately attractive, wearable style.

In the world of couture, the economic slump meant, not no clothes, as one might expect, but *new* clothes. With a radical change of silhouette, slim fitted lines replaced those loose, low waists of the 'twenties. It is still something of a puzzle to understand how these new styles were financed. In the first season after the Wall Street crash, not a single commercial model buyer came to Paris from the USA. Even though the technique of the American buyers over the years had been to 'steal what they could and buy what they had to', their sudden disappearance was a catastrophic loss

92

Louiseboulanger's exquisite long afternoon frock of printed chiffon shows the total reversal in hemline length which was achieved by the end of the 'twenties. The dress was shown in April 1930.

left
Maggy Rouff provided *Art, Goût, Beauté,* with an exquisite cover for its April 1931 issue; the cardigan jacket and the loose, fine pleating of the skirt became typical of fashion styling in the early 'thirties, which was more sportive and out-of-doors.

to the Paris houses and it was not until 1932–3 that they returned in forces France was less immediately affected by the Depression than either the UK or the USA, being so much less industrialised. Staffs of the couture house. were large, but were mostly women earning small wages, and as willing to go on half-time as they had previously done overtime. Buttons and trimmings were made by small independent ateliers, and in this and other ways the loss was spread. Couture houses were then, as now, the shop windows for French fabric manufacturers, themselves a mainstay of the national economy; they were prepared to supply materials on credit, recouping their profits when the models were purchased and copied. The sale of perfumes also provided the houses with an additional source of income.

Fortunately, these lean years came after the fat years of the 'twenties – those boom years which enabled most of the more prudent houses to put enough by to carry them through at least a short part of the Depression. It is known, for instance, that the accounts department of that most respected of Paris houses, Molyneux, had difficulty in coping with the sheer volume of money that passed through their hands. Chanel owned her own premises in the rue Cambon, and there were always those jewels . . . but even she, usually one of the most expensive of the houses, cut her prices by half in 1932.

The seriousness of the crisis can be gauged by looking at the order books of the house of Vionnet, again an important and respected name throughout this period. In no way did that house lose either respect or prestige, yet by 1938, when the severity of the economic crisis had passed, Vionnet was making only half the number of dresses she had been making ten years earlier. The only casualty was Augustabernard, who had been successful during the 'twenties with her graceful and understated clothes, those marvellous foils for jewels which remained popular from 1919 to 1934. She had won a *Concours d'Elégance* in 1930 with one of the first trained dresses. In 1932, her pleated, classically draped gown made *Vogue*'s most beautiful dress of the season. Augustabernard had just moved into her new and superbly appointed salon at 3 Faubourg St-Honoré when her clientèle, mostly South American, were hit by the currency crisis and were unable to pay their bills. The shortage of money was less apparent after 1932, and although *Vogue* referred haughtily to 'peculiar if passing conditions', the easy days had gone forever. Besides the increase in labour costs, employers also had to cover the social security payments for their employees.

Dresses were using larger quantities of material, at least five yards where two would have been used in pre-crisis days, while the classic draped styles of the latter part of the 'thirties in which Alix and Vionnet specialised used very large quantities of double-width fabric. Tariff walls made materials much more expensive, especially those from England, but the two stars of couture, Chanel and Schiaparelli, used them frequently.

In 1930, *Femina*, the French magazine, attempted to promote the use of artificial silk as a unique material with decorative possibilities of its own, not merely as a poor relation of real silk. To use it was almost a patriotic duty. It was invented by a Frenchman, the Comte de Chardonnet and manufactured at Vaux and Velin – 'the work of French hands'. It was a pity that its wearability was so unpredictable. Throughout the period printed silks grew steadily in favour, and *Femina* notes in an unguarded moment that they would last longer and look fresher than a plain material. Cotton, which was a very economical material, enjoyed a vogue, but the fashion did not last long.

Many of the haute couture customers bought the less opulent clothes. Even Vionnet's clients preferred black crêpe with a black suede belt to her rich, renaissance-patterned evening dresses. Since she numbered among them the richest women in the world, possibly in their case it was the modish 'l'art de paraître de pauvre'. Even by the standards of their own time, couture clothes were not extraordinarily expensive. A plain Vionnet dress in 1938 cost about 3500 francs (about £19).

L'Officiel, the professional journal of haute couture, suggested in 1930 ways in which couture might set its own house in order and encourage orders from overseas: precise dates published in advance would make it possible for the buyers to get their schedules organised; spacing out the shows to cover twelve rather than six days would give time for buyers to see more collections and cover fashion accessories as well. The collections themselves were much too big. Showing four hundred outfits twice a year, with two mid-season collections of ninety each, was a waste of resources. A hundred outfits at a time was quite sufficient. Buyers could not concentrate on such quantities and in any case most tended to buy the same dresses. The introduction of press handouts would serve as useful advertisements and prevent the misrepresentation of ideas. To deter the wrong sort of buyer – the cheap copyist – they suggested a bureau for the registration of models, controlling quality and providing royalties, with a visitors' book to assist in keeping out undesirables. The majority of these proposals have been adopted by the couture since, and many are supervised by the Chambre Syndicale.

The couturiers also devised means to help themselves. Thus, one of their obvious sources of loss was the long credit traditional in couture, which was more than unusually ill-advised in a period of violent currency fluctuations. Another was the time and money spent on numerous fittings. Some of the couturiers developed other aspects of their businesses in compensation: Lucien Lelong introduced an *'editions'* department, where ready-made or partly made-to-measure clothes could be purchased, and Schiaparelli set a trend with her boutique, full of irresistible novelties.

Elsa Schiaparelli brought a completely new and original talent to the world of haute couture, and was the most successful new couturier to cope with the often trying circumstances of the 'thirties. She was born in 1896 in Rome of an academic, professional family. Her father was an expert in oriental languages and a coin collector, her uncle a famous astronomer.

left
A Schiaparelli model, shown in February for the mid-season and summer collection of 1933, shows the exaggerated proportions which the shoulders had reached by that year.

right
A characteristic Schiaparelli model for the early 'thirties demonstrates her skill in combining a severely tailored line with ultra-feminine accessories.

left
Schiaparelli's winter collection for 1936 included this checked coat, set off with a typical innovation from the couturier – buttons shaped like coffee beans.

right
A supremely elegant, casual trouser suit designed by Schiaparelli in May 1935.

94

She had an intense adolescence, wrote poetry, modelled and painted, in a amateur way. She married young and unsuccessfully and went to the USA. After the birth of her daughter Mariza (or Gogo as she was known) Schiaparelli was left almost without resources, and so she became a small antique dealer. As a child she had always loved clothes, but her first direct contact with couture was when she met and became a friend of the great Paul Poiret. She attempted dress design, but an approach to Maggy Rouff was repulsed with the statement that she would do better planting potatoes than trying to make dresses. Her break into fashion came in 1928, when she designed a sports sweater quite unlike all the others available at the time. It was in black and white with a child-like scrawl of a bow on the front, the knitting unusually soft, yet elastic, the product of a small factory run by Armenian peasants. She launched it herself and orders followed thick and fast, her first from the American firm of Strauss. Anita Loos, the small, piquant authoress of *Gentlemen Prefer Blondes* was her first private customer. Schiaparelli moved to an attic in 4 rue de la Paix, and within the next few years was in a position to take over the whole house. In 1934 she moved to the Place Vendôme where she stayed till her retirement in 1954. Sweaters with futurist, negro, skeleton and tattoo designs were added to her range. She made skirts to match the sweaters, other types of sports clothes, and her first evening dress in black and white. It was, she says, unique: the first dress with a matching jacket. It was the forerunner of the evening suit, and the greatest success of her career. Her original and amusing ideas caught the fancy of the smart world. She made a tremendously successful tour of the USA and in 1934 opened her establishment in London at 36 Upper Grosvenor Street. She had launched herself from boutique selling into haute couture.

Much of her originality comes from the work she put into the materials of her craft. She worked very closely with fabric manufacturers and her name is associated with ranges as diverse as 'Viyella', even at this period desperately trying to lose its nursery image, and Colcombet's glass fabric, 'Rhodophane', which was considered the height of sophistication in 1935. She extended the range of tweeds, working with the Macleods of Skye to develop new colours, and with the Irish tweed manufacturers in the Vale of Avoca. She also experimented with prints, persuading Colcombet, more or less as a joke, to make a fabric printed with a mélange of her press cuttings.

She was equally as tireless in her pursuit of original fastenings. In 1930, she used zip fasteners on the pockets of a beach jacket – their first appearance in high fashion. They were still rather a shocking novelty when she used them for dress fastenings in 1934 and even in 1936 it was still big news to the fashion press that she was using the 'Lightning fastener on all suit skirts'. There may have been some reciprocal agreement in her arrangement with Imperial Chemical Industries who made the Lightning fastener, for there is a certain mutual congratulation about their advertisements.

96

right
Country clothes, designed by Vionnet, from British *Harper's Bazaar*, January 1934.
A page of sketches from Paris, in British *Harper's Bazaar*, November 1938.

over page
Examples of the work of Mme Sonia Delaunay, artist and wife of Robert Delaunay, one of the most original designers of clothes and fabrics in the 'twenties. Like Dufy, she was a link between the worlds of art and fashion. The Dadaist poet Tristan Tzara wrote descriptions and a 'Poème Pour Une Robe de Mme Sonia Delaunay', which accompanied these designs:

L'ange a glissé sa main
dans la corbeille l'oeil des fruits.
Il arrête les roues des autos,
et le gyroscope vertigineux
du coeur humain.

The illustrations were taken from a folder of prints and writings, which were published in France to coincide with the '*Arts Décoratifs*' exhibition of 1925.

On these pages, indisputable evidence that Paris is plaid-mad.

Molyneux. A tight little
jacket and a deep-pleated skirt

Paquin's dark brown
antelope sports coat
lined with plaid

Alix. A plaid blouse under
a mulberry suit, and over
all an off-white coat

SK7 38

Also at Alix, a great coat
of rainbow plaid with all
the fulness swept to the front

Schiaparelli was sometimes helped in her work by the artist Salvador Dali, who designed the fabric for this evening dress. The 'torn' effect was printed onto the pale blue dress with blue, red, black and purple, and appliquéd to match, on the stole. (1937.)

Most novel and decorative are her buttons, their inspiration coming from each theme of a collection. Stars and moons fastened clothes in the astrological collection; clowns, circus horses and acrobats, those in the circus collection. Others are inspired by the atmosphere of the times. There were 'buttons of gold sovereigns and French Louis to mock the next French devaluation'. She gives full credit for the invention of these delectable novelties to those who created them: they were 'men of extraordinary talent. One of them was Jean Clement, a genius in his way, a real French artisan, who would work with such burning love that he was almost a fanatic. He would arrive at the last moment when we had given up all hope of having anything to fasten our clothes. There would be a smile of triumph on his face while he emptied his pockets into my lap.' At a later period her buttons were made by Jean Hugo. Even Aragon the poet and his wife designed for her a necklace that looked like aspirins.

She always enjoyed the company of avant garde artists and designers. Jean Michel Frank was a friend of long standing. He designed her first apartment and her boutique so successfully that on occasion it stopped the traffic in the Place Vendôme. She collaborated with Salvador Dali, an arrangement of mutual profit: she dressed his wife for free, while he provided inspiration for some of her designs. His 'City of the Drawers' and the 'Venus de Milo of the Drawers', became, in Schiaparelli's fashion-conscious hands, a neat and wearable *tailleur* with a delightful eccentricity about the drawer-shaped pockets. He inspired the scarlet lobster and

Her hat designs were often extreme and very difficult to wear, but this page of hats from the sketchbooks, dated summer 1937, are flattering and even a little coquettish.

scatter of parsley that is splashed across the skirt of a romantic, full-skirted white evening dress, but the dress is otherwise so simple and well balanced that it merely surprises, but it does not shock. The 'mad hats', like the befrilled lamb cutlet, or the high-heeled shoe, have the same quality. A Jean Cocteau head with streaming hair decorates the shoulder of an evening cloak, and the influence of Bérard is omnipresent. Small wonder press and clients relished each collection as a unique and exciting experience.

Chanel called Schiaparelli 'that Italian artist who makes clothes'. She intended it derisively but it can be interpreted as a compliment. Schiaparelli herself stated that her inspiration was architectural, 'that the body must never be forgotten and it must be used as a frame is used in a building. The vagaries of line and detail or any asymmetric effect must have a close connection with this frame. The more the body is respected, the better the dress acquires vitality' – a profound and valid comment on contemporary dress design. It is true of all Schiaparelli's models, and so great is her creative vitality that she must have been ruthless in her elimination of motifs. Even when she used flamboyant, encrusted embroideries, she was restrained. They enhanced the structure and she was careful not to allow them to distract from the line of the garment.

The body Schiaparelli preferred to enhance was one with broad shoulders and slim hips. Much ink has been spilt on deciding whether it was she or Marcel Rochas who initiated this silhouette but it would seem that many designers were attempting to provide a small decorative focus at shoulder level, although most concentrated the emphasis at the elbow with drapes or capes. Schiaparelli's particular contribution, so *Harper's Bazaar* said in 1930, was to pad the shoulder and 'handle it exactly as it used to be in a man's coat'. Throughout the 'thirties, she continued to promote this feature in the most imaginative ways, and was among the forefront of the designers who made the stressed shoulder so fashionable.

Apart from the evening suit, which was her particular contribution to fashion, Schiaparelli's evening clothes are pretty rather than breathtakingly original. She was experimenting with the pleated bustle, the forerunner of the new romanticism as early as 1932. She dallied with the oriental sari in 1934 and went on to the high-busted Empire line, claiming credit for the introduction of '*La Belle Poitrine*' introduced so disconcertingly between the spring and autumn collections of 1934 and immortalised forever in the rounded contours of her 'Shocking' perfume bottle, designed for her by Eleanore Fini.

On the eve of World War II, she had been in couture for just over ten years. Her models were the apotheosis of hard-edged chic and were much appreciated by women who liked to make an impression with their clothes. Her novelties were so widely copied that any good idea, whatever its origin, is almost always ascribed to her. From an attic atelier she had become the head of an enterprise employing 600 people, not perhaps the largest in Paris but certainly the most influential. Contemporaries

Schiaparelli's advertisements for her new 'Shocking' perfume, which also became the name of a particular shade of bright magenta-pink. (1938.)

98

A classical tailored suit designed by Marcel Rochas, showing the emphasis on the square shoulder, which both he and Schiaparelli promoted. (March 1930.)

thought she drew inspiration from the air, but in retrospect the source was rather her own rich and individual cultural heritage.

Marcel Rochas worked in the same genre as Schiaparelli, and during his 25 years in couture was often the centre of controversy. He had opened in 1925 and in 1930 became notorious overnight when eight *élégantes* at a smart party found themselves wearing the same model. He was Parisian born and bred, and took his métier as couturier very seriously. From his salon at 14 avenue Matignon came a multitude of ideas, all defended with passion especially when they coincided with those of someone else. His first affray was with Schiaparelli and concerned the origin of the emphasised shoulder. Adjudicating 40 years after the event is a chancy business, but *Femina*, writing retrospectively in 1933 on the origins of the fashion in 1931, came to the conclusion that each couturier had the same idea with significant differences: the result a draw. Rochas states that the origin of his inspiration was the Javanese and Balinese dancers he saw at the '*Exposition Coloniale*' in 1931, and throughout 1932 he provided many charming variations on this theme.

Rochas was never short of original ideas, but he was also capable of an elegant restraint. Three arum lilies twined at the neck of a dark dress make a rich and subtle decoration. Sometimes his designs were so original that they were almost prophetic. In 1932, he designed a gray flannel trouser suit and in 1939, a plain white lace shirtwaister, simple, straight, and uncluttered, which looked forward 20 or more years. He was very popular in the USA and his multicoloured striped 'gypsy' evening dress had the dubious compliment paid it of being judged the most copied French model in that country for 1938.

Mainbocher came to couture in 1931. He had been a sketch artist at *Harper's* and went to French *Vogue* to become fashion editor, and later full editor. Born, Main Rousseau Bocher in Chicago, 1890, he was a disappointed opera singer with a talent for sketching until his real career was developed by Edward L. Mayer, one of the USA's great dressmakers. Mainbocher had been very successful in his journalistic career, and was now tasteful in his choice of models and tactful in his dealings with the couture. From the first he was successful. He aimed at a youthful elegant simplicity and by intention he followed in the tradition of Molyneux. In retrospect, he was responsible for several important innovations of cut.

In the late 'thirties when most couturiers were growing tired of the possibilities of a gathered sleeve, puffing put at the shoulders, Mainbocher added a new dimension to the style by putting extra padding at the top, and deepening the armhole so that the sleeve fell straight and wide from a broad shoulder: a silhouette very characteristic of the 1940s. A three-quarter length, half-belted jacket with a bloused back which he designed in 1937 was another innovation and presaged post-war styling. His afternoon clothes had a graceful prettiness, with a rustic flavour. In 1938, this styling provided Mainbocher with one of his firmest successes, which French journalists called the '*malheurs de Sophie*' dress – or as the Americans

One of the earliest influences of workmen's clothes, which has been revived periodically ever since. By Mainbocher, in 1934.

right
Another of Mainbocher's designs for the Duchess of Windsor's trousseau, 1937.

described it, the '*Little Women*' fashion. It was actually a daytime version of the romantic mid-19th-century mode for evening wear, with a neat, high-necked, tightly fitting bodice, and a wide short flaring skirt, trimmed around the hem with white embroidery. Couturier Robert Piguet showed the same idea at the same time, but Mainbocher is usually given credit for the design.

Mainbocher is said to have had his first success with the introduction of strapless styles for evening wear, but in the main, it is Chanel rather than he who retained it most consistently throughout the 'thirties. He experimented with the decorative potentialities of bead and sequin embroidery, and in 1938 his embroidered, pink crêpe Edwardian dress, with heart-shaped neckline and long sleeves puffed at the shoulder, the whole entirely pailleted in gold beads and sequins, was hailed as 'one of the most sensational dresses in all Paris'. The best known, if not the most decora-

right
In September 1939, on the eve of war, Mainbocher designed this corseted evening dress, which perfectly captured the silhouette which Dior was to launch so successfully two years after the end of hostilities as the famous 'New Look'.

Mainbocher's sketch for a blouse to match a suit designed for the trousseau.

tively exciting of his beaded models is the striped sequin bolero and sash, in a long, light crêpe evening dress immortalised by Sir Cecil Beaton in his wedding photographs of the Duchess of Windsor, who was Mainbocher's most famous client. In another photograph she is seen in one of his slim-fitting evening dresses, which he introduced in the last pre-war season with the revolutionary wasp waist that so startled his contemporaries. This was taken up of course by Christian Dior eight years later, as the starting point for the 'New Look'. Encased in their back-lacing whalebone *guêpières*, made by Warner's, his mannequins lost three inches around their waists, and it was with the profits from these models that Mainbocher, an American in Paris, had to leave at the outbreak of World War II. He settled his affairs, and started again in the USA.

The house of Lanvin continued unchanged throughout the decade, still under the personal direction of Madame Jeanne Lanvin who at the opulent and social evening openings took her place behind the desk at the door, personally checking her contribution to each year's fashion. She was an enthusiast for modern design, and in early years she stayed with the decorative influences of the 1920s much longer than the rest of the couture. Her 1930 collection has an almost archaic 'art deco' look, but she soon began to produce clothes of a rich and truly feminine elegance. Her *'robes d'ange'* must have been among the most comfortable and lovable clothes of the decade, with their straight and sweeping lines. The technical excellence of her dressmaking detail gave an extra dimension to her styling. An evening dress of 1934 in purple of an almost drunken richness, a mere slither of satin, incorporates the two typical fashion features of the period: lapels to broaden the shoulders, and a cape. The former was stiffened with close, regular rows of impeccable seaming, and the cape of rich velvet textured with dense and precise ruching. (The dress is now in the Victoria and Albert Museum, London.)

Jean Patou who had also risen to prominence in the 'twenties, continued to contribute new ideas. He had led the way in 1929 by raising the waistline to natural level, as well as lengthening and levelling the skirts. Patou lowered the waistline again in 1932, but his 'mediaeval dresses', their long skirts sweeping from the hips, failed to catch the fancy of an age reluctant to lose the waists which they had so recently found. He died in 1936 and the house continued to produce clothes in his style under the business-like direction of his brother-in-law, Raymond Barbas.

Edward Molyneux was now installed in the rue Royale, where he showed his clothes against a luxurious pale gray background. (He was the only couturier in Paris to insist that his staff wear uniform, also in pale gray.) His clothes were the mainstay of the wardrobes of the majority of women who wanted to dress well without causing comment. The shoulders of his impeccable suits, dresses and jackets are never overstressed, the waists never constricted. A jacket with a pleated skirt seems an anonymous enough outfit, but to contemporaries his signature was immediately apparent. One his clients, Madame Ralli, in 1939, wearing a neat gray belted suit with a pleated skirt and a spotted turtle-neck blouse with a bow at the neck, could have worn the outfit without noticeable affectation from that day to this. Always within the limits of good taste, his clothes were never boring. In 1934, he introduced the collarless peasant jacket and began to experiment with boleros and gay combinations of contrasting colours. Two years later he was one of the first to bring in the shorter full skirt. He preferred to create for the slim and natural woman, and is commemorated best by the unostentatious elegance of Princess Marina. With Chanel he shares the credit for the creation of modern but classic couture.

His evening clothes of the early 1930s were slim and straight, trimmed with flowers and feathers, but in 1935 he introduced a new fullness into the skirt and by 1937 his evening dresses were considered 'the most romantic in Paris'. He himself was a more than competent amateur artist and a collector of Impressionist paintings. In his clothes, the ladies of Renoir live again. He made a dramatic hooded black *faille* evening coat, crinolines with festooned skirts, and in 1939 the quintessence of Second Empire romance: a wide-skirted full-length velvet evening suit, its neat, fitted, hip-length jacket trimmed with astrakhan and bunches of violets. Molyneux's clothes, more than those of any other courturier, can only be judged by their illustrations in the magazines of the period, and from the reminiscences of happy owners. Few survive, for they have been loved to death, and the records of the house were destroyed during World War II.

Another well established house with much still to contribute was that of Vionnet. With increasing success Madeleine Vionnet worked through to 1939, when she retired leaving her personal tradition to be carried on by Marcelle Chaumont, Mad Carpentier and Jacques Griffe. Her house retained the affections of its clients over the years. She made clothes for the Queen of the Belgians and the wealthiest and most established of European society. The Rothschilds, Mme Clemenceau, Mme Citroen, Mrs Harrison Williams and Mme Martinez de Hoz took the places reserved for them at each of her crowded, yet well-organised openings.

Madeleine Vionnet has always avoided personal publicity but her unique contribution to fashion has made her an immortal of the couture during her own lifetime. Edna Woolman Chase, a hard headed and experienced critic described her as 'unique . . . perhaps the only true creator on the art of couture . . . she was an artist in fabric as Picasso is in paint'. Frederick Yoxall notes her 'development of the bias cut . . . gives to her dress a new dimension . . . as important as the discovery of perspective to painting. Bias cut not only gives the model greater subtlety; it also enhances the characteristics of the female form.' It is no coincidence that to Vionnet goes the credit for the first nipple to appear on the chaste pages of *Vogue* – outlined by cross draping satin in 1932. Her feeling for the counterpoint of female body and clothes is extraordinary, and the dresses look best on a well-built woman.

In the early 1930s, Vionnet made many wearable, slim-fitting afternoon

Patou's revolutionary dropped hemline transformed Paris in the autumn of 1929.

Three magnificent evening gowns from Madeleine Vionnet:
winter 1928.
winter 1931.
winter 1937.

Three day outfits from Madeleine Vionnet:
winter 1932.
summer 1935.
summer 1939.

Three coats from Madeleine Vionnet:
winter 1929.
summer 1934.
summer 1935.

All these photographs were taken by the house of Vionnet at the time of the collections, as contemporary records.

102

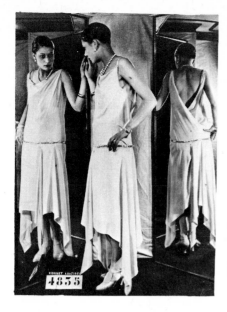

dresses and snug wrap-around coats, but her unique contribution to the history of fashion is the pale coloured heavy silk crêpe rosalba dress which all her customers wore to summer race-meetings. The top cross cut, falls softly away from the neck, moulding shoulders and breast. Its only trimming is a simple design in hem stitching. It is controlled at the side with a unique triangular seam, and then flows softly into an easy bias skirt. At the waist is a contrasting coloured leather belt. These dresses need no fiddly fastenings, nowhere do they cling, and they can be adapted to almost any figure with only the slightest alteration at the hem.

When, after 1933, fashion demanded an exaggerated shoulder line, Vionnet devised her own way of dealing with the problem, using drape instead of shoulder pads. She was always secretive about her methods, and since none of these drape dresses have survived, her method must remain unclear, though to judge from photographs, it was both graceful and effective.

For evening, she preferred dresses in sheer floating fabrics. Her clients liked white, or pale shades, but for shows she made them in vivid colours, sending them out three at a time. A dazzled viewer said they looked like summer butterflies. The bodice shadowed the body, often leaving the back bare, and the circular skirt swayed with every movement. In the hand, the dresses are mere cloudy wisps and in 1932 it was doubted whether her very respectable clientèle would agree to wear them without an additional underslip. For those with more luxurious tastes, she provided the acme of opulence – white velvet and black mink (her particular innovation) or black velvet and white mink.

The trend to more romantic styling in the second half of the 'thirties seems to have found her unprepared. In the autumn of 1934, within two weeks of her opening, she scrapped her entire collection and made another. She triumphed. Vionnet 'opened on the dot with her phenom-

It is interesting to note that for this *directoire* dress, designed by Vionnet in lilac and gold lamé, with a circular skirt, the mannequin wore no bra: the gown was a sheer stream of shining sex appeal in fabric. (1938.)

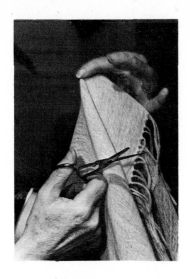

The hands of Mme Grès.

Two ball gowns designed in the Winterhalter style by Alix, later known as Mme Grès. (1938.)

enal 1880 models cut with a modern dash . . . as a result Vionnet stands today . . . not for self-effacing crêpe de chine but for conspicuous stiff bustles, picture dresses and triumphs in taffeta'. Only when these clothes are held in the hand can one appreciate the skill with which Vionnet has made materials bounce instead of slinking, without resource to buckram or *crin*. In 1937, she made her greatest dress. It had a high-waisted bodice with a halter strap, and from it the tightly swathed pleats of gold lamé fell in a shower of gold. Shining through the years, it still has an archetypal sex appeal . . . truly, her range was staggering.

The potential of double-width draping fabric was extended yet further by a new couturier in Paris, Alix, later to be known as Mme Grès. She was the daughter of an intellectual family, and trained as a musician and as a sculptor before turning to the career of couture. She opened her own establishment in 1934, when still only in her twenties. In 1935 she experimented with new versions of the draped, straight cut dress as an alternative to the bias cut with which she had become a little bored. At the time it was thought that her new methods of designing would lead to a new school in couture, but this has not proved to be so. Alix made these dresses in the 1930s, and Madame Grès continues to make them now, but only she – they are her unique contribution to couture. True to her training, she sculpts in the material, taking her inspiration from Greece of the golden age. The designs have slightly formalised over the period but remain basically unchanged. Probably only Madame Grès herself can tell with certainty a magnificent long-sleeved pleated jersey dress from 1938, from one made yesterday. There seems no reason why they should not continue. They are fashion, and yet they transcend it, demanding an impeccable dressmaking technique. These miracles of fine and regular pleating are products of very personal concentration. Small wonder that Alix's openings in the 1930s had an intense quality lacking in other houses. Bettina Ballard describes them as 'long drawn out, tense psychological struggles . . . we would wait and wait and wait . . . while Madame Alix pinned her last dresses together. Finally a beautiful Indo-Chinese girl would weave into the room draped skintight in jersey. Eric the artist would . . . make animal sounds of pleasure as the exciting exhibitionist figure undulated through the salon.' The models were often made in deep and vivid colours though probably they were most popular in white. A short version in dark wool was much in demand as a '*robe d'intérieure*'. At this early period, Alix was almost as well known for her exotic mode. She travelled widely in the east, and in 1936 triumphantly brought to Paris a westernised version of a Javanese dancer's tunic in Bianchini brocade, her 'Temple of Heaven' dress, launching a most satisfying version of the three-quarter length tunic with peplum.

An aspect not often stressed by her appraisers is her ability to cope with large scale patterns. One of her first successful models in 1934 was an evening coat of ciré satin embroidered to suggest Renaissance pattern leather. She was equally able with large-scale checks and in 1938 made an overcoat in a large and brilliant tartan, short and flared with the fullness swept forward to the front. A recent example epitomising several of her talents is the simple rectangular tunic in blue and black squares on white, made in 1969. It embodies the structural simplicity and consummate skill in sculpted, large-patterned fabrics which are the trademarks of a Grès model.

The reader may be intrigued by the amount of detailed knowledge which has survived from the period of the 'thirties, about French couture, for which there is one most important explanation. The previous two chapters have chronicled in brief the early developments of photography, of fashion sketching and reporting, but it is not until the 'thirties that these activities became a major force in the world of fashion, when the magazines widened their appeal and catered for the mass market more professionally than ever before. In this decade, fashion writers became much more accurate and up-to-the-minute with their information (one season's report was actually broadcast by radio from Paris), and the art of the photographer acquired a sharper style and definition of the mode. The 'glossy' magazines became valuable records of the social tastes of the time, and their contributors gave considered opinions, which were noted, if not always enjoyed, by the haute couture.

Silhouettes for evening wear in the late 'thirties.

Vogue, the most reasonably priced of the fashion magazines with pretensions to an almost popular circulation, started a section on 'The well spent pound', and helpfully assessed budgets of débutantes, working girls and ladies about town, but not unfortunately, the *haut monde*. Advice was given on clothes suitable for the fashionable day: *tailleurs* or neat suits for shopping; dresses and jackets for lunch; and the new late-day dress, which by the early 'thirties was beginning to be called the cocktail dress and had lengthened to just above the ankle. This fashion could also be worn for simple dinners and even for that new way of spending an evening – going to the cinema. As the decade progressed, the 'glossies' showed ball and gala dresses of an ever-increasing splendour. They also showed large numbers of dresses for country and sport, in which some of the younger couturiers like Jane Règny specialised, although an old-established house such as Worth was, in 1930, still refusing to use the term 'sports clothes', referring to them merely as 'out-of-town wear'.

The magazines laid the world before their readers. Resorts became even more exotic. In addition to Deauville and Biarritz, there was the south of France, Venice, and even Yugoslavia where hundreds holidayed in the wake of the Prince of Wales and Mrs Simpson. North Africa was added to the tourist map and Djelabas and Turkish trousers appeared on the least exotic beaches. With the popularisation of the ship cruise which was reinforced by the impact of the *Exposition Coloniale* of 1931, came the fashionable discovery of the Pacific and the Far East. Jacques Heim introduced the *pareo* to the beach, Alix her 'Temple of Heaven' dress, and Mainbocher his minaret drapes to the smart drawing-room. In Europe, Germany and Austria became popular for holidays but though the maga-

A sheath of satin was designed by Edward Molyneux for Gertrude Lawrence, in autumn 1934.

zines concentrated on Rhine castles, never visiting Munich beer cellars, nevertheless they promoted the peasant fashion which became popular in the late 1930s. The full gathered *dirndl* skirt of 1938 was disowned by *Harper's Bazaar* the following year – 'we loved the *dirndl* well, but not too wisely, for it was essentially a peasant fashion'. The onslaught of war made peasants of everyone, happy to have a gay skirt from just over a yard of gay material. The USSR was added to the fashionable scene for a fleeting moment when Schiaparelli and Sir Cecil Beaton went to Moscow for *La Foire D'échantillons de l'Industrie légère de France* but the effect was minimal on all sides.

The Paris weekend became a commonplace for the English, while to reciprocate, the houses of Molyneux and Piguet, Schiaparelli and Maggy Rouff opened in London. Though the Paris houses never moved to New York, nevertheless the big shops like Bendel's, Altman's, Saks, Bonwit Teller and Marshall Field received a regular supply of French models. Paris fashion had become truly international, and by the end of the 'thirties only half of the top couturiers were French; Schiaparelli was Italian, Mainbocher American, Molyneux English and Balenciaga Spanish.

The internationalism of the couture went further than the expansion of tourism, which the magazines promoted. Hollywood, with its world-wide film industry, set its own styles, and encouraged that love of dressing-up which had always played its part in Paris fashion. A number of houses, such as Schiaparelli, Rochas, Molyneux, Alix, Patou, and Lanvin, designed costumes for films. The couturiers had always enjoyed their work for the theatre, as far back as the days of Sarah Bernhardt; now, this new impetus brought about a taste for fancy-dress balls, which became ever more elaborate as the decade progressed. In 1937 came that apotheosis of dressing-up – the Coronation of George VI.

In the small and ruthlessly competitive world of haute couture, the importance of the glossy magazine was paramount. *Vogue*, *Harper's Bazaar* and *Femina*, together with the more trade-oriented *Women's Wear Daily* and *L'Officiel*, could make or break couturiers by the publicity they accorded. Edna Woolman Chase, Bettina Ballard and Frederick Yoxall of *Vogue*, M. D. C. Crawford and John Fairchild of *Women's Wear Daily*, have each given individual accounts of the period. Together with Carmel Snow of *Harper's Bazaar* and Martine Regnier of *Femina*, they showed an integrity and rare flair in their pursuit of talent. At a quick glance, the magazines seem to show most of the same dresses for most of the time, but personalities are rife and differences of emphasis, small in themselves, are important to the general view of the period. In the early 'thirties Vionnet was suspicious of *Vogue*, so it is *Femina* and *Harper's Bazaar* which give the more complete picture of her work. Carmel Snow and Martine Regnier were quicker to publicise the new star Balenciaga than was Bettina Ballard. The rivalry between Patou and Chanel is described in the chapter devoted to the latter.

Schiaparelli was every journalist's dream, for in every collection there was something memorable and amusing. In 1938 her spring theme was the circus. In her memoir, *Shocking Life*, she calls it her 'most riotous and swaggering . . . Barnum and Bailey, Grock and the Fratellinis, got loose in a mad dance in the dignified showroom, up and down the imposing staircase, in and out of the windows. Clowns, elephants, horses, decorated the prints with balloons for bags, spats for gloves, ice-cream cones for hats.' It was reported in all the magazines, but Christian Bérard drew it for *Vogue* and its impact was immortalised.

The journals depended on the quality of their photographers and artists for their effect. There was temperament, there were arguments, there was poaching, and the vituperations resound through all the memoirs. Editorial attitude at its purest is stated by Edna Woolman Chase: 'I'm sick and tired of having women say to me "How is this dress made? What is it like?" . . . Concentrate completely on the dress, light it for this purpose and if that can't be done with art then art be damned' – a policy which only *L'Officiel* has followed without deviation.

At the beginning of the 'thirties, fashion photography, although thirty years old, was only just emerging from its adolescent stage. *Harper's* had poached from *Vogue* a late survivor of this early period in Baron Adolph de Meyer. To be photographed by him was a social accolade. Schiaparelli had arrived in 1930 when she was recorded by him in her black and white reversible satin dress. He also commented rather ponderously on the more traditional collections. By 1933, his photographs of static, pure, profiled ladies, one elbow and one foot turned out, looking at least half a stone heavier than they would ever look again, had disappeared forever. Edward Steichen, a painter who turned to photography in 1923, made a virtue of realism and gave his pictures a quality of dignity without intrusive artifice. He worked well with Marion Moorhouse, the first of the great fashion models, whose slight smile enlivens the elegantly furnished backgrounds in *Vogue*. He liked Vionnet dresses perhaps because they reminded him of his photographs of the Isadora Duncan entourage, taken in the Parthenon! Baron Huynigen Huene and his disciple Horst Bohrmann – usually known simply as Horst – contributed some of the most memorable fashion photographs to *Vogue* and *Harper's*. Again they are at their best with the classical drapes of Vionnet and Alix. Man Ray, too, served his time as a fashion photographer, and his experimental colour plates were truly memorable.

Day clothes and accessories never received the emphasis they deserved until Sir Cecil Beaton entered the field. He is unique in his fidelity to *Vogue*, which put him under contract in 1928, and also in his ability not only to photograph, but to sketch and to write. Henry Yoxall states firmly: 'He made . . . a greater contribution to the reputation of *Vogue* than any other artist of the period.' An anthology of his works is a social history of the *haut monde*. His photographic style changed throughout the period; gleam and reflection characterised his earlier work, of which his portrait

The Coronation of George VI: Princess Marina's robe for this event was designed by Edward Molyneux. (May 1937.)

Jean Patou designed the gowns for many society weddings during the 'twenties and 'thirties. This was for the marriage of the Countess Henri de Castellane, in 1931.

Another exposition of the Winter-halter theme came from Balen-ciaga in October 1938; the gown on the left was in shimmering pink moiré, the one on the right in heavy white satin, tight-bodiced and decorated with bright yellow, tasselled velvet. The photographer was Baron Huynigen Huene.

of that impish and talented couturier Charles James, reflected three ways in the lid of a grand piano, is a particularly fine example. He experimented with bizarre but pretty props: hats with heads pop out of hat-boxes, through paper screens, and sit under glass domes. His use of surrealist backgrounds was most effective when he recorded the Dali-inspired Schiaparelli suits against a deserted Dali background. Period, imaginative atmosphere, are there, and you can still see the clothes.

Artists were placed under contract as eagerly as were the photographers. They carried on the early fashion-plate tradition, but with much greater

Mme Grès, a study by Sir Cecil Beaton, seen in the background.

freedom of expression. 'Eric', Carl Ericsson, a Swedish–American, who was formerly a painter, brought a graceful but almost full-blooded realism to the genre. Count René Bouet Willaumez began as an engineer but later turned to fashion illustration. His 1939 sketch of a rust crêpe Vionnet flaring in finely controlled tucks from a beaded halter neck, shows the flow and states the effect with great charm, while absolutely concealing the cut. Vionnet, who hated being copied, must have been very pleased.

Almost every decorative artist of quality was called on to contribute at least a drawing, if not a cover, to the magazines of the decade, but the glamour and gaiety of the later 'thirties are best captured in the sketches of Christian Bérard. A neo-romantic painter, he first became known in 1924, and by the 'thirties he was turning increasingly to stage design and fashion illustration. From 1934 he worked more or less continuously for *Vogue*' inspiring and illuminating the whole of haute couture. No opening was complete without him, no *toilette* acceptable without his approval. His drawings are unmistakable: brilliant, spontaneous suggestions and impressions in sweet, rich, and strangely contrasting colours. Editors might derisively call him 'faceless Freddy' and ask with despair how any reader would recognise the clothes he drew, but the sketches evoked brilliantly the fantasy of the fashions of the period. Diabetic, an opium addict, gross and dirty, he had a charm that endeared him to the most jealous of couturiers, the most harassed of editors and the most impeccable of the *haut monde*. Everyone loved and trusted him. He passed freely between the warring camps, an inspiration to all in that ruthlessly competitive world.

Throughout the 'thirties, both the cause of creativity, and a good deal of the finance of the couture industry, still came from the private client. Couturiers of the old school made for their customers and not for the press. Bettina Ballard termed them '*les dames de Vogue*' and '*les dames de Femina*', and their charm and chic were acknowledged wherever the glossies were read. Most lived more or less constantly in Paris, buying regularly from the same couturier, an arrangement probably to their mutual advantage. Mme Jean Ralli, small and charming, was Greek, and a Molyneux disciple. It was she who brought him his best known client, Princess Marina of Greece, who later became the Duchess of Kent. Mme Martinez de Hoz, a South American, dressed at Vionnet. She had a superb dark beauty, and an impeccable elegance. In the Jean Seeburger *actualité* photographs of smart Paris racegoers she is recognisable even

A delightful sketch capturing the fanciful, joke details which were typical of Schiaparelli's otherwise classical designs: a suit, with small handmirrors as enormous buttons. (1938.)

below left
Mme Martinez de Hoz, **(right)** the famous Parisienne hostess and beauty, dressed by Vionnet, and photographed by Seeberger at Chantilly in June 1935.

from the back in her large brimmed Reboux hats and the unmistakable drape of her Vionnet dresses. Princess 'Baba' de Faucigny Lucinge had a fey, almost other-worldy charm, and dressed mostly at Lelong.

Daisy Fellowes, heiress to the Singer sewing-machine fortune, half American, half French and of an impudent and immaculate elegance, was Schiaparelli's most publicised customer. She wore extreme models with confidence, and even managed to carry off with elegance the notorious 'lamb cutlet' hat. Her 'roi soleil' cape is now a gift from her executors to the Carnavalet Museum, Paris. Sometimes, she and Schiaparelli worked together on her clothes. In 1934, she persuaded a slightly reluctant Schiaparelli to make her a dress inspired by the Bérard costumes for the ballet, Mozartiana. 'What fun it was at the next big gala to wear an angelically demure navy-blue front and demoniacally scarlet back', she commented.

Prominent among Schiaparelli's many American clients were Mrs Reginald Balcombe, later Millicent Rogers, and dynamic Bettina Bergery, who had been her first assistant. Less well known as a client was Mrs Wallace Warfield Simpson, later Duchess of Windsor. Her incisive tapering silhouette and neat dark head made her a pure Schiaparelli type, for, like Chanel, Schiaparelli worked best with women who looked more or less like herself. At the time of her engagement to King Edward VIII *Femina* published eighteen of her Schiaparelli outfits, chosen mostly from the more graceful and less extreme styles; but for her trousseau, and after her marriage, she went to Mainbocher.

Couture, with all its individuality is illustrated in a suitcase if not in a nutshell by Bettina Ballard's choice of clothes for her return to the USA in 1937. She was young, slim, her judgement impartial and professionally trained. She was also determined to impress. 'I concentrated on a handsome black Schiaparelli suit with fancy buttons, a Creed suit and a Molyneux navy dress and jacket for day, with no less than twenty of the most conspicuous hats in Paris. Chanel lent me from her closet two sublime evening costumes . . . soft long skirts pleated onto bare bodices and their own waist-length bolero jackets – simple and very elegant . . . for a real shocker I took Schiaparelli's gold embroidered black monkey jacket, a long black skirt and a matching high chechia hat.' With the exception of Creed, she brought nothing from the more traditional couturiers – her clothes are those of young Paris.

Among the couturiers themselves two main groups emerge – the traditional, which carried on in the same way as they had in the previous decade, and the newly arrived, like Alix, Schiaparelli, Mainbocher and Balenciaga. Of the older type of couturier, the house of Worth was the most traditional; by this period it designed mainly for the rich and middle-aged, and for those daughters who were too young to choose for themselves.

A good contemporary mirror for the couture of the 'thirties is its contribution to the *Exposition International des Arts et Techniques* in 1937. The

Mainbocher's most celebrated commission was to design the trousseau for the Duchess of Windsor in 1937. This evening suit shows the couturier's characteristic skill with beaded, sequined formal clothes.

left
A sketch by Christian Bérard for *Harper's* designed by Lanvin for the Vicomtesse de Noailles: a dress in white velvet with mosaic print in black. As accessory to this evening gown. Lanvin introduced a Chanel brooch of diamonds, like a fern, which was pinned across the hat. (1935.)

exhibition, which was held in Paris, was a triumphantly elegant enterprise. The couture, under the direction of its president, Mme Jeanne Lanvin, organised the *Pavillon d'Elégance*, a chaste little building by the architect-designers, Aillaud, Kohlmann and Vibert, which housed the models of the 120 exhibitors in a fantastic, Chirico-like interior, of blue and terra-cotta. On the roof of the building was the 'Club des Oiseaux', a nightclub and restaurant which staged a show of live elegance in the afternoons with mannequin parades, and rivalling display of society's splendour in the evenings, which was organised by a committee of the fashionable élite. Within the pavilion the clothes were shown on models designed by the sculptor Couturier, and made by Segall's, the Paris model manufacturers. They were elongated, dreamlike, formalised creatures; featureless heads mounted on bodies in formal, declamatory poses. To some commentators they were a '*synthèse des Aphrodites des Artemis . . . une Greta Garbo, une Marlene Dietrich*'.

The couturiers seem to have found them rather a problem and dressed them in clothes more glamorous than strictly contemporary. Patou made a wonderful evening coat covered with lacquered feathers, and Vionnet, the arch-dressmaker, painstakingly sprayed lace to look like plaster. The most successful exhibit from all points of view was Alix's classical drape. Schiaparelli, ever the individualist, found the models frankly hideous, laid her flat, covered its nakedness with flowers, and slung up a clothes line on which she hung the entire wardrobe of a Schiaparelli fashionable. She says her corner was mobbed. If only there had been a photograph!

In 1939 came the World's Fair in New York and again the couture were called on to contribute. Committee, designers and architects were much the same as they had been two years before, but this time they did not show any dresses. Their stated reason was that any clothes shown in the USA would be out of date (or copied?) within a month of their arrival, and they consoled the visitor with the statement that so many of their clothes had in any case been sold to Americans that they were more or less on view anyway. Around a statue of Venus were arranged bas reliefs by Mme Anny Vibert, symbolic of the ideals of each couturier. Alix showed a classic draped robe, Lanvin a '*robe d'ange*,' Worth, an opulent '*robe de style*', Molyneux an Empire dress, and Patou was still loyal to his stillborn long torso line of 1932. Chanel symbolised her contribution by writing her name in block capitals across a classical arch, and it would seem that this time Schiaparelli never bothered to show anything at all. After all, a good many of the clothes sold to the Americans were hers. Only posterity can confirm their choice.

Iris Ashley

5COCO

Mademoiselle Chanel, in the 'thirties.

There are a great many people who hold the opinion that the whole business of French haute couture is simply a vast confidence trick. They suggest that all the members of the Chambre Syndicale de la Couture Française get together and decide just what new ideas in fashion they will impose on waiting (*sic*, gullible) women of the western world. No doubt this theory might have a certain plausibility if the designers were not artists, and in deadly competition with each other. Also, if it had not been proved beyond question, that it is not possible to impose any change of fashion except in response to a corporate need. The timing must be right. In 1947, Christian Dior's 'New Look' with its extravagant use of voluminous material, was an obvious counterpoint to the boredom of wartime restrictions and the dreariness of clothes in which the absence of any charm or frivolity was considered a positive merit. Dior's success is history. However, a few years later, Pierre Balmain tried to introduce a return to

114

the styles of the 'twenties and early 'thirties: fashions that are now sweeping the 'seventies. He was too early. The collection was lavishly presented in Paris, to a packed house of foreign buyers and journalists. They came, they saw, but they were not conquered. Alas, they were right, the collection was a total flop. All the same, Balmain is one of the great designers, and I am glad to have written at the time that 'Anybody can make a mistake. But Pierre Balmain likes to make women look pretty, and I'll lay odds that his talent will be around when many other names have faded from the scene.' He is still a name to draw Queen Sirikit of Siam halfway across the world to get her clothes for great occasions. His private customers are both numerous and rich enough to give him economic security. He is indeed among the very few who have stayed the course.

How then, against such a background of cut-and-thrust competition of difficult timing, and even more difficult finances (it takes up to £150,000 to produce a collection), how then did Mademoiselle Chanel sweep the board to become a legend in her own lifetime?

She achieved an internationally wider, and in her own lifetime, longer lasting, fame than any other figure in fashion history so far. Her genius was for a very special kind of simplicity. She found a formula for making women look extraordinarily elegant and at the same time comfortable, therefore easy and relaxed. Anybody who is scornful of the suggestion that fashion designing can be considered an art would do well to give a little time and study to Chanel. Her eye for proportion: just how high above the wristbone should a sleeve end; how long a jacket should be in relation to the skirt and how wide in the same context, were things she knew by instinct. Her sense of colour; wonderful blends of colours woven into what the French call 'tweeds', but which are as much like British tweeds as rice pudding is to a soufflé. Pure silks and shantung or softest jersey used in combination with the tweeds, all unique to Chanel, added up to a way of dressing which was very feminine in effect and gave out an aura of expensiveness difficult to define. Cecil Beaton has summed it up as looking 'expensively poor', which is paradoxical, but accurate. In the hands of Chanel, fashion designing was an art. She could be, and was, copied line-for-line in reproductions of her clothes, all over the world, much as prints are made of famous paintings. But nobody has ever produced an original design that could be passed off to an experienced eye as a 'Chanel'. A minor art it may be, but it is art for all that.

Mademoiselle Chanel held that a woman's face mattered much less than her figure from the point of view of dressing. 'An ugly woman with a bright mind can turn herself with make-up into a "jolie-laide" . . . clothes will do the rest', she said. As a woman who in her hey-day was remarkably good-looking it was perhaps a view she could afford to express. But it is true enough that she did make older women look much less than their years, and gave to young and beautiful girls a grace and dignity that made for a formidable combination of attraction. In the late 'fifties and early 'sixties, when every female in the USA was striving to look like either Grace

Kelly (now Princess of Monaco) or Jacqueline Kennedy (Onassis), it is easy to understand why Chanel had such a fantastic success.

Gabrielle Chanel was born to a peasant family in Auvergne in 1886, give or take a year either side of that date. Nobody can be quite sure and Chanel was not one to help on such a subject. All her life, she foxed would-be interviewers by not answering their questions, and merely told them what she pleased, frequently varying the stories. Such a personality could not have had a pedestrian beginning, and the little Chanel obliged the demands of the romantic-celebrity syndrome by being born in a railway-station waiting room. Inevitably, one had hoped that like Oscar Wilde's Ernest, she was found 'in a hand-bag', but no. The waiting room is all. The story of her childhood is in the true sad tradition. Her mother died of tuberculosis when she was six years old. Then, her young father, adored by the pretty little Gabrielle for his gay, light-hearted character, was moved by those very attributes to take himself off to seek his fortunes in the USA. He left his daughter in the care of an elderly aunt.

A sensitive child, she felt herself abandoned, no proper family to lean on and call her own, taken in at obvious inconvenience from sheer pity by the aunt. In later life, Gabrielle Chanel made it clear that it was at this moment, at eight years of age, that she made herself a promise. She swore that never again would she evoke the pity of anyone. Somehow she would become the most beautiful, the most loved, the most celebrated woman. Envied she would be; pitied never. But the Fates had not finished with her. When she was about eighteen, her elder sister, of whom she was fond, committed suicide. Then, the first love of her life, an Englishman called Boy Capel, was killed in a car accident. Each loss she not only mourned but looked upon as a personal treachery. Each loss was a new kind of abandonment which began to drive her towards the lonely, solitary character she ultimately became.

Chanel was always loyal to her affection towards her father. She told people he was a wine merchant in America. He was in actual fact an itinerant salesman, a sort of commercial traveller. By nature a rover, it is clear that even before he left, his daughter saw him seldom. He was hardly ever there. Chanel had inherited this restless nature. 'I do not care much for places. I prefer the routes that lead to them', she said.

Legend has it that the infant Gabrielle was inclined to cut up her aunt's curtains to make clothes for her dolls. Knowing the French peasant's attitude towards the sacredness of all property, it would have been a brave child who attempted anything so reckless. Certainly, she would not have done it twice. It is also said that the boy Dior used to dress cardboard dolls and that Hubert de Givenchy offered practical advice on fashion to his mother when he was seven years old. These winsome stories do of course help to bridge the gap of childhood of celebrities, when, since nobody realises the fame which lies ahead, all are calmly indifferent to the daily sayings and doings of the genius in their midst. For my part, winsome stories are apt to produce a slight feeling of nausea and if there was a thing

Chanel could not abide, it was sentimentality.

Somewhere around the age of nineteen or twenty she became a dancer and got a job in a night club in Pau, in the Pyrenees. Here, in best Dornford Yates style, she met a young Englishman who fell madly in love with her. With the recent example of his own king, Edward VII, to encourage him, what more natural than that the young man should take his inamorata off to Paris and set her up in business. Chanel had her own shop as a modiste, a designer of hats in the days when hats were a very important item of fashion, at 23 rue Cambon, only a few doors away from the famous salon of mirrors she was later to make famous at number 31 in the same street. She must have had some success from the start, for in a fashion journal of 1912 there is a picture of the actress Gabrielle Dorziat, wearing a new spring model and beneath it the caption reads: 'Hat by Gabrielle Chanel.'

The 1914 war effectively removed her English backer, and Chanel went off to Deauville to work for the Red Cross. How much was pure luck and how much that weird instinct which seems to lead determined people towards their ambitions, no one can say. True, the Red Cross did ask her to go to Deauville, but equally true that Deauville was the most fashionable seaside resort in France, war or no war. A new, and it is nice to imagine by now a more perspicacious 'ami' provided her with a small but elegant shop just where those aiming for a morning stroll along the famous broadwalk by the sea were bound to pass.

Early evidence of the influence of the great outdoors in fashion (which Mlle Chanel made elegant) is seen in these fashion sketches from *Gazette du Bon Ton*, in 1913 and 1920.

She now produced her first stroke of unmistakeable genius: the genius for sensing just what women wanted a split second before they knew it themselves. The ability to sense and provide for a corporate need. She realised that more and more women were taking on work of all kinds, to enable the replacing of men now at the Front. And the clothes they were wearing were ludicrously unsuitable, often even dangerous in their new activities. She decided that the straight jersey jackets, such as Marines wore, or men's woollen pullovers, would be far more practical and look much less silly. She bought sailors' jackets and men's pullovers. With only slight adaptation, a little trimming and single well-placed brooch, she herself wore them above a pleated skirt on the promenade at Deauville. They were a sensational success. Orders poured in to the little shop and she began to have jackets and pullovers made especially for her customers with individual 'Chanel' touches which identified and gave them cachet. She had found her true métier and there was no holding her. She had entered the ruthless field of fashion design and its fascination held her like a drug or like a lover for the rest of her life.

The days of Paul Poiret's feathers and furs, his elaborate frills and furbelows, were numbered. Chanel and Chanel alone, was propelling women's fashions from the 19th century with its atmosphere of time and leisure into the frenzied world of the 20th century.

She returned to Paris, and in 1920 a reporter to one of the more serious French newspapers wrote of a collection shown by Chanel: 'It is like

117

seeing clothes which an amazingly talented and artistic woman has had made for her own use alone. Furthermore, made by a dressmaker who works solely for her.' There were suits of jersey wool with short sun-ray pleated skirts, pullovers, simple jackets trimmed with fur (she even used rabbit), with pockets meant to be *used* and not merely as trimming. Real buttons and buttonholes were intended to fasten, as against the old haute couture idea of using buttons as ornaments, with concealed hooks for real fastening, a 'fidgety fussiness' Chanel abhorred. There were straight-lined evening dresses and crêpe-de-Chine capes. Everything looked uncluttered, with simple lines, and mostly in dark or neutral colours. During the next few years, Chanel hardly altered these lines at all, and in this attitude lay her great strength. Part of her genius lay in the intuitive recognition that women were bored with the fussy dressing and trimmings that had constituted the height of fashion for so long. She realised ahead of time that even rich and fashionable women would be riding in subways, jumping in and out of taxis, travelling casually and for brief visits. All of which made nonsense of elaborate clothes or the mountains of luggage needed to transport such things. She looked for and found the real woman hiding beneath all those exaggerated clothes. She decided that a woman's breasts and buttocks would look far better gently concealed, rather than have her puffed up fore and aft like a pouter pigeon. Ruthlessly, she stripped off the conventional finery. The talent, the genius, lay in converting this drab-seeming basis into a 'look' or 'fashion' of brilliant simplicity, which was exactly what Chanel achieved. She hated the way the hairdressers of the day set and waved hair into rigid ruts. She quite often grabbed a pair of scissors and sheared the heads of favourite clients. When she had dressed them in a simple jersey jacket and skirt, or a dress entirely plain, when they looked 'chic on the edge of poverty', then she allowed the jewels. Then and then only did she hang them about with costume jewellery, with brooches and rings and earrings, with great lumps of rubies and emeralds, with ropes and ropes of pearls. 'It does not matter if they are real', she remarked. 'So long as they look like junk!'

One could be forgiven for supposing that any little dressmaker of reasonable talent could have made passable imitations of such uncomplicated clothes as Chanel's, but her simple lines were far harder to catch and re-create than the more elaborate creations of a designer such as Poiret. She understood how to give her clothes a superb and matchless chic. Her complete refusal to add anything superfluous resulted in an effect that was the epitome of elegance. Balzac's theory of 'luxury through simplicity' was brought visually to life.

The artistic temperament does not as a rule go hand-in-glove with financial acumen. In this Chanel was something of an exception. Her French peasant background, combined with her horror of ever again being dependent on anybody's charity, gave her a shrewd and provident approach to money. All her life she fought to be paid what she felt she had justly earned. She fought for her worth, and she won a life of material

An early Chanel model, dating from spring 1922.

luxury at least.

The simplest suit or dress from the house of Chanel cost as much as gold and silver embroideries of other designers. As Anny Latour remarked in her book, *Kings of Fashion*, Chanel was well qualified to write a book herself which could have been called: 'The art of dressing simply . . . and paying a great deal of money for the pleasure.'

By 1922, Chanel was back in Paris and well established at 31 rue Cambon, where the luxurious salons bear her name to this day. A new beau came on the scene in the person of a rich English peer, whose assets included a large and beautiful yacht. By now too, she had acquired the nickname of 'Coco' and was never again called by any other name. Coco went for long cruises with her Prince Charming in his lovely boat and quite by chance, she became very sun-tanned. A sun-tanned skin was unknown at the time. Already a famous and much-imitated personality, Chanel walked off the yacht and into the Carlton Hotel in Cannes, dressed in a white jersey suit trimmed with navy that set off quite beautifully the golden glow of her sunburnt skin. Overnight, a sunburnt skin became fashion, and a great many people did indeed burn themselves to a crisp before learning how to acquire a sun-tan by gradual degrees. The Prince Charming was already married, but he was willing and anxious to divorce his wife in order to marry Gabrielle Chanel. However he made one (in the circumstances understandable) condition. She must give up her career and live her life according to her new station as the wife of a rich peer of England. Emancipated well ahead of her time, Chanel could not face this prospect. To give up all she had fought for, to lose her independence, however wealthy, to spend the rest of her days simply as 'somebody's wife', was an idea which she found suffocating. The idyll was over. She continued to run her fashion house, which was by 1924 one of the most important in Paris. Each new collection was hailed with enthusiasm and praise from the fashion writers. New storeys were added to the house at 31 rue Cambon, and the workrooms were extended. Then the houses on either side were added. Her models were bought by American buyers for reproduction and her concept of fashion was a great success in the USA. Chanel's fashions were a constant feature in *Vogue* magazine.

About this time, in the late 'twenties, the young Edward Molyneux was the first (and only) Englishman to storm the bastions of French haute couture in Paris. And Jean Patou was a distinguished and well-recognised couturier. Both these designers were akin to Chanel in that they designed clothes to make women look like elegant ladies, rather than any attempt to cause a sensation. There was no friendship between Patou and Molyneux, but Patou felt that his real blood adversary and enemy was Chanel. It was a rivalry that later resulted, as we shall see, in one of the major revolutions of the fashion industry. Each season after the collections had been shown, Patou used to watch for the special edition of *Vogue*. He would count the pages illustrating Chanel, and compare them in number to the models shown from his own new collection. If Chanel outnumbered him to any extent, he would write off in furious protest both to the editor and managing director of *Vogue*. At that time the editor was the famous Edna Woolman Chase, and she bore with this brouhaha with great patience. Finally however, when a protest came because Patou found himself on a page actually facing Chanel, a propinquity he could not endure even on paper, Mrs Chase had had enough. She wrote to Patou saying that she had given him important publicity over many years without as far as she could discern ever receiving a word of thanks from him, that *Vogue* reported the collections as a whole and not of a single designer, and that in future she would find it more peaceful to omit the name of the House of Patou from the pages of *Vogue* entirely. This brought a prompt and gentlemanly apology from M. Patou and friendship was restored. But he and Chanel would not sit down in the same room. Whoever spotted the other first, always left as ostentatiously as possible.

Another fierce rival at the top of the same ladder was Elsa Schiaparelli. 'The Italian artist who makes dresses', Chanel called her. 'Schiap', as she was always known in Paris, arrived on the scene eight years after Chanel: she was a little younger, and therefore all the more to be hated. The Hotel Ritz in Paris occupies a whole depth on the block between the Place Vendôme and the rue Cambon. Schiap's salon was in the Place Vendôme, almost alongside the main entrance to the Ritz. Chanel's salon in the rue Cambon was almost opposite the other entrance of the hotel, inside which was the famous Ritz Bar, and which for the sake of clarity in making dates was often called the Back Door. 'Poor Chanel', said Schiap. 'I use the front door of the Ritz . . . she must use the back.'

It was in the beautiful and elegant Ritz Hotel that Chanel got her own back for that remark. The great fashion photographer Horst happened to be lunching with Elsa Schiaparelli in the Ritz when Chanel came sweeping in with some friends. Seeing Horst, she smiled at him radiantly and as she actually approached his table towards another obviously reserved for her, Horst made a fatal mistake. He rose to his feet intending a courteous, and brief greeting. Chanel stopped dead, and completely ignoring Schiap, she kept Horst on his feet while she chatted non-stop for more than half-an-hour. It was only when a red-faced Mr Horst glanced desperately at his watch and murmuring something about '. . . being late for another date . . .' fled from the room, that the trap was sprung and Chanel proceeded to her own table with a happy smile. The story does not tell whether or not Schiap sat out a lonely luncheon or went hungry.

These bouts of childish jealousy, the intense rivalry, the occasional exhibition of appalling bad manners, may sound absurd. That they were also at times extremely funny, I was at a later date, able to vouch for personally. But they were not hard to understand. The top designers of Paris were creative artists, and the harnessing of artistic talents to commercial demands calls for a rigid form of discipline. There was not only the necessity for a new collection to be right *in* time, it had to be right *on* time as well. To fail in either could mean a failure with no chance of a

An expressive sketch, dated 1925, by Etienne Drian, of the shingle, which Chanel launched.

comeback. Small wonder, that in this forcing house of elegance, this hot-house of good taste, the exponents themselves sometimes felt the need to let off steam, even if the noise carried farther than they actually intended, and the resultant vapours smelled a touch less fragrant than their own exclusive perfumes. It was not in the last resort a really vicious rivalry. I never saw any actual blood.

It was in the late 'twenties, about the time that Chanel was invited to go to Hollywood to design for films, that she launched her now famous perfume. Having been born on 5 August, she considered five to be her lucky number. She always showed her new collections on 5 February or 5 August, and she decided to christen her perfume simply *Chanel 5*. Like everything she did it had the Midas touch about it. It had an international success from the beginning, but no one could have foreseen the fantastic demand for *Chanel 5* which came about towards the end of World War II. American GIs in Paris wanted naturally to take home something essentially French to their wives and sweethearts. Perfume was a natural, but the GIs were shy of attempting the French language. However, even a middle-west cowboy-soldier could manage the one word 'Chanel' and hold up five fingers to the shop assistant. It worked like a charm. It seemed that the whole of the USA must be smelling just like the air of 31 rue Cambon . . . and Mademoiselle Chanel moved into a luxurious suite at the Ritz Hotel on the proceeds.

When Chanel went to Hollywood for the first time, she had a success which surprised the film moguls as much as it did Chanel herself. The film stars had always been dressed for what then was thought to be 'glamour'. It was quite usual for a star such as Jean Harlow, Joan Crawford, or others of the period to appear in what looked like full evening dress at 10 o'clock in the morning in the films of the time. They did not wear clothes, they wore 'costume'. Chanel thought they looked wrong and started to dress them as she believed all chic (and rich) women should look. Films began to acquire a new veracity. The actors looked more convincing. The success was great and far-reaching: so far-reaching that when drastic changes of fashion took place twice almost overnight (in 1929–30 and in 1947), the film world took a terrible beating with pictures still not shown to the public but rendered obsolete by the change of hemline. If Chanel had never influenced Hollywood and they had pursued their fancy-dress ways, they could have been saved a lot of money.

On Broadway, it was the blonde Ina Claire, herself a slim, leggy version of the basic American ideal of looks, who put the Chanel-look across the footlights. She did for Chanel what Gertrude Lawrence later did for Edward Molyneux, and, later still, Audrey Hepburn did in the designs of Givenchy, and Katherine Hepburn when dressed by Balmain for the play *The Millionairess*. The idea of actresses appearing on the stage in clothes that the audience themselves might like to copy, was an entirely new concept when Ina Claire was first dressed by Chanel. When set against the elegance of Miss Claire, 'theatrical' clothes began to look tawdry, exaggerated, and often vulgar. The box-office appeal of the star gave Chanel, quite literally, a stage from which her whole philosophy of fashion was seen by thousands of women who might otherwise have taken much longer to get the idea. This philosophy, which always seemed to convey itself to the wearers of Chanel's fashions, was the clear implication that clothes must not appear to matter at all. It is the whole way you look that counts. A nihilistic attitude for a dress designer, if it had not also contained the subtle addition that only the most beautiful and understated clothes could in fact create the right effect.

The reader might perhaps be wondering just what is meant by all this

Ina Claire, one of Hollywood's first stars to be dressed by Chanel. Her sophisticated casuals marked a new era in dressing films, and made other 'costumed' actresses look out-of-date overnight.

emphasis on the words 'simplicity', or 'understated' when used in reference to fashions. It was the complete absence of any kind of distortion either to the fabrics or to the general outline. It was the absence of any obviously-imposed trimmings. No coat collar was wide enough to dwarf the wearer, no shoulders seen to be padded, no waistlines belted tightly. No buttons were in danger of popping, no seams showed the slightest strain. The Chanel ideal was a woman who wore her clothes with grace and effortless ease. It was an effect which the fashionable women of the 'twenties began more and more to acquire. Later, it became a standard look with American working girls. And chic women of today have it still.

In the late 'twenties Gabrielle Chanel herself clocked up her fortieth birthday. In those days women dreaded becoming forty much as they dislike achieving the age of sixty now. Always subjective, Chanel naturally began to devise ingenious ways for making women look twenty years younger than they actually were. She realised that a young and pretty woman whose clothes shrieked money might look like a *poule de luxe*, but a middle-aged woman in the same circumstances just looked like a rich old bag. She dressed her clients in velveteen jackets such as workmen wore and topped them with apache-like caps. She gave them plain black cloth overcoats, and it was only when these coats were removed that you discovered they were lined with mink or even sable. (This was an idea followed up by Christian Dior in the 'fifties, when he lined ordinary Burberry-type rain-

Mlle Chanel produced these exclusive pages of designs for British *Harper's Bazaar* in September 1938, conveying the humour and femininity of her accessories.

over page, left
Two sketches from the house of Patou, for 1930-1, show the intricacy against which Chanel reacted with her casual clothes.
over page, right
Classic examples of Mlle Chanel's easy elegance, both in jersey, and photographed by the Baron Demeyer in 1930.

coats with mink, to stunning effect.) She invented suits with little cardigan jackets, blouses with soft pussy-cat bows, and she took the hemline above the knee. The result was to make women look younger without looking foolish, and they loved her accordingly.

Chanel, long before the days of the mass market of ready-to-wear, had no objection to being copied. She was comfortably aware that a copy was at best – a copy. She held that fashion was not created by one person or even a small group. It must be widely popular with a large number of people before it can rightly be termed 'a fashion'. In essence she believed that the term 'fashion' meant the favoured mode of behaviour and dressing in any given era of time. She was responsible for the innovations of many 'fashions' which fulfilled these requirements. She popularised the wearing of enormous horn-rim glasses by women whose eyesight was in no need of help. She invented the sling-back pump in black and beige, still worn by Chanel addicts to this day. She made shirtwaister dresses in lace, a more sporty look than this material had ever known; she made trousers which ended at 'pedal-pusher' or calf length. Her mind was logical; there was reason in all her designs, which may account for the fact that so many of her creative ideas are still around. (The glasses were to protect the eyes.)

It was in the month of January 1930 that *Vogue* magazine published a double-page spread of drawings by Cecil Beaton that were hardly credible. On the one page were the fashions of winter 1929, with skirts well above the knee and waistlines somewhere around the behind. Opposite were the new fashions already successful in winter 1930, with long flowing skirts to the ankle and waists at normal level. The metamorphosis was complete.

As has been said, there is no question of the Paris designers collaborating to produce a change of fashion. Their ideas are evolved and brought to life in the utmost secrecy. But time has proved that there is usually something in the air, some kind of antennae, that leads them to new ideas that are at least consistent with each other. It is very rare indeed for one isolated house to produce designs so different from the others that they could scarcely be worn at the same period. Towards the end of 1928 and early in 1929, the tendency to a longer hemline had already been seen with handkerchief-points at the hemline or skirts to the knee at the front, but dipping almost to the floor at the back. So it was perhaps to be expected when, in the summer (for winter) collection of 1929, every house in Paris sent their hemlines plummeting with the unanimity of the window-blinds in a street at night-fall.

The other most important designer in Paris at this time along with Chanel, was Jean Patou. (Still a very big name in the haute couture and the ready-to-wear worlds of 1972.) In the matter of the dropped-hemline revolution of 1929, it is generally agreed that it was Jean Patou who fired the first salvo. The story goes that he was galvanised into action by sitting across the room from a group of women, all of whom had clearly been dressed by Mademoiselle Chanel. The brevity of their skirts exposed a good deal more of the wearers than Monsieur Patou found attractive in the circumstances. He is reported as having put a hand to his brow, and crying, 'My God, my old, I can no more', rushed off to his workroom where he started feverishly designing dresses of floor length.

Patou's own previous collections had been equally short-skirted, but his sudden repugnance had been brought about happily for him, by somebody else's fashions, and by Chanel at that. No doubt this added to the flame of his inspiration. At all events, after the most hideous attack of stage-fright, when he was utterly convinced that he had been quite mad to attempt such a radical change, the collection was a wild success. It was said that before the end of the show, the audience were already tugging at their skirts trying to cover their knees. A member of Patou's staff rushed to where he was hiding from view and told him gleefully, 'They are embarrassed by their skirts . . . already they feel démodé!'

If Patou showed the first completely revolutionary collection, Chanel was only a hop-and-a-skip behind. She raised the waistline and lowered the hemline, but only to ankle length, maintaining that floor-long

dresses got dirty hems which was an obvious antithesis to elegance. The time was exactly right. Women were bored with looking like boys, no breasts and no buttocks. The 'garconne' look had had its day. Every house in Paris went flat out for the lines of flowing femininity. And in the USA they followed suit to the last detail. So the comic situation arose wherein women had cupboards full of clothes they could no longer wear. The new long dresses not only made the short skirts look out of date, they also looked extraordinarily vulgar, a word which has lost much of its meaning today, but then had an unattractive connotation. In Hollywood, producers wept over the fashion consciousness they had acquired through Chanel. New films as yet unseen by the public had to be shelved, because the newly long-skirted audience would not tolerate their favourite stars looking out-of-date. In fact, at the mere sight of the old short skirt and low belt, they were apt to break into peals of laughter. The film world caught a cold in precisely the same way in 1947 when Christian Dior introduced his 'New Look'. It is hard to see how it could have been avoided, but perhaps they can derive some comfort from the completely undefined outline of fashion as it is today. It may be hard to harness it to any great effect, but if you have no definite outline at least you cannot have a definite revolution.

It was a strange paradox that women adopted a way of using more materials for their clothing just at the moment when money became more scarce. The Wall Street crash of 1929 had natural repercussions in London, Paris and Berlin. The legend that all Americans were automatically rich vanished overnight. Private fortunes went up in smoke; women did not spend as they had before either because they did not have the money, or because it was in bad taste to fritter on a single dress the kind of sum a man and his family could have lived on for a month. Unemployment was everywhere.

This is not to infer that life came to a stop. History tells that it did not. Paris fashion was a supply in response to a continuous demand, and so continue it did, but in a much lower key than the gay 'twenties. Countries, as always in times of economic struggle, became more chauvinistic. People were urged to 'Buy American', 'Buy German', and 'Buy British', in terms of patriotic endeavour. Far less private customers went to Paris for their clothes, and very, very few buyers for the big stores. For French couture, the 'thirties became something of a twilight period. In London, a group of young designers began to enjoy recognition and success. Such names as Lachasse, Digby Morton, Hardy Amies and, of course, Norman Hartnell, acquired the prestige previously only accorded to Paris fashion houses. That in the end Paris outlasted them in terms of haute couture and took back the ruling reins, I think is really more attributable to the artistic climate of Paris than to any lack of talent among the British houses.

Mademoiselle Gabrielle Chanel survived all this and more. Longer hem-lines and all, her philosophy of fashion remained unchanged. Her lovely, easy-to-wear clothes had a constant following of clients that kept her not only in business but at the top of the tree.

Not that Chanel was having it all her own way and all to herself. She was used to the distinguished Jean Patou and the elegant Edward Molyneux, but now she had to accept the considerable success of Elsa Schiaparelli. Just why Schiap with her baroque designs, her 'shocking' pink (an adjective still used today to describe a particular shade of magenta) and her use of rough fabrics such as hessian, was such a success is dealt with in another chapter. She was the counterpoint to everything that Chanel stood for. It says a great deal for the basic logic, the practicality of Chanel, that she endured alongside the flamboyant Schiap, and remained a big enough name to conjure with. She was able to *se reculer pour mieux sauter*, to come back from retirement in the 'fifties to create an even greater success for her designs than she had had before. She reached a far bigger audience. Chanel was still up there, a bright star, when her hated adversary, Schiaparelli, was done and she had disappeared like a meteor from the sky.

Through the 'thirties, the life and career of Chanel kept a fairly steady course, as far as can be ascertained. It must be added that it seems odd to apply the word steady to such a volatile character, but she was in many ways a living contradiction in terms. Though her designs were simple to the point of austerity, she herself lived in almost bizarre luxury. Her apartment above the salons at 31 rue Cambon was filled with Louis Quinze tables with gilt and crystal, with chairs covered in coffee-colour suede, with Coromandel screens, and to quote Cecil Beaton: 'With too many dark red roses'. When I interviewed Chanel myself, later in the 'fifties in that very apartment, I thought how wonderfully it epitomised the meaning of the word luxury combined with intellectual taste. If only Chanel's drawing-room were to be reproduced on stage or screen, the audience would know exactly what kind of play they were about to witness before a word was spoken. Intellectually too her life was rich. She was not merely a social success, but poets and artists were among her closest friends. She enjoyed the artistic acclaim from designing beautiful sets and clothes for a ballet by her friend Jean Cocteau. In her turn, she was constantly being drawn, sketched, painted and photographed by the most successful artists and photographers of the day. Looking at the results, particularly Cecil Beaton's refined and delicate drawings, it is easy enough to understand how that alive and witty face, that slender, angular body, the perfect summary of all that Chanel herself stood for, would attract an artist. He would long to capture such a spirit of the times on canvas, or on paper, for eternity.

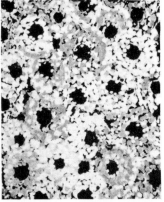

In the early 'thirties, Gabrielle Chanel was invited to England by Messrs Ferguson to help promote cotton as a fashion fabric. Her cotton evening dresses, beautifully cut and of delightful simplicity, were seized upon by all the débutantes of the day whose parents could foot the bill (a surprising number managed it). Lady Pamela Smith (now Lady Hartwell) was sketched by Drian wearing a long dress designed by Chanel for Ascot

Chanel's famous beret, accessorising a superbly-tailored suit dating from 1938.

This *tailleur* epitomises the severity and inconvenience of line against which Chanel reacted in the 'fifties. (Balmain 1955.)

left Examples of Chanel's favourite silk patterns for 1939, which she designed for the store, Harvey Nichols, in London, to be sold over the counter.

races. It was of white cotton piqué, trimmed with little flowers of the same material. Other dresses for the same occasion were of similar fabric, but ornamented with small Royal Worcester china flowers around the décolletages. Most of these dresses were slim fitting from the bust to the knees, with frilled hems and sometimes matching frills at the shoulders. But a few broke away to give a clear trend of a new epoch, and showed wide, almost crinoline-shape skirts, with stiffened petticoats beneath. By the time the war came in 1939 evening dresses were all reminiscent of that worn by the Empress Eugénie in the famous Winterhalter painting (which original dress was of course designed by Worth), with bared shoulders, small tightly fitting bodices and wide, wide skirts to the ground. Even at the time though, romantic, they did look rather like fancy dress as the girls clambered in and out of the small sports cars so popular at the same time. Chanel herself is reported as having expressed regret at the success of these dresses. She had only intended to promote cotton!

As Britain declared war on Germany in September 1939, it comes as a mild surprise to discover that the French haute couture houses showed their collections in Paris in January 1940 much as usual. They were the last coherent collections to be seen for the duration.

What happened to Chanel herself during the actual German occupation of France seems to have been nothing very dramatic. There are those who say she was friendly with the Germans and others equally vociferous who say she was not. At around fifty-five years of age there does not appear to be any reason why she should have behaved with any more or less heroism than most of her compatriots who had to go on living as best they could.

When hostilities were ended in Europe, Gabrielle Chanel was still a rich woman from the sale of her perfumes alone. She lived in retirement in the rue Cambon, with her salons given over entirely to the presentation and sale of those perfumes. It was not until 1954 that she descended into the arena for the second time. This bold gesture was prompted by two motives. The sales of her perfumes in America were falling off, and her financial advisers were of the opinion that a successful re-opening of her *salons de couture* would give the perfume sales a new boost. The second and probably more telling motive was that the fashions in favour in 1954 were very similar indeed to those she had so successfully knocked for six at the outset of her career. Dior's 'New Look' of 1947 had evolved into an hourglass silhouette, or 'figure of eight'. I started my job as a fashion writer and columnist of a British national newspaper (the *Daily Mail*) in 1949 and I have good reason to remember those fashions. Suits had skirts which were 'pencil slim' and the hemline was lower-calf length. If you had long legs, to walk any distance in such a restricting garment was tiring beyond belief, so much so that Dior invented a little slit at the back known as a 'Dior pleat' which helped, but not much. Jackets were so tight-waisted that every time you sat down, the centre button popped off!

Evening dresses were so whale-boned and petticoated that they would virtually stand up by themselves. There was even a small waist-corset (invented by Jacques Fath) called a *guêpière*, which was known evocatively in English as a 'waspie'. This was luckily only worn with evening dresses, for it pulled in the waist to such an extent that it was a choice between not eating, or suffering from acute indigestion until it was possible to retire and undress. Mademoiselle Chanel is reported to have remarked that such a pulled-in waistline was '. . . an exaggeration, even on a wasp'.

When at the age of sixty, Gabrielle Chanel was encouraged to return to the fray, she must have reacted like an old war-horse to the sound of bugles. The call was irresistible. Looking around her she must have been reminded of Paul Poiret, of all those boned dresses, of all the frippery and restriction of those fashions, and surely she thought: 'Plus ça change . . . plus c'est la même chose.'

In my years as a fashion writer and reporter, I was always fascinated by the way all Paris seemed to involve themselves with the biennial showings of the haute couture collections. Taxi drivers knew the names of the designers with familiar ease and would inquire with interest as one came out from this house or that, as to the length of the new hemlines. The man at the corner *charcuterie* would joke about a new waistline after the first day of the reports. People of intellectual and artistic talents and interests, as well as the expected socialites, would find the new fashions worthy of serious discussion at any gathering or party. All of which was quite un-imaginable in London, where fashion was always spoken of as something rather silly and only of interest to women (except of course by those actually concerned with the design or production of fashion), as though fashion had nothing to do with sex.

So it was, that when Mademoiselle Chanel announced that on Friday, 5 February 1954, she would show her first collection since the war, *tout Paris* was in a ferment of excitement.

The name of Chanel was famous, but it was a fame of the past. American money was making itself felt very keenly in France at this time, and the French themselves did not entirely enjoy the way it was being spent. Lavish spending, and lavish tips from the American visitors, did not always make up for the works of art, the paintings and various *objets* that were being purchased for, it was said, less than their worth (since the French were very hard up and in no position to bargain), and carted off to the USA. The Americans are not to be blamed for acquiring what they could, but it did not endear them to the people of Paris. And it was known to be American money that was backing the return of Chanel, in the hope that if she succeeded, the sales of Chanel perfumes would recover their previous popularity. That Chanel was going to get big support from the American trade fashion newspaper, the popular *Women's Wear Daily*, and from American *Vogue*, was virtually assured. Unless she produced an absolute dodo, they wanted a new story and a new name to promote, and after all, big business is big business. However, all the rest of Paris re-minded one forcibly of those ladies who sat knitting beneath the guillotine, waiting with pleasureable interest for somebody's head to roll.

Chanel was a loner. She scorned to join the select band who belonged to the Chambre Syndicale de la Couture Française, the syndicate which kept tight control over all comings and goings of outsiders to the other couture houses. As has been explained in the first part of this book, a special identity card was issued only to accredited journalists, and without it there was no possibility of getting in to see the collections. As all Paris was dead set on getting in to see Chanel's first new collection, and as my employers expected me to report on it instantly, I was a bit unnerved to discover that Chanel was not a member of the Syndicale and so my pass was not automatic. In fact, by what process of elimination I do not know, an invitation did arrive, which was lucky, for on the day I saw the door closed on the packed salons, and some of my colleagues, to say nothing of an Ambassador and his lady, were turned ruthlessly away.

Naturally, with all this build-up every journalist who descended on Paris to cover the collections as a whole, wanted to interview Chanel. Nobody succeeded. It was in fact some time before she would receive anyone for an interview for the press. She neither understood nor really liked publicity as such. Which was where Madame Helène Lazareff, the brilliant editor of the now famous magazine *Elle,* scored over her professional rivals. Chanel heartily disliked worldly women, in fact she had small time for women in general. 'Women cannot be friends', she said, 'you can love them or hate them, you cannot *like* them' (with the few rare exceptions, amongst whom was Madame Lazareff). Of her, Chanel said: 'She is *Somebody* . . .' adding the supreme compliment, 'and she is not a fake.' So it was *Elle* magazine that secured the first interview, and for the most part the best pictures from Chanel.

When I took my seat that February afternoon, I was, I think, prejudiced in a way I have never been before or since in anticipation of a collection. I had failed to get an interview with Chanel, or any kind of co-operation towards a story; I knew her reputation had been for making women look younger, but had not yet personally arrived at an age when that talent seemed very exciting; I thought of Chanel (whom I had never seen) as 'an old woman of sixty', and could not conceive that such a person would have anything really vital and interesting to contribute to modern fashion. I expected and I am sorry to say I think I also hoped for, a flop. It would have been a far easier story to write than the one I actually sent to London.

My about-face was complete. I was absolutely confounded in all my preconceived ideas. Along with almost every other fashion-writer of repute in that room, I thought that Mademoiselle Chanel had started another revolution of fashion. Just how she put this across was hard to define in writing. The clothes were so undramatic.

The shapes were all the same: the neat collarless cardigan-style jackets, the slightly-flared skirts falling from a small but not overly-tight waistband, the pretty blouses, with the soft 'pussy-cat' bows. It was chiefly the colours, the fabrics, the sheer feminine softness of outline, that made you realise how hard and forced the silhouette of fashion had become. I would not say that I liked it straight away, but I was somehow convinced that I and millions of other women were going to learn to like it. In the attempt to explain the metamorphosis to readers who had as yet seen no pictures, I said that, 'The figure-of-eight outline will give way to a fashion based on a rectangle. If you draw those two symbols side by side on a piece of paper and then add little heads and arms and feet at the appropriate places . . . you will see more or less what I mean.' It was near enough to the truth. Chanel's clothes always did look good on a hanger.

It was that same February afternoon in 1954 that I first set eyes on Coco Chanel, and I use her nickname in this instance with intent. The packed salons had fallen silent as the arc lamps were switched on and the first model girls appeared, and began their swift walk along the E-shaped aisles. At this moment there was a slight movement at the top of the stairs leading straight out of the salons up to Chanel's private apartment, and Mademoiselle herself slipped into a seat on the staircase itself, near the top and half-hidden by shadow. For all that, I saw her very clearly. She wore one of her own suits in navy and white, her shoes were the now-famous sling-back court shoes in black and beige. On her head was a *canotier* or boater-shaped hat, and I caught the glimmer of ropes of pearls. She

A delightful portrait of Mlle Chanel by Paris photographer André Ostier.

130

crouched on that stair, in her elegant clothes, looking completely comfortable, a feat she could not have achieved in any other fashionable clothing of the time. Her face was sun-tanned and rather like a bright monkey. She was ageless. The phrase, 'an old woman of sixty' flew out of my mind, and as applied to Coco Chanel, it never returned.

That collection, on 5 February 1954, without any fireworks, without any dramatics like the radical change of hemline, but with a sublime subtlety of understated elegance, started the ball rolling for another decade of fantastic success for Chanel.

By the autumn of that same year, she had become a cult in Paris. Every young and chic woman who could pay the price, was wearing a suit by Chanel. By the following spring, it seemed that every smart woman you saw had at least a copy of a similar suit. A strong change in fashion takes about five years to percolate through to the mass market. The reason for this is obvious. Mass-produced fashion naturally becomes cheaper and therefore available to more people; but the wholesalers and retailers of the vast ready-to-wear fashion industry cannot afford to adopt a new line too quickly and so render all their existing stocks obsolete. Equally, the public are not willing to jettison their current wardrobes. And so it was, that it took five years for Chanel to reach into the far corners of the western world. That she should have a degree of success at this moment of time, was as has been seen logical. But the size of the success in terms of sheer economics, and the length of time it lasted was in the circumstances of the fashion world at that time, astounding. The ready-to-wear fashion industry had grown to gigantic proportions. In order to keep this vast wheel turning, the wholesalers had to look to some authentic and acceptable source of supply of new ideas. It seemed that only Paris had both the talents for such needs and the panache with which to present their talents. The French government lent a hand with very substantial subsidies to their top couturiers, and the result was that French high fashion became the second largest export industry in France (steel being the first). To support this claim to be the only true source of original new, high fashion, Paris produced a number of excellent designers whose names, in the course of time, became world famous. The greatest of all was probably the Spaniard, Balenciaga, though Christian Dior achieved a wider fame (possibly because his name was so easy to say in any language).

Dashing around reporting the collections twice a year was a murderous stint. In your seat by 9 a.m., right on through lunch (with a sandwich if you were lucky) often with a late show taking you on till midnight. In between you had to get your story and some kind of pictures over to London or wherever. The names that went over the ticker tapes were numerous and each one had an importance of its own. Dior, Balenciaga, Cardin, Givenchy, Dessés, Grès, Balmain, Laroche, Heim, Lanvin, Ricci and of course Patou, to name only a few. It was against this kind of competition that Chanel carved her second meteoric way to the top. She refused to join the official syndicate. She showed her collections at 4.30

p.m., which meant leaving the previous collection before it was finished, or having the doors of Chanel shut in your face. On one occasion a colleague who was too late was heard to be hammering on the door and crying loudly: 'Let me in . . . let me in . . . it's *The Times*, do you hear? It's *The TIMES!*' Mademoiselle Chanel was seen to give a single slight shake of her head. And *The Times* remained outside. Chanel did things her way. She fought the world on her own terms, virtually single-handed. And she won.

It is a fair analogy to say that by 1959–60, the Chanel suit was the equivalent of the ubiquitous trouser suit of the early 'seventies. There were

Chanel's success with film designing continued throughout the decades: here she dressed Romy Schneider for her role in 'Boccaccio 70', (1962).

other fashions, of course, alongside her. But when in doubt what to wear, everybody tended to fall back upon 'my Chanel'. She was a godsend to the fast-growing ready-to-wear market because she never altered her basic outlines. Practical as ever, and with a large private clientèle, she thought it patently ridiculous to make any change strong enough to make her previous models out-dated. Women wanted something new from Chanel simply because her colours were so beguiling – her fabrics were the only thing that changed. The snob value of a really new Chanel, identified by the unique new material, was enormous. In London, one man understood the subtlety of Chanel so well that it nearly ruined him.

Geoffrey Wallis, of the firm of Wallis Bros., a man of taste with a real love of fashion, felt that Chanel ought to be reproduced in as near facsimile as possible or not at all. He managed to corner the market in materials from her actual source. He paid heavily for this privilege. He then retailed suits and coats 'Chanel inspired', for prices ranging between £20 and £50,

Chanel's influence on the couturier Saint Laurent is clearly seen in this suit designed by him in 1971.

Romy Schneider dressed by Chanel in 1964.

which were so good that only an experienced eye could tell they were not direct from Chanel, Paris. They sold like hot cakes, but Geoffrey Wallis' idealism cost him too dear. It was not an economic business. But rather than try to copy Chanel with anything less than the real fabrics, Mr Wallis moved to other designers. As a matter of interest, he is the quickest and best off the mark with the successful Yves Saint Laurent designs now.

Yves Saint Laurent, the fashion darling of the moment, has much in common with Gabrielle Chanel, in that he believes that clothes should be easy and pleasant to wear, and he is intensely logical. His designs evolve, they do not leap wildly from one idea to another. He is the first to admit that he has been greatly influenced by Chanel. It is significant that one of the most successful outfits in his collection shown in January 1972 is remarkably reminiscent of Chanel. It seems as if every twenty years Chanel could rise like a phoenix and carry all before her. Only sadly, even Mademoiselle Chanel was mortal.

She died on 10 January 1971 at just about eighty-six years of age. She was alone in her suite at the Ritz Hotel. She had been to the races that day with a friend, Claude Baillén, who had accompanied her back to the door of the hotel. With a new collection scheduled for 5 February, Chanel had been working hard, and she remarked rather wearily that January evening, that she would be back at work early the next day. She prepared for bed, and gave herself an injection, which was usual since she could not sleep without. She slept, never to wake again. With her way of dressing, with her pearls and her little boaters, with her witty (often cruel) tongue, Chanel was a legend long before she died. A legend too glittering, a death too solitary, for one not to stop and ask, what manner of person was she? What kind of human being behind the façade she so carefully maintained?

Few people knew her. The questions have no complete answer, but there are a few clues.

When I finally arranged an interview with Mademoiselle Chanel in 1958, I was told sternly by her press attaché that I might have half-an-hour: 'No more, if you please. Mademoiselle does not like long interviews.' With this rather unpromising beginning, I was agreeably surprised to find Chanel in a chatty and relaxed mood. I would not say she was attempting to answer my questions; she hopped about from one subject to another. She also amused herself by trying to turn the tables and cross question me about my job, about life in England at the time, and whether or not the Duchess of Windsor was to be received at Buckingham Palace. I do not think she had the smallest interest in my replies, for her eyes were sparkling with mischief. Then quite suddenly, she rose from the sofa and threw herself down onto a beautiful rug on the floor. 'Look!' she said, 'one should always be able to do this in clothes without damaging them.' I asked her why, but she did not deign to answer. When the half-hour was up, I honoured my agreement and rose to go. 'Unless you are in a hurry?' she said, 'Why not stay and take a glass of something . . .?' At the end of two hours, I felt that I had at least learnt a little of Chanel's philosophy of life, even if the time was too short to tell much of the woman herself.

She held that the look of love in a lover's eyes is essential to the beauty of a woman. With such a regard she needs no beauty-parlour. Without it, the beauty-parlour can do little. 'A woman needs to be caressed from her head to her toes', she said. 'Otherwise she feels frustrated . . . I am not a frustrated woman. I have had lovers . . . But that was a long time ago.'

Her recipe for elegance was a blend of austerity and natural purity. It was to do away with everything unessential. Not a superfluous button, or floating panel, or frill. Colours must be drawn from nature; beiges in skin tones, pinks of roses, blues from the sky at night or mid-day, red (if at all) in the deep tone of blood. Any colour not found in nature, jarred.

She thought that imitation was the sincerest form of flattery. Quite aware that her designs were copied (as best they could) by many who had not paid for the privilege, she merely smiled. There were enough good customers coming in to the rue Cambon and paying good money. But more than that, to see countless women walking along the streets in 'Chanel' outfits gave her a sense of being loved and admired.

Perhaps because of the lack of parental love in childhood, it was clear that she placed great importance on being loved for the rest of her life. She was like a young girl always waiting for romance, for a telephone call, a surprise visit, a new love. 'I never looked so much for someone to love, as for somebody to love me', she said. In this was a hardness, a wariness, a fear of giving, which produced an emptiness around her.

Why did she not marry when she had so much opportunity? A shrug of the shoulders: 'Perhaps because I did not find another name as pretty as Gabrielle Chanel!' Certainly she clung firmly to her name, and to the 'Mademoiselle'. If anyone was careless enough to think it a compliment to address her as 'Madame' they were soon corrected.

She disliked all thought of change. Her basic style of fashion she had dreamed up to suit herself at thirty years of age, when she was beautiful, slim and supple. Her slender agile body she kept always. Her way of dressing too remained unchanged. To alter the form or the materials, would have been to concede that time passed, that beauty and youth passed. For Chanel this idea was unthinkable.

All of which, tells a little of what Chanel was like, but does not explain how it happened that a woman who was rich, famous and sought after, came to die all alone, in a room where if she did indeed utter a small cry for aid, nobody was there to hear. Like some small animal, thrown out by the pack who goes off to die by itself.

This strange, sad ending is explained to some extent through a friendship formed late in Chanel's life. A young student of medicine, Claude Baillén walked into the rue Cambon one fine day with her books under arm, to have a casual look at some of Chanel's scarves on display. Mademoiselle herself happened to be right there, on the ground floor of the salons. She noticed the blonde, poetic looks of the young student, who was very like Botticelli's painting of 'Spring', and invited her to luncheon. This was the

One of Mlle Chanel's famous 'little black dresses', dated autumn 1960.

start of a friendship which lasted up to the day Chanel died. Claude Baillén, by now an established psychoanalyst, had accompanied Chanel to the races and then back to the door of her hotel. And it is in Claude Baillén's book *Chanel Solitaire*, from which Claude Berthod wrote an especially revealing article, for *Elle* magazine, in November 1971, that clues are to be found as to how and why Gabrielle Chanel was, in the last resort, so utterly alone.

She never recovered from that insecure, loveless childhood. All her life, she was protecting herself against the hurts and the disappointments that only people can inflict. 'Between the three types of men in my life . . . the Prince of Wales, Dimitri of Russia, and the Duke of Westminster, I chose the one who offered me the greatest sense of protection.' But she married no one. She was a solitary who actually hated to be alone. Sundays were a kind of nightmare limbo of time to her. She waited always for the telephone to ring; she answered and went gladly if and when it did ring with an invitation. But never, never would she be the first one to make the call. In the end the number of callers dwindled away.

The only women she liked were those who strongly resembled Chanel herself. She enjoyed transforming them into a kind of replica, with similar hairstyle, the delectable little suits, and the inevitable ropes of pearls. She prepared them for seduction as if it was for herself. But without the terrible risk; without the fear that after the conquest would come the desertion.

In her work she was not only an artist, but a driving professional. A perfectionist. 'What is tough, is never to be careless for one moment', she once sighed in between collections. 'When work is there, you must get on with it. If you don't put your heart into your work, you will get nothing back from it.' She was irritated by holidays, and by the fact of her workrooms being closed on Saturdays and Sundays. The making of a suit for her created the framework of a drama. 'My life is one long battle', she announced on one occasion as she tore out an offending sleeve, cut out a buttonhole newly sewn. She vilified her 'premières', often accusing them of 'Sabotage'. The fight was incessant. But in her work, it was really herself she was whipping, herself she punished with words, herself she tormented. At these times she forgot her other ghosts, she forgot to be afraid, forgot to feel alone. She was waiting for nothing. In her work lay the only refuge in which she felt nothing was missing. In the untiring demands she made of herself, lay the secret of her eternal youth. 'I have an eagerness, a greed for life. It is the one force of which time cannot rob me.' Her ambition was limitless. 'Each and every dress that I create for a woman, is with the idea that on the day she wears it . . . she might meet her Destiny.'

Chanel had met her own destiny, her own fate, and she had long come to terms with it. With her eyes open, she chose solitude. She disliked being alone, but she disliked even more the suspense created by human relationships.

'One acquires everything in solitude . . . except character', said Goethe.

Perhaps if there is almost too much character there already, a degree of solitude is the only answer. It was General Lord Wavell who said that many people felt impelled to try to climb the trees of life, but he wondered if they would try quite so hard if they understood how lonely, '. . . how very lonely, life can be at the top'.

A modern version of the Chanel 'little black dress' from the spring 1971 collection: an evening suit in black crêpe, printed with gray, orange and black patterns, mingling with beaded embroidery.

Thelma Sweetinburgh

One of Dior's most beautiful
'New Look' models.

All through the German occupation of France, Parisian women liked to
think that one look at their hats was enough to throw the enemy off
balance. In size and composition, these hats were so stupendously inco-
herent that German soldiers twisted their necks to stare at the flowered
parterres drifting along the Paris streets atop of their cycling wearers in

billowing knee-high skirts, with clog-soled feet pushing at the pedals. 'Whatever would they have worn if they had won the war', the Germans were known to have remarked. When not crowning the wearer's head, the hat was enclosed in a hat-box balanced on the bicycle's luggage rack at the back. What were these hats made of? 'Oh just nothing', would be the answer. 'Only bits of feathers, ribbon, artificial flowers, tulle, veiling, lace, velvet, wood shavings and even newspaper.' 'One feathered bird at the time, not two', ordered the Germans, who controlled everything. But of course the second one was re-installed as soon as the control had been passed. Of felt there was none, nor straw, nor fabric other than *fibranne*, an artificial product obtainable with points, on the rationing scheme. A yardage of real wool material was harder to find then than a dose of LSD today, and procured a far more lasting enjoyment. Parisians were convinced these rarities sold on the black market came direct from London and were parachuted by the RAF along with a few other trinkets destined to the Underground forces. It was only just before the war that the book *Gone With the Wind* had come out in Paris and visions of Rhett Butler forcing the English blockade with precious silks from abroad were transposed to fit into the present context. Anyway, the idea stirred the imagination. If during the war years pure wool materials were available in England, fashion itself had come to a standstill since 1939, the majority of women being in uniform.

No wonder when, in summer 1945, the very handsome wife of the new French ambassador, Madame René Massigli, appeared in London in a long waisted jacket over a knee-length billowy skirt and one of those unde-pictable hats, she caused a stir. Wildly elegant, she looked as if she had landed from another planet. During the first couple of years of the occupation of France (later on they were otherwise engaged), the Germans had formed the project of transferring the Paris haute couture to Vienna. Defending couture and its right to remain in France was Lucien Lelong, then president of the Chambre Syndicale, who had been appointed head of the official 'Women's Clothing Department' with Paul Caldaguès as general delegate. After a good deal of haggling with the Occupants, they obtained a derogation from clothes rationing for haute couture and a special contingent of points based on pre-war figures. This, of course, being far from sufficient, the Chambre Syndicale thought up a remedy, and Daniel Gorin, then General Secretary, and until recently President of the Chambre, used to recall with great amusement how they concocted a bank of false points to meet the requirements and cheat the Germans. Clients were asked to bring in old clothes which were exchanged for points. M. Gorin also told how the Germans broke into the Chambre Syndicale premises in 1940 and discovered a few English-speaking method books as well as a Union Jack kept for window decoration on specific occasions. The invaders gathered the books in shape of a catafalque, spread the flag over it and placed a placard with the following inscription: 'It is German you should have studied.'

139

Approximately twenty couture houses managed to remain open and keep their work-people if not warm at least busy enough to prevent them from being sent to forced labour in Germany. Collections were presented twice yearly all through the occupation. When Grès (new name for the famous pre-war Alix) and Balenciaga were both ordered by the Germans to close their houses for two weeks because they had exceeded the authorised yardage for some of their models, the rest of the couture joined forces to finish their collection for them so that they could present on time. Lelong had engaged two young beginners as designers, Pierre Balmain and Christian Dior. Paquin had Antonio del Castillo just away from Piguet. Jacques Fath managed to move out of the courtyard rooms where he started just before the war, doing all the cutting and sewing himself with his future wife Geneviève as mannequin, and settle in much improved premises on rue François Ier. Marcel Rochas, designer in 1938 of the most reproduced model in the USA, a gypsy dress, kept his house among the leaders and was soon to marry his third wife, Hélène, one of the Paris fashionables yet. In spite of reduced means of expression, Paris couture was actually reeking with young talent. Very few of the pre-war elegant women came close to haute couture during those dark years, whereas an entirely new and recently moneyed class had emerged and formed the new 'de luxe' clientèle. The short, gathered skirt worn by Parisian cyclists was a continuation of the 'country girl' silhouette shown in 1939 by Molyneux and Mainbocher, but behind the scenes a new and more feminine silhouette was ready to emerge. Already the waistline was being tightened, the skirt flared over a stiffened petticoat, the bust emphasised and, last but not least, the hips were being rounded. Balenciaga was particularly responsible for the latter feature, by far the most premonitory of future developments.

It was all in the air already, women aspiring to be beautiful and feminine again, men longing to see their companions other than as their uniformed equals. There was a general urge for softness, tenderness and beauty. A man as sensitive as Christian Dior felt this urge perhaps more deeply than anyone else: he who had been deprived of luxury for so long and who had always in his mind the vision of his mother as she appeared to him when he was a small boy, and how beautifully dressed she was. The time was right to turn away from the makeshift war fashion with its flashy overtones, and Christian Dior, influenced by his good-mannered background, wished above all to present a well-mannered fashion and to render women beautiful once more. The scene was set, waiting for someone to raise the curtain. Christian Dior, shy and reserved, who dreaded nothing more than to be in the limelight, was the one to do it when he fathered a revolutionary silhouette christened, the 'New Look'.

One of the first and strongest resolutions Christian Dior formed in his early youth was never to lead the same life as his father, that is, never to set foot in a factory or an office, never to 'go into trade'. Although he had great respect for his father, who ran a family-owned concern in Normandy producing chemical fertilisers out of guano imported from Chile, it was not the life of which young Christian's dreams were made. His parents were prosperous and the house they lived in overlooking the sea just outside Granville was comfortable enough, and, though in Christian Dior's own words, 'it had all the ugliness of the typical turn-of-the-century Anglo-Norman buildings', he loved it. He described his life and home background in *Christian Dior and I* (1957). He grew up in a dècor of Japanese panels, embroidered silk screens, and a winter garden which inspired his life-long love for green plants and flowers, shared with his mother. He day-dreamed in front of treasures enclosed in glass vitrines, shepherdesses and dainty marquises in Saxe porcelain, lavish feather fans and many other tokens of an obsolete past. The room he liked best, however, was the dining-room, for young Christian already had a keen interest in food. Next in his preferences came the linen-room where he loved to watch the maids ironing and sewing while they made him shudder with spine-chilling tales of the devil. Above all he worshipped his mother. All this took place before World War I: Christian Dior was born in 1905, when nothing, it seemed, could happen, to deter the even course of a well-to-do family in those golden days of *La Belle Epoque*. The Dior household emerged unscarred from the 1914 war and Christian became a student in Paris where his parents had taken a flat in the residential neighbourhood of the 16th arrondissement. This time the décor was typical Louis XVI–Passy which always remained his favourite and influenced his choice of gray and white Louis XVI panelling for the walls of couture salons. Without a care in the world, Christian Dior's life consisted in small part of studies and in a large part of amusement. Paris in the 'twenties was paradise on earth for a young man with eclectic tastes, and Christian Dior plunged headlong into a world whose gods were Picasso, Matisse, van Dongen, Stravinsky, Erik Satie and his '*Groupe des Six*' who composed the music for Jean Cocteau's *Les Mariés de la Tour Eiffel* and *Entracte* by René Clair. The new music-hall stars were Mistinguett, Maurice Chevalier, the Dolly Sisters, and Josephine Baker. A world where women cut their hair *à la garçonne*, wore outrageous make-up, smoked in public and danced the Charleston and the Black Bottom. Together with his friends, the artist Christian Bérard, the composer Henri Sauguet, Pierre Gaxotte, an eminent historian today, and the fashion designer Jean Ozenne – to whom he was later on to owe his salvation, Christian Dior played charades, listened to modern music and to the recently introduced 'Negro Spirituals'. They rushed to see the latest films, the Russian ballets and the avant-garde Swedish ones, and danced at the fabulous balls given by Count Etienne de Beaumont, a most elegant figure with a high shrill voice and regal gestures, extremely avant-garde in his artistic preferences.

When the choice of a career could no longer be postponed, young Christian met with a veto from his parents when he suggested architecture. So to please them he put his name down for *L'Ecole des Sciences Politiques*,

141

a school for future diplomats, then more of an elegant pastime for young men about town, and everything went on as before – keeping up with the newest German Expressionist films with Conrad Veidt; the latest theatrical creations with Dullin; rushing to the art galleries to view the discoveries in primitive art, or to see the Negro, Peruvian, and Chinese exhibitions, the 'Dada'-inspired sculptures by Lipschitz, the paintings by artists of the Surrealistic school led by André Breton, such as Picabia, Miro, Dali, Jean Hugo. Architecture springs to the fore with Le Corbusier, and the whole concept of interior decoration was upturned at the *Exposition des Arts Décoratifs* in 1925, introducing geometrical forms and lacquered panels. All these subjects were passionately discussed well into the night by Christian Dior and his friends, when they met at the *Boeuf sur le Toit*, a night-club run by Moyses, who was to befriend Dior when the lean years arrived. Meanwhile, with Jacques Bonjean, Christian Dior had opened a small art gallery, in a very inconspicuous blind alley off the rue La Boetie, which made quite a promising start. It was in 1928 and speculation had just discovered art. The 1929 slump in the USA had but a faint echo in Christian Dior's private world, but when in 1930 a large mirror in his home crashed to the ground, Christian Dior, who was deeply superstitious, knew that disaster was imminent. Shortly after, his mother fell ill, underwent an operation and died within a very short time. The following year his father, who had invested all his capital in real estate, was faced with bankruptcy. The family was ruined, and everything had to be sold. Nothing was left of Christian Dior's picture gallery, and his best paintings, today worth millions, were practically given away as the USA crisis reached Europe and buyers grew more and more scarce. He joined forces with a friend, Pierre Colle, after separating from his partner, Jacques Bonjean, but things went from bad to worse and the Surrealistic paintings they showed scared away the best-intentioned customers. (Surrealism made a bouncing entrance in the fashion world a few years later with Schiaparelli.) Only his friends remained. Staunch and generous, they housed him, fed him, and cared for him when he fell ill from despair. Moyses lent him an attic room and provided an evening meal regularly. Soon began the darkest hours, scurrying through advertisements in the morning papers, and rushing out job-hunting day after day, all without any result. Until one day, his friend Jean Ozenne took him to live in his flat and taught him how to sketch. Another friend, Max Kenna, an American artist, taught him how to use colour. Christian's first efforts were not up to much, but on one occasion, Ozenne presented them with his own and sold six at twenty old francs each.

Christian Dior was beside himself with joy and decided he could improve his drawings if he put himself to it in earnest. He set to, and for two years peddled his sketches up back staircases and down long gloomy corridors into uninviting waiting rooms, for hours and days on end. His hat sketches sold best. The milliner Janette Colombier bought quite a few, but his dresses were not much liked. Then one day a decorator friend, Georges

La tenue classique 1938 : Pantalon étroit et long.
Veston droit ou croisé.

Manteau-capuchon

Christian Dior sketched models of his own invention for *Figaro*'s fashion page on Thursdays, at the start of his career as a designer and before he became a couturier, in 1938–9. (See signature at the bottom right-hand corner.)

Geffroy, presented him to the couturier Robert Piguet who, although unable to design clothes himself, knew enough about fashion to recognise talent when he saw it. He asked Dior to draw a few dresses and liked them enough to have them made up. The following year, 1938, when Piguet moved to new premises at the Rond Point des Champs Elysées, he took Dior on as a regular designer. Meanwhile, a journalist friend, Paul Caldaguès, working at the daily newspaper *Le Figaro*, and Geneviève Perreau, editor of the woman's page, had procured him a regular fashion page where he sketched models of his own invention. Some were very 1900 in feeling and foretelling of the 'New Look' he developed later. Others showed women in trousers and piped blazers, such as are in

143

fashion again now. A gifted designer, Dior knew nothing about cutting or sewing, and never did learn either, but he had a great sense of proportion and knew exactly where the seams should be. 'The less a dress is cut, the better it is', he used to proclaim.

The models he designed for Piguet met with great success and once again fate seemed to smile at him. At last he was able to move into a flat of his own, at 10 rue Royale, at first with furniture borrowed from friends until he could afford to buy some and thus re-create his most cherished period, very *fin de siècle*. He met important personalities such as Marie-Louise Bousquet, one of the wittiest women in Paris, whose Thursday afternoon 'salons' were already famous, and she introduced him to Carmel Snow, the all-powerful and astute editor of *Harper's Bazaar*. One of the dresses he designed, called 'Café Anglais', particularly applauded, was in small black and white checks with white trimming, very reminiscent of *Les Petites Filles Modèles* in Countess de Ségur's book for children which takes place in the mid-19th century. But fate was only grinning at Christian Dior.

World War II was round the corner, and very soon the promising young designer was snatched away from frills and flounces by the army and dumped in a far-off spot called Mehun sur Yèvre in the centre of France, not far from Bourges. Here he spent the 'phoney war' period, living with peasants, dressed like one of them, wearing wooden shoes, and working in the fields. Dior, surprisingly, was not one bit unhappy, discovered he was a country man at heart and, for a year, forgot all about fashion. As soon as he could, after the armistice, Christian Dior joined his father and his sister, now absolutely penniless, who had taken refuge in a tiny little village called Callian in the South of France, not far from Grasse. Christian, who had now become quite an experienced farm labourer, decided that the small patch of land surrounding the house could be profitably turned into a kitchen-garden. So, together with his sister Catherine, they planted French beans and green peas which they exchanged for olive oil or sold at the nearby market. At the time, everything was scarce, even water, and brother and sister would get up at night to water the vegetables. Then one morning arrived a letter from Paris. Robert Piguet wrote that he was ready to welcome Dior back as a designer. However, Dior lingered too long over the vegetable patch, and, when he finally turned up at the Rond Point des Champs Elysées, it was to learn that Piguet, tired of waiting for him, had engaged another young designer, a Spaniard previously at Chanel, called Antonio del Castillo. Again, friends came to the rescue, and Paul Caldaguès introduced Dior to Lucien Lelong, who suggested that he might be co-designer for the collection with another young man just out of the army, named Pierre Balmain. The salary was 10,000 old francs a month.

Lelong, who had opened his house in 1923, was not a designer himself, but had established a great tradition for workmanship, which he had entrusted to the guidance of Nadine Cassandre, another one to join the Dior

Nina Ricci

Jacques Heim   Velours de Bucol

Maggy Rouff

Paulette

Harmonies Poétiques
dessinées
par
gruau

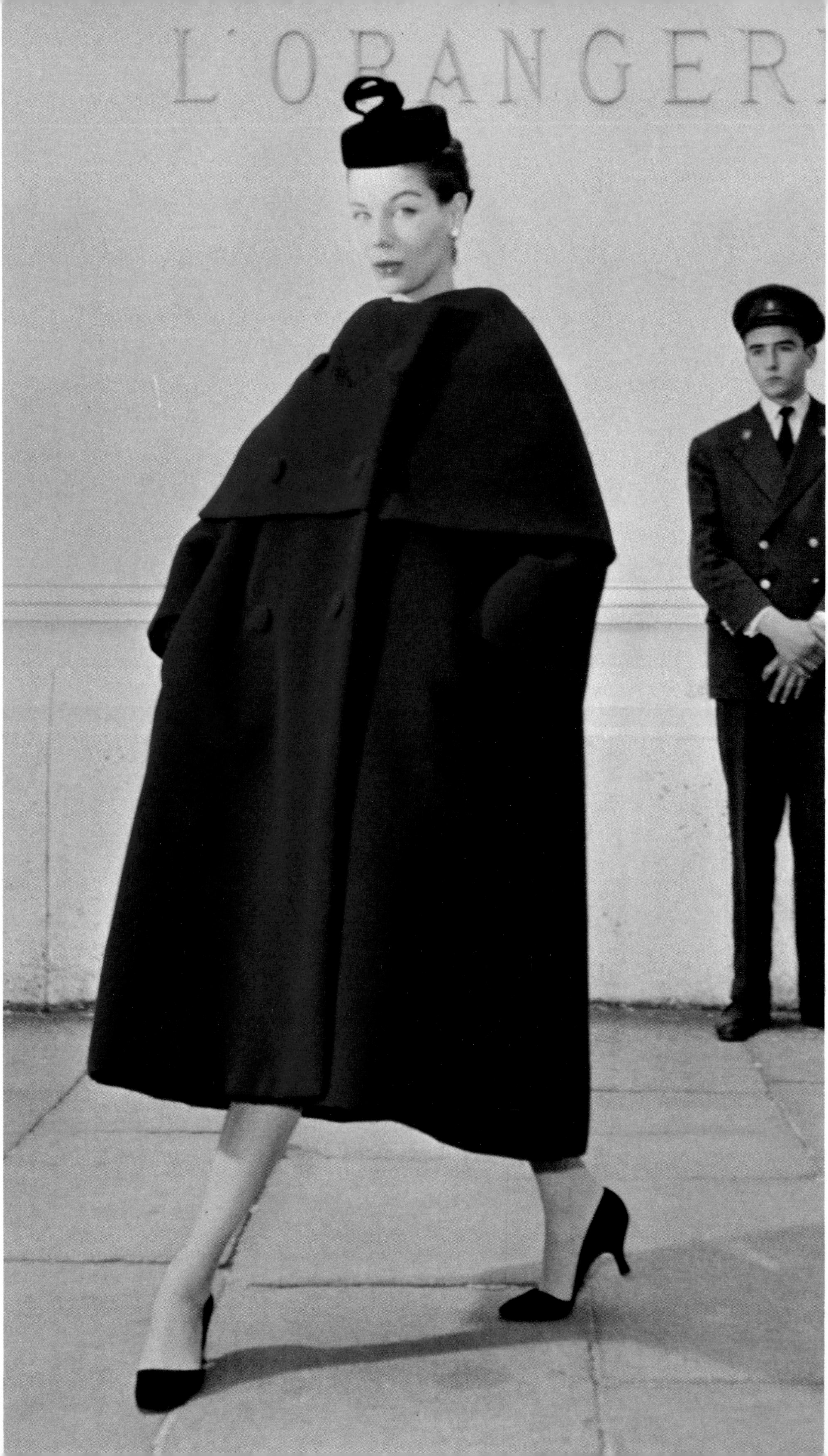
L'ORANGER

team later on for ready-to-wear. Lelong's intention was to create a school after the war for young designers. Meanwhile, all together they managed to cope with the textile restrictions and the German demands till the liberation of Paris in August 1944. There was at Lelong's a long-timer, who had entered in 1924, called Raymonde Zehnacker who was rapidly to make herself indispensable to Christian Dior before becoming his confidante and closest friend. Ever alert and ready with an answer to any problem, she immediately knew where to find the right belt, the newest button, or the exact shade of fabric requested. Above all they shared the same fortune teller, the famous Madame D— who had repeatedly said that Christian Dior's dearly loved sister, Catherine, would return safely

Christian Dior at his farmhouse home, Milly, where he grew beautiful flowers.

left
One of Dior's last designs, a beautiful full-backed wool coat from the autumn 1957 collection.

from the Nazi camp where she had been deported. From then on Dior was never to make a move without consulting Madame D—. For Dior, the lean years were over at last. He felt safe, protected and once again was happy. At Lelong he was free to design the clothes he liked and free to remain in the background because his name was never mentioned, which suited his shy nature perfectly. A few people still remember one of his evening dresses, a beautiful orange dress with a definite 1913 flavour.

But once again destiny knocked at his door. Three times running on his way home to the rue Royale, Dior ran into an old friend from Granville who was the director of a couture house called Clarence owned by the cotton tycoon Marcel Boussac. 'The house was in bad need of a designer',

145

said the friend, 'did Christian know of one?' It was not until the third meeting that Christian Dior took an interest in the question and casually proferred: 'Why not me?' Meanwhile, at Lelong, Pierre Balmain had decided to try his luck and open a house of his own. Dior could not picture himself following suit and breaking the news of his own departure to Lelong, who had befriended him so. However he was a little hampered in his designing. He felt something quite different was becoming necessary and that he could provide it, but not without outdating everything in existence. But it meant a new venture, a new risk, and Dior knew too much about hard times already not to appreciate the moral and physical comfort he was enjoying at Lelong's. So it was quite light-heartedly that he met Henri Fayol, Boussac's right-hand man, and then Boussac himself, to whom he declared that he was only interested in the possibility of opening a house of his own and that Boussac must look elsewhere for someone willing to breathe oxygen into the badly ailing house of Clarence. He thought that by exposing such an ambitious project he would be rid of M. Boussac and free to remain in the shelter of the maison Lelong. Such an inflexible attitude could only have the inevitable, though entirely unsought-for, effect on a business man of M. Boussac's calibre. A man of figures and horses, obviously a gambler at heart, he reacted by doubling the stakes, which meant accepting to finance Christian Dior's plan to start a couture house under his own name. Marcel Boussac was not long in grasping what he expressed in his own vivid terms: 'Dior was a tree to be planted, not just grafted.' Meanwhile, the designer, remembering that a fortune teller had, in his Granville days, once predicted, 'You will become penniless but women will be beneficial to you and a source of great profit', which had hardly made sense at the time, began to see a meaning in these words and set off to consult Mme D—. Without a moment's hesitation, Mme D— declared that this was the opportunity of his life and that an unbelievable success was ahead of him. Little by little, the idea grew in Christian Dior's mind. He confided in Mme Raymonde, who had now become an intimate friend, and who encouraged him whole-heartedly, promising to follow him. Finally, he broke the news of his departure to Lucien Lelong, offering however, to design another two collections. Lelong, who was already planning to retire, was anxious to keep Dior at all costs and offered to make him his successor. But Dior was already on his way to 30 avenue Montaigne, where he had heard the milliner Coralie, occupying the first, second and ground floor, was giving up her lease, to retire. This was in 1945 and Christian Dior was forty years old.

Then started a period of drum-beating when Dior summoned all those he thought qualified enough to form the team with which he was anxious to work. Mme Raymonde he brought with him from Lelong. He called her 'his other self'. Mme Bricard, who had assisted Molyneux for ten years and 'to whom elegance was all', in Dior's own words, he chose as 'counterpart to his too-rational self'. Technical ability was personified by

Mme Marguerite Carré, discovered by the decorator Georges Geffroy, then designer at Patou, where she was an experienced *première*. For her eagerness and devotion to the task Dior named her 'Penelope' and for her fresh, chubby looks, he compared her to a Renoir. To a childhood playmate, back in the Granville days, Suzanne Luling, who was spending a summer holiday precisely at Granville, Christian Dior sent a telegram: 'Can you meet me in Paris August 11th at rue Royale.' She knew right away what it meant, as Dior had confided in her several months before and told her that if all went well she would be the directrice of the new couture house. Among all her qualifications for the job, Suzanne Luling knew how to make friends, with her warm, hearty disposition, and the experience she had gained, first in advertising, and second working at a milliner's called Maud Roser, gave her the required business background. But above all, she was unflinching, dedicated, and never, never, gave the slightest sign of fatigue. A look at her had the effect of a bottle of Dom Perignon on staff and clients. Again from Granville came Serge Heftler-Louiche, a life-long friend and an old-timer in the world of scent, ready with an offer to start the Christian Dior perfume company which came into effect as early as 1947. Another figure from the Granville days was among the first to enter the team of *vendeuses*, Nicole Rousseau. 'As close to me as a sister', said Dior of this pretty blue-eyed and rather Greuze-like young woman, with a sweet smile. There was something of *Time Regained* in this regrouping of characters of bygone days, and *Remembrance of Things Past* too, but without an atom of melancholy. On the contrary, they were all governed by a common will to create something great, and a tremendous drive to force success along the Dior way. Another driving force was the sprightly Yvonne Minassian, as pretty and typically Parisienne in chic as she turned out to be unyielding in business. She was to become head of the export sales. At the end of the war, Yvonne Minassian had made up her mind to go to the USA to find herself a job as adviser to prospective American buyers coming to Paris. She was spotted by Suzanne Luling, then at the milliner Maud Roser, when she walked in to buy some hats for this proposed trip. Suzanne Luling, always on the alert and already dedicated to the Christian Dior cause, immediately sensed Yvonne's possibilities and declared: 'You must go and see my friend Christian.' This is how Yvonne Minassian (today Mme de Peyerimhoff) describes the interview: 'I was wearing a Legroux hat and in my pocket was my ticket with the dollar currencies for my trip. We got on from the word go, and at the end of the interview I had signed a contract. Dior offered to make me three dresses for my visit and I went off on a troop-carrier (all there was available in 1946) to announce the opening of the maison Dior to the New York fashion world.' This is a typical example of Christian Dior's art of convincing, and the irresistible aura that drew people to him all his life.

However, across the ocean, the power had not yet begun to operate and Yvonne Minassian was met with remarks such as, 'We have our own designers now, why should we go to Paris?' adding, 'Why did you take this on?' All Yvonne could say was: 'I could not resist such an exceptional man.' But to Christian Dior she wrote her fears: 'I am not at all sure they will come.' However, for the first showing in February 1947, eighteen buyers were gathered in the salons and benefited by a free entrance – the one and only time. Next season, caution fees had been established on the strength of the smashing success of the 'New Look'. It was like a tidal wave. Those already in Paris bought up to forty dresses, like I. Magnin. Other stores – Bergdorf Goodman, Bendel, Marshall Field, Eaton, Holt Renfrew – took all they could manage, and a steady flow of buyers kept arriving from the USA.

The Dior staff worked relentlessly eighteen hours a day. Buyers came as late as midnight and stayed till 2 a.m. Suzanne Luling remembers a fifty-four hour stretch, a record. Nothing was ready for such a success, not even the order books. By the next season all that was seen to, including the percentage for the sales-people which had been settled at random by the management, with no idea of the figures it could reach. Christian Dior himself had no fixed salary, but had signed up for a percentage on the sales, a contract he was able to maintain, which explains his rapid prosperity and accumulated possessions in the ten years of his short career.

From Mainbocher, who enjoyed a great reputation of refinement as a person and as a designer in Paris before the war, came the perfectly experienced *première vendeuse*, Suzanne Béguin. She was ready for the arrival of the world's most elegant women, who had been reached by the rumour of this new king of fashion and his overthrow of all they had seen in the past. The Duchess of Windsor made her first appearance at Dior in October 1947, and Eva Peron ordered two models as early as July 1947. The greatest success of the season was the model called 'Bar', a tight-fitting natural silk shantung jacket over a widely pleated black skirt. The price for private clients was 59,000 francs (of 1947). Mademoiselle Béguin, who now lives a life of leisure with painting as a hobby, loves to rattle off the great names: Lady Marriott, who ordered forty models each season; Mrs Thomas Biddle, who would have the same dress repeated in three or four different colours; Mrs David Bruce; Mrs Douglas Dillon; Baronne Leo d'Erlanger; Princess Liliane of Belgium, and in Mademoiselle Béguin's own terms: 'All those beautiful English women victims of the currency restrictions in England: Lady Beatty, Countess Kenmare, Lady Peek, Lady Peel.' Of the French elegant women, the first were Madame Pierre Michelin, Madame Pierre Champin, Baronne Alain de Rothschild, and Madame René Massigli. Other internationally celebrated beauties who came were Brazilian-born Madame Martinez de Hoz and Mexican-born Madame Jean Larivière, a great friend of Christian Dior.

Everyone to take part in the new Dior machinery was selected with the same care. Even the search for a suitable doorman was not one of the easiest, and Ferdinand, there to this day, only just growing gray with the years, was tracked down in Normandy and chosen for his very proper manner, corresponding to the general atmosphere Christian Dior wished to convey of the house. As for models, with his ultra-feminine silhouette in mind Dior chose six young girls whose contours often needed artificial curving to identify themselves with this newborn woman. Out of this original group, Tania and Marie-Thérèse were to be the stars, later on joined by Sylvie, Renée, Allah, Lucky and France, until the day Dior made a Left Bank turn, and engaged Victoire who looked unruly, aggressive and 'kitsch' long before the word came to Paris. She already impersonated the 'tough chic' of the 'sixties. When presenting the collec-

Dior, with two of his most distinguished clients, the Princess Paul of Yugoslavia and her daughter. (She was cousin to the Duchess of Kent.)

tion, all the girls had the 'Dior walk' which Michel de Brunhoff, editor of French *Vogue* and intimate friend of Christian Dior used to say reminded him of Shakespeare actresses at the 'Old Vic' theatre in London who advanced with a backward slant. Kuka's back tilt was so extreme she became an oblique figure. Under the technical guidance of Madame Marguerite, sixty work-girls were crowded into a small space under the roof top. Six tiny fitting rooms were set up, and there was only one showroom, not very large at that. For himself, Christian installed an exiguous studio. The entire staff ready for the opening added up to eighty people, each one of which proved to be inured to fatigue, to lack of sleep or food, and absolutely dedicated.

Once this great effort was achieved, Christian Dior turned to M. Boussac to supply the business head able to co-ordinate all the activities of a house which was to grow beyond all expectation. Marcel Boussac provided a solemn figure in black named Jacques Rouet, who turned out to be the human computer capable of dealing with the rapid, octopus-like, developments of the firm in a big-business manner which had never before been applied to couture.

To set off his dresses to their best advantage, and not compete with any colour effect, Christian Dior chose what had always been his favourite style in decoration, Louis XVI: not period, but a 1910 vintage such as he had grown up in at his parents' home in Passy. Victor Grandpierre was the perfect interpreter of Dior's dreams in gray and white with sparkling crystal chandeliers and boudoir-like *appliques* on the walls. Christian Bérard, the artist and faithful friend, hugging his miniature Ténérife dog Jacinthe, pranced around in glee and insisted on having the ground floor boutique hung with toile de Jouy. The boutique was the realm of a delightful young woman with premature gray hair, Carmen Colle, wife of Pierre Colle, Dior's partner in the unsuccessful picture gallery enterprise before the war. It was at the home of these two friends at Fleury-en-Bière, near Fontainebleau, that Christian Dior retired in December 1946, having just left Lelong, to put on paper the silhouette that was to become a world famous landmark in fashion.

Christian Dior fits one of the toiles in his workrooms.

Piercing the thunder of applause following the passage of the wedding dress, on that famous day in February 1947, historical phrases were uttered. On Dior: 'Yesterday unknown, today famous.' On the overwhelming success that put Paris back on the fashion map: 'It is the battle of the Marne once again.' The only discordant note was provided by a Princess reputed for her elegance and for wearing a different dress every day, who piped out, 'Another designer who will only last one season', rather like the Marquise de Sévigné, who predicted the same fate to coffee when it was first introduced to France in the 17th century. But unlike the sharp-tongued Marquise, the Princess was quick in changing her mind and in ordering herself a couple of 'New Looks'. From her observation post, near an emergency bell in the salon where she was always to stand during showings in the future, Mme Raymonde made her way through the cheering crowd, now calling for the designer, to seek for Christian Dior in the mannequin's cabin. He emerged from behind the gray satin curtain, smiling through tears of emotion, overcome by his success, and followed by Mme Marguerite and Mme Bricard, both as moved as he was. Mme Luling, the picture of happiness, beamed on everyone. There was a rush of friends who hugged and kissed Dior, and a firing of flash bulbs.

Then began for Christian Dior a period of undreamt-of success and fame. He was invited to Dallas by Neiman Marcus to receive an Oscar, the first ever given to a French couturier. This was the occasion of a grand tour of the USA, once the second collection had been presented. All Americans were not favourable to the New Look and, in Chicago, Dior

Dior with his hand-picked staff, photographed on the stairs of his salon.
First row: from left to right, Mme Marguerite Carré, Christian Dior, Mme Bricard. *Second row:* Monsieur Jacques Rouet, Mme Raymonde Zehnacker, Mme Suzanne Luling, Mme Minassian. *Third row:* at left, Mlle Suzanne Béghin. *Fourth row:* at right, Mme Carmen Colle. *Fifth row:* at right, Mlle Nicole Rousseau.

was met by mobs of revengeful females brandishing posters saying 'Burn Mr Dior' and 'Christian Dior Go Home'. But New York, which he compared to a 'village' on account of the small area in which 'café-society' people live and move, delighted Christian Dior, who made many friends and immediately began thinking of designing clothes adapted to the American way of life, and of opening a New York house. The Dior collections themselves began touring the world's largest cities with fabulous showings at the different French embassies. Twice they were invited to Blenheim by the Duchess of Marlborough. To widen the circle of admirers and clients, a new public relations person joined the house in 1954, the very charming Greek-born Lilia Ralli, who gathered in a number of royal highnesses when she accompanied the collections abroad. Today she is a frequent companion to Marc Bohan in his social activities.

Back in post-war Paris there was a new *joie de vivre*. Balls were conceived like works of art and the refinement of costumes for the fancy dress *Panache* ball given by Christian Bérard was an enchantment, as were the feathered masks worn at the *Bal des Oiseaux*. Count Etienne de Beaumont, famous for his pre-war receptions, gave the *Bal des Rois*, where Christian Dior appeared as the king of animals, a thick-maned lion. Stupendous receptions were given everywhere, by the Viscountess de Noailles, whom the *tout Paris* referred to as Marie-Louise, and by Mr and Mrs Arturo Lopez-Willshaw who had reopened their lovely home in Neuilly. But nothing equalled the splendour of the ball given in Venice by Mr Carlos de Beistegui in 1951, at the Palazzo Labia, decorated with the famous Tiepolo frescoes. This time Christian Dior, mounted on stilts, took part in a fancy dress entry named 'The Entrance of the Giants'.

Dior himself loved to entertain his friends and gave many delightful dinners and parties with music in his Paris flat on Boulevard Jules Sandeau, which had replaced the smaller one on rue Royale, and where he had the joy of possessing a winter garden which brought back memories of his youth at Granville. Here he gathered all the art treasures he was at last able to buy and enjoy, in the surroundings he had always craved for. The accomplishment of his dream was to be the house *La Colle Noire* in the south of France, his retirement dream, but which alas he hardly had time to become acquainted with before fate caught up with him for the last time. Christian Dior was a delightful host, full of charm and fantasy, firing off witty remarks, jumping up to play the piano for his intimate friends, or masquerading with anything on hand – curtains, tablecloths – to amuse his guests. The food was delicious. Rare dishes were always one of his favourite topics and pastimes. He invented recipes himself. Indulging in all these delicacies had a disastrous effect on Christian Dior's figure and he soon began to worry about his increasing corpulence. He tried dieting but it had very little effect on his weight, it only depressed him, so he gave it up. In the same way, he tried to alter his outward appearance, which he found too conventional for a couturier, but never got any further than adding an occasional flower to the buttonhole of his conservative lounge suits. He was a born worrier, always carrying a bag of pills and consulting doctors as well as the fortune-teller Madame D— on every

Christian Dior at a party, conversing with Mme Bricard (left) and French actress Madeleine Renaud.

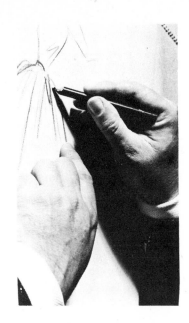

The hands of Christian Dior.

move he made. Mme Raymonde became more and more indispensable to him, organising his private life, his dinner parties, and accompanying him everywhere. To his friends, so kind, so generous and so loyal to him always, he was true till the end. He always kept a level head and, when at last success came his way, he never really believed that it had actually happened to him, the same Christian Dior. But no one was able to warn him against going to Montecatini to take a cure, and it was to Mme Raymonde that befell the sad task of putting through a call to Paris on that fateful November night, in 1957, to impart the tragic news of his sudden death.

Twice a year Christian Dior would return from his period of country retirement with at least 600 sketches for the coming season. First called in to see them was Mme Marguerite who describes the scene: 'Monsieur Dior was an expert at dosing effects, the best sketches were underneath so that enthusiasm went crescendo'. 'Shape guides me first', Christian Dior always proclaimed. It was only much later that fabric and colour intervened, when the shape had been definitely established in muslin form. Even a muslin form has to be fitted on a manikin that is shaped like a woman and not like a tree trunk as were the ones in use at the time', states Mme Marguerite, who questions with as much conviction as twenty-five years ago, 'How can one make a voluptuous dress on a tree trunk?'. And that is why she set about battering those wooden shapes, hollowing out the waist, raising the breasts for a long torso effect, rounding the hips with stuffing, slimming buttocks and eliminating that nightmare of all couturiers, the dreadful inward curve just below the waist at the back. 'I even rounded the abdomen, as on Greek statues', adds Mme Marguerite, 'and there at last was a voluptuous figure to pin the muslin shape to, and ready to express the New Look.'

Once the sketches had been dealt out to the workrooms, Mme Marguerite set herself to decide on the cut of the pleats – straight or on the bias. 'Some of the models required 30 metres of cloth in 1 metre 30 width', tells Mme Marguerite, 'and if it was wool something had to be done to lighten the look and the weight borne by the wearer'. 'To begin with, the muslin shapes, when presented to Monsieur Dior, were lined with a stiffened gauze, called tarlatane, which stands alone. There is a snag in a muslin shape. It flatters the model and takes the form beautifully, much better than wool, which can sometimes droop pitifully. To render the same effect it is necessary to increase or reduce the volume according to the material selected. Once a muslin is accepted, it is sent to the workrooms and taken apart so that the ultimate material can be cut on it piece by piece.' But Mme Marguerite, ever cautious and too afraid of losing an indication or the exact proportion between each operation, insisted on one half of the muslin being left intact. 'It is so easy to lose the right expression of a model', she says. And that was her main concern when she asked M. Dior: 'Have I expressed you correctly, Monsieur?'

153

She continues: 'Then the scaffolding was put up under the dress itself. First the famous no. 132 tulle from Brivet, then a very sheer organza from Abraham. To prevent the tulle from scratching and making ladders in stockings a very fine silk pongé was added to line the skirt. But that was not all', pursues Mme Marguerite, as if reliving the entire experience: 'There were the tulle corsets made to give women the shape we wished them to have.' At this point, Mme Marguerite produces one of these corsets, an absolute masterpiece made of two thicknesses of black tulle, in opposite weave direction to prevent any stretching, with slim and supple narrow boning all around. It served as a low strapless bra, trimmed the waist and ended just below the hipbone. It differed from the *guêpière*, a creation of Marcel Rochas, which was bra-less and only made to pull in the waist. Evening dresses were actually built on a corset of this type, and the wearer just slipped into the mould, needless of anything else. A corset was required for every dress and, since made in the Dior workrooms, was worth a fortune.

The entire procedure of the New Look was actually borrowed from sculpture, even the materials were sculptured into shape with a hot iron. 'You have a sculptor's thumb', Christian Dior would say to Mme Marguerite, who gives this explanation for the fundamental difference between haute couture and ready-to-wear. 'Shaping materials is something ready-to-wear could not do, they put darts instead. Not even darts exist in today's fashion' adds a trifle wistfully the guardian of this precious, bottled-up technique who now lives graciously at home. Commenting on how fleeting inspiration can be, Mme Marguerite recalls how next season's silhouette was already in the budding of the one in preparation, how things had already evolved before even the showing, and how Christian Dior would exclaim: 'If we had another two weeks we could start everything over again.' But now and then he would insist: 'If I cannot have this dress the collection has no meaning, besides there is still one night left.' And so the dress was made and presented. One of the most eager for an overnight job was a young tailor named Pierre Cardin, who began his couture career at Dior's the season of the New Look. 'A perfectionist, he spent the night doing and undoing', remembers Mme Marguerite. 'The next morning he looked like Jesus Christ, a hippy before the time.'

Amongst all the roles imparted to Mme Raymonde, described by Christian Dior as 'the bond in periods of strife', and 'method within imagination' which he summed up in his own formula 'my exact complement', was the task of producing the appropriate materials for the models. Post-war cloths were very poor in quality and the crisp materials Christian Dior was looking for to express the 'New Look' were rare. But among her other gifts, Mme Raymonde was a remarkable conjurer. She could produce anything from anywhere. A natural silk shantung was discovered at Bianchini for the jacket of the famous model, 'Bar', which identified the 'New Look' together with 'Macadam', for which a light gray woollen was found at Dumas Maury. Staron provided 'Alaskine', which was to

Pages from *Harper's Bazaar* (July 1947) explained to readers the elaborate technical processes which lay behind the famous 'New Look'.

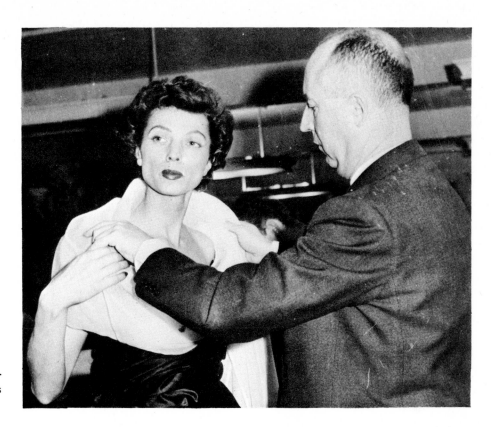

Christian Dior makes a last-minute adjustment to one of his mannequins.

become a classic in wool at Dior, and 'Starella', a delicately grained taffeta. Once she had registered the master's choice from all the muslin forms, and his decisions as to whom was to wear what, Mme Raymonde established a detailed chart with divisions for coats, suits, day and evening dresses. Then she added the fabrics, each one selected after numerous tests because, in Christian Dior's own words: 'The shape of the model depends nearly as much on the way the cloth reacts as on the cut itself.'

The delivery of the materials always proved to be a headache, and is to this day. At last, when all the pieces of the puzzle had been assembled, came the day when Christian Dior was faced with the first fittings in cloth on the mannequins. Armed with a long cane, like a schoolmaster's, he sat in his studio surrounded by his immediate staff, all wearing the same white smock, all very eager and tense. In a dead silence the announcement was made, 'Monsieur, un modèle', repeated each time a new model appeared. The cane served to point out a fault, indicate desired alterations or to emphasise proportions and volume. Mme Bricard, of whom Christian Dior would say 'her point of view is that of the Ritz, she is the achieved model of cosmopolitan style', made frequent interferences which the couturier considered the best of stimulants. He particularly consulted her on the hats. 'Shape and volume have to balance the silhouette of the dress', he stressed, adding, 'even if no one wears them eventually'. Never to be overlooked was the little spray of lily-of-the-valley present each season on one of the models and which became Dior's keepsake and token of good luck.

The final rehearsal took place before an enlarged audience, with

155

Suzanne Luling, directrice of the salons, Mme Linzeler, who supervised the fittings, press attachés Robert de Maussabré and Jean-Claude Donatti, Roger Vivier, designer of the Dior-Delman shoes, and Michel Brodsky, who sold them. Even M. Rouet and M. Chastel slipped away from their management duties to take a peek now and then. Each model had still to be christened. Every season there was a suit named 'Bobby' which turned out to be the best-seller. Models meant to be show-stoppers and intended for magazine covers were known in the house as 'Trafalgars'. They generally had their place toward the middle of the showing, to rekindle the flagging attention of the audience after an hour or so of concentration.

The press release was Christian Dior's own composition, as was the slogan invented each season to describe the new silhouette. The name he chose for his revolutionary silhouette in February 1947 was 'Corolle' but the one that went down in history was coined by the ever-fertile American press. The expression 'New Look' branded the image and toured the world. The following season, in August 1947, Christian Dior developed the 'New Look' to the maximum of its possibilities. Nothing was too wide, too long, too sumptuous, or too costly. Happy times were back with a new abundance of luxuries of which everyone wanted their share. The season's best-seller was a dress in light pink wool called 'Bonbon'. The price had to be readjusted in a hurry from 29,000 to 32,000 francs, because of miscalculations in the cost, which was rocking the profits. But the glorification of the 'New Look' was the dress named 'Chérie' which required 80 metres of white silk faille.

For Christian Dior, gone for ever were the days when he could retire into a shell and indulge in a peaceful life with his intimate friends. His basically anxious nature caused him to live perpetually on tenterhooks,

The couturier views his collection and makes suggestions, aided by his colleagues, Mme Bricard, on his right, and Mme Marguerite, on his left.

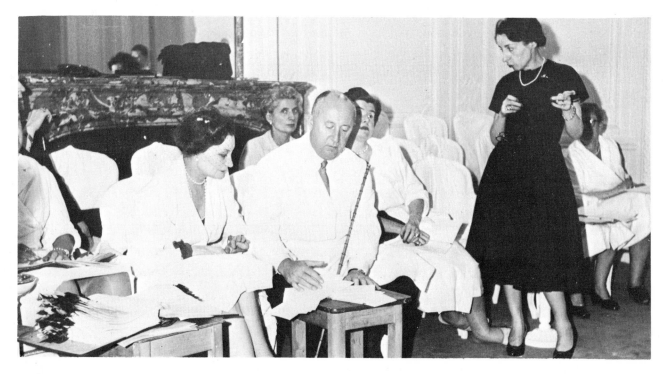

156

Mannequins from the house of Dior make a secret exit for an official photographing session in the avenue Montaigne, outside the salon.

eyes scrutinising, ears quivering to capture signs of appreciation or criticism on the part of clients, journalists, buyers and, of course, friends. Ever on the alert and ever present, he was to stop a showing one day and step out to chastise a clandestine sketcher. Like God Almighty chasing Adam and Eve out of the Garden of Paradise, he stood in front of the shameful culprit and pointed a wrathful finger toward the door until she got up and left. Professional buyers and private clients were left to the care of Mme Luling and Mme Minassian. The seating of each one according to importance was always a delicate problem and full of meaning. Reduced buying one season meant a less good seat the next time. Eyes needed to be watchful to spot the buyers quick to unsew a lining for a better view of the seaming on a dress, or to snatch off a piece of jewellery. Still smiling into the middle of the night, Suzanne Luling would gather up the late-comers, once the orders were registered, and carry them off to some other aspect of Paris night-life. The parties she gave in her lovely home overlooking the Seine, with a good dosing of buyers, press and friends, were famous and the genuine 17th-century parquet floor nearly collapsed with the dancing, led on by the mad beat of the band from Jimmy's night-club.

By 1952, post-war euphoria had subsided, life was becoming more serious, and so should fashion, thought Christian Dior, who was gradually designing a silhouette with a freer waistline. It was a season of blousons and sweater tops, all in grays and natural colours. Skirts, still at the 'New Look' length were being pulled in and made stricter. Followed a regular and subtle progression toward total freedom of the waist, starting with line 'H' in August 1954, which *Harper's Bazaar* editor, Carmel Snow, named the 'Flat Look'. Lines 'A' and 'Y' in 1955 stressed lengthened

157

torsos and gave an indication of rising hemlines. That season there was a much-noticed black and white evening dress with a distinctly high waist, emphasised by a white satin front-bowed sash with a trailer to the floor. But there was also the appearance of a perfectly straight midi-top over a straight, matching, long satin skirt, which did away with the waistline completely. In 1956, Christian Dior showed the first of his tunic dresses, double breasted, slim, and unfitted down to the narrow underskirt, still at mid-calf. In 1957, he introduced the 'Free Line', and presented a perfectly straight unfitted chemise dress in wool, a small herring-bone pattern, with crew neck and long narrow sleeves, raising the hemline to calf top.

This was the beginning of a long era of loose shapes developed by Yves Saint Laurent in his famous 'Trapeze' line in February 1958, when he was promoted designer of the collection after the sudden and tragic death of Christian Dior, to whom he had been assistant for four years. As dresses became fuller and looser under Saint Laurent, with skirts ending just below the knees, a new technique was developed for body-shaping under the dress which was allowed to fall freely from the shoulders. In this manner, the body was outlined when the wearer moved. It was a technique which gave birth to a long-lived series of transparencies over body-shaped foundations. Parallel to the bulky coats which followed the loose unfitted silhouette, Saint Laurent began to reintroduce the waistline by belting the dresses with wide leather belts, which gave an extra bounce to his flounced or rounded skirts with knee-level pull-in. This was in 1959. Before leaving the maison Dior, for much-debated reasons which are explained in another chapter, Saint Laurent presented the following year a premonitory, though at the time totally unsuccessful look. Turtle necks and sleeves in heavy knit on wool outfits were forewarnings of the sportive look and the chasuble dress, sleeveless over a high-necked sweater, which was worn for years, and ended up by being a classic. But it was all too early. Courrèges had not yet come to blast the walls of fashion, and haute couture was not mixing with the hippies in the streets yet. In fashion, good timing is essential.

Once the Dior ball started spinning it was rapidly put in orbit to proliferate. Christian Dior himself, who was not indifferent to figures and had a good business head, proclaimed: 'Behind all the frills, figures are the ones that talk.' According to the information given out by the house today, the original 10 million francs invested by M. Boussac in 1946 were increased to 100 million within three years. Success was so immediate and orders so overwhelming that an eight-storey building had to be put up rapidly in the courtyard to house eight workrooms, quickly followed by a twin building for more workrooms and warehouses. The maison Dior was soon to outgrow the initial building at 30 avenue Montaigne, which to this day is still only rented, and was in a position to buy the neighbouring house on the corner, at number 32 of the avenue, as well as the one next to it at 13 rue François Ier, to make room for the perfumes and

An impeccable *tailleur* in the 'H' line designed by Dior, and modelled by Diana Massie, one of his house mannequins.

right
One of Dior's most successful models, 'Allah'. (1959.)

158

Zika Asher's rose-printed silk, 1954, broke away from the small, scribbled, abstract designs which had dominated fabric design since World War II, and was used by Christian Dior to make this beautiful double-skirted summer dress.

furs, and larger offices for various branches. The staff has increased from 85 in 1946 to its present number of 1200, a figure which includes the workers of the ready-to-wear factories at Blois and Orleans. The Dior empire was not long in extending abroad and it was Christian Dior himself who in 1949 insisted on establishing a Christian Dior firm in New York with the purpose of making and selling ready-to-wear 'de luxe' specially designed for America.

Christian Dior was a perfectionist and wished to create an overall image of woman. He took an interest in every detail of a woman's appearance. 'Christian Dior Perfumes' and 'Christian Dior Furs' had both been launched in 1947. In 1949 the first licence programme was signed for ties, and in 1951 was started a department co-ordinating the different wholesale and licensing operations for stockings, gloves, scarves, ties, girdles, hats, knitwear, and lingerie. A licence is a contract between two companies whereby one of the said companies grants the other the right to use its label and models for reproduction and distribution in a chosen country, the goods being manufactured in that same country. Dior gives the name, the model and the right to sell within territorial limits against a minimum guarantee and the payment of royalties. Licences are profitable when custom duties are high, for example, in South America, where they can reach up to 300%. Within the Common Market it is preferable to manufacture and to export oneself. There are other points which make a licensing programme the best choice. For climatic reasons it is sometimes better to choose fabrics and colour locally. Taste may differ totally from one country to another, and important morphological differences appear, such as between American and Japanese women in the case of girdles and bras. A good licensing programme depends primarily on finding the right manufacturer and the right material. The largest number of Dior licences are for the USA. Figures given by the house show a progress of 70% between 1969 and 1970 for the licensing programme with Japan. One licence signed with the firm Kanebo, in Osaka, Japan's first textile concern, covers fourteen different articles ranging from town clothes to beachwear, girdles, and so on. Approximately eighty countries are concerned with the Dior licensing programmes, and twenty-eight items. 'Christian Dior Stockings' are manufactured in twenty-two different countries, ties and accessories for men in thirteen countries, girdles and bras in six countries. Shoes, costume jewellery, gloves, scarves, handbags, are manufactured by various French and foreign firms for Dior who exports them to different countries, but not to the USA. On the other hand, 'Dior–New York Ready-to-Wear' is manufactured in the Dior–New York workrooms and so are the 'Dior–New York Furs'. Other landmarks include, in 1954, the inauguration of the 'Boutique' on the corner of the avenue Montaigne, in 1955, the opening of 'Christian Dior–London', a collection designed by Marc Bohan from 1958 to 1960, when he was offered the top job in Paris, and today by Jorn Langberg. In 1959, a ready-to-wear and half-to-measure shoe department opened. In 1967, it was the launching of the ready-to-wear 'Miss Dior', now designed by Philippe Guibourgé, for many years assistant to Marc Bohan, and the opening of the boutique 'Miss Dior'. 'Baby Dior' opened also. In 1970 the boutique 'Monsieur' was enlarged by three new departments: custom-made and ready-to-wear clothes, and shoes. The men's clothes are designed by Marc Bohan.

A most profitable operation, the selling of toiles and paper patterns, was rapidly set up in connection with the caution fees paid by the buyers, as early as the second Christian Dior collection. The present day conditions stipulate that every European buyer paying a caution of 3500 francs·has the right to one or two paper patterns according to their country of origin. Americans are about the only ones left to buy muslin patterns priced at 7000 francs, which are too expensive for Europeans. American manufacturers are charged a caution of $2000, which gives them the choice of one model in fabric exact to the original. The buying of a

right
The first mini-skirted suit, in Courrèges' favourite colouring, from 1965.

Marc Bohan and the stork of scissors.

left
A display in the Dior boutique.

A sketch by Marc Bohan given to the author to illustrate this book.

pattern concedes total rights in each respective country, but prohibits selling it outside that country. Some firms sign up for so many patterns over so many seasons. However complicated the system and the diversity of its applications (for example, in Italy one firm has total exclusivity), the result represents a regular income for the maison Dior.

Christian Dior furs are designed by Frederic Castet, a long-timer in the house, who started in 1952 as head tailor, at the age of twenty-three. He had the best possible training: three years at Balenciaga and seven years with Christian Dior himself, then three years designing the London collection when Marc Bohan took over the Paris collection. Finally, he returned to Paris, and succeeded Monsieur Manteau as designer for the furs, in 1968, and works under the supervision of Marc Bohan so as to

160

One of the first suits designed post-Dior in autumn 1961 to be copied by the London ready-to-wear firm of Wallis.

A pretty checked suit from the Dior collection of spring 1963.

left
A coat (with matching dress beneath) in satin, designed by Ungaro in 1966 for the winter collection.

maintain the same fashion mood. He likes to treat furs like fabrics, and thinks nothing of cutting up minks into a plaid pattern or combining four species of spotted furs in a patchwork coat. The Dior fur shows are now fashion events in their own right which, once a year, and for one hour, make you think it might be nice to be the favourite spouse of one of the Arabian oil kings.

'Christian Dior Perfumes' was a separate company started in 1947 on the impulse of Serge Heftler-Louiche, one of Christian Dior's oldest and closest friends from the Granville days. For Christian Dior, it was not enough to dress a woman, he wanted to create the total effect including the fragrance surrounding her. M. Heftler-Louiche, who had been deputy-manager for Coty Perfumes, was at the time owner of Cadoricin, a famous hair cosmetic firm which enabled him to immediately contribute a factory at Monte Carlo and a distributing organisation, all in perfect working order. Owing to these advantages, the initial capital needed and provided was modest: 2 million francs (of 1947). The shares were divided in the following proportions: 40% for M. Boussac, 30% for M. Heftler-Louiche and 30% for M. Dior. The couturier put all his creative and business abilities into this new venture. He designed the bottles, in Baccarat crystal, and the packaging as well. With Serge Heftler-Louiche he selected the fragrances. *Miss Dior* was the first-born, and 283 bottles were put out the first year by a small factory at Courbevoie, on the outskirts of Paris, where six work-people had been grouped for the production. To give an idea of the development of the business, in 1971 eleven million bottles were turned out, and the turnover was 24 million dollars, divided into 60% perfumes and 40% cosmetics.

There are 700 employees in the Dior–Perfumes organisation today. The entire production was grouped in a new factory at Rueil-Malmaison in 1961, and there is a plan to move all the services out to near Orleans in 1975, where they will cover 75 acres. When Christian Dior died in 1957, his shares were divided between M. Boussac and M. Heftler-Louiche, proportionately to their existing holdings, which gave M. Boussac a total of 60% and M. Heftler-Louiche 40%. Shortly after, M. Heftler-Louiche died, and his shares remained in his family till the coming-of-age of his children. They were then bought up by M. Boussac, who in turn sold 34% of his total holding to Moët & Chandon, in 1968. Further sales were to follow, and the group, now become the Moët-Hennessy holding, was to acquire 50% in 1971 and be the owner of 99% of the total shares in January 1972. M. Boussac has now become M. 1%, which he wishes to remain, in order to attend the assemblies, though he resigned from his presidential seat, now occupied by Bernard T. Picot. Otherwise, everything continues as before, with the Christian Dior perfumes, *Miss Dior, Diorama, Diorissimo, Diorling* and the toilet waters *Eau Fraiche* and *Eau Sauvage* being sold all over the world, except in China and Albania, but including Siberia. Dior was among the first firms to step behind the Iron Curtain for business, in June 1959. Since the success of *Miss*

Dior it is the toilet water *Eau Fraiche* which has the largest sales in Europe of all existing perfumes for women or for men. The cosmetic man is Serge Lutens, to whom make-up is an element of decoration which must follow the evolution of fashion. His most striking manifesto, for the image it gave, was the multicolour striped face photographed by Guy Bourdin and published in all top fashion magazines. The latest project is to add a wide range of beauty treatments, which is expected to raise the sales proportions to 50% perfumes and 50% cosmetics and beauty treatments.

The Société Christian Dior today is above all a colossal business complex. Never before has such a frivolous topic as haute couture been taken so seriously. Through the ability of the management, concentrated in the hands of Jacques Rouet, who has steered the house to safety through many a storm, overcoming internal crises and ever ready to adjust to new conditions, while disconnecting press rumours of a shutdown following the selling of the Perfumes, the house has survived profitably with an official turnover of $51,200,000 for 1971 – a figure that applies to all the Dior activities of couture, ready-to-wear, furs, licences and so on, but does not include perfume sales.

Marc Bohan, designer of the Dior collection today, has actually outlived every other designer in the house, including Christian Dior himself. During his eleven years career he has been faced with many difficulties and has managed to steer clear of all of them. He did not benefit by the extraordinary post-war period and the fascination exerted on women by the return of luxury and beautiful clothes. By 1961, when he arrived in the house, clients had become more realistic, more demanding, and were no longer inclined to spend madly. Money was more restrained. That explains why his first collection, christened the 'Slim Look' was perfectly timed. It met with great success because it was exactly adapted to women's way of life, and at the same time it was very pretty. It stressed a slim silhouette with a slightly flared hemline. 'It was in a dancing mood', says Marc Bohan today as he sits in his upstairs studio, a slim figure himself with a high brow and beady brown eyes, wearing a white belted smock. Facing him is a huge metal stork made of all different sizes and types of scissors, a very spiky bird which Marc Bohan picked up from the ground floor window decorations when Jean-François Daigre, who invents them, decided on a change. Bohan says this in a kind, good-humoured way, as if he meant that 'he couldn't let the poor thing starve to death' (of affection, no doubt).

Marc Bohan had met Christian Dior once or twice, had been invited to his private house on Boulevard Jules Sandeau. At that time he was designer for Patou. Christian Dior had asked him if eventually he would like to assist him for the New York collection, a plan which never developed because it was within a few months of Christian Dior's death. It was only after a year that Marc Bohan was asked by the house to design the Christian Dior London collection, which he kept up until the

Three of the 'A' line coats, designed by Dior's successor, Marc Bohan, in autumn 1966.

The coats covered skirts at a new short length – an innovation which achieved the greatest success that season.

year of the 'Slim Look', in February 1961. His path had nearly crossed with Christian Dior's once before. He, too, started his fashion career at Robert Piguet's, but after the war, instead of before it, like Dior. There were two other beginners at the time, Hubert de Givenchy and the American Jimmy Galanos. This is how Marc Bohan describes the scene of his débuts: 'Hubert and I were each seated on a footstool and asked to participate in the making of the models. We could not just sit, we had to make appropriate remarks.' One day, Bohan was asked by Piguet to design two or three models. 'I drew a little black crêpe dress', he tells, 'with a trapeze neckline and a draped effect on one hip. It sold one hundred times.' Bohan was then nineteen years old. Then followed a period, when, still at Piguet's, he worked with the actor Louis Jouvet and the artist Christian Bérard on the stage costumes of the play they produced together, Molière's *Don Juan*. After his military service, Bohan went to Molyneux's until the closing of the house in 1951. From his period at Piguet's, Bohan remembers the principle this designer imparted to him on which he had thrived himself for many years: 'When you have designed clothes women are tempted by, then you have succeeded.' Bohan adds: 'It has remained my motto ever since.' For himself, Marc Bohan favours close-to-classic styles, with accents on accessories and colour, except at weekends and on holidays where he ventures on more out-of-the-way clothes. Where he really lets off speed is when he drives a sportscar. He lives around the corner from the maison Dior; can feel the Dior buildings looming up behind his screened windows. His daughter, eighteen year old Marie-Anne, lives with him. The décor of his home is modern, the furniture a combination of period and contemporary with one of Niki de Saint Phalle's very obvious and colourful 'Nanas' towering over the scene in one corner.

Another good vintage year for Bohan was when he brought coats down to mid-calf and gave them a 'Tin Soldier' look, slim, with epaulettes, high boots and a slanted beret. Skirts underneath were still short to kneecap. This was in July 1966. The following year, Bohan was all for African art and totem prints covered day and evening dresses, while suits turned safari style with Baden-Powell chin-strapped hats. He did well too with his 'Radjah' collection, and when he brought the djellabah back from Morocco.

Back to charm and prettiness today, Bohan, who has a subtle sense of colour and knows how to choose materials, says: 'Today women come to couture for what it specialises in, all the delicate workmanship, the intricate pleating, the fabulous embroidery. All that is inspired by fashion off the street they hate. I must confess that, led on by the press, we all went right off the deep end for a while recently. Women are not faithful as clients, they come and go according to whether they have heard the collection is good or bad. We can count on an average of four to five models per client when the collection is a success, but gone are the days when a customer would order the same dress in five or six different colours.' According to the Chambre Syndicale, there are still between four and five thousand women who buy haute couture clothes. Marc Bohan gives a warning on designing clothes such as the current batwing sleeve developed by ready-to-wear. 'It is a mistake', he says, 'it never looks right, it is heavy, droopy and ageing.' He thinks that the safest way for couture to survive is 'to offer women what they want'. And under these conditions he believes it will survive.

Everyone at Dior agrees with everyone else in the haute couture field that conditions have changed drastically in the past ten years. There are fewer foreign buyers, and those that come buy less. Private clients, scared by rocketing prices, buy more sparingly and look to ready-to-wear to complete their wardrobe, often ready-to-wear sold in the couture boutiques and well-adapted to their needs. The maison Dior, like the rest of couture, is going through a period where it is necessary to advance with great caution. However costly, haute couture is indispensable to the image of the house and to the numerous side industries operated under the Christian Dior label. Whether the timing of couture collections can be adjusted to fit in with the presentation of ready-to-wear is one of the yet unsolved questions that interests buyers and press who hesitate to make four trips a year to Paris. But one point appears irreversible – the radical change in the way of living and what women want out of life today.

Three models from the Christian Dior London boutique collection for spring 1972.

7 Jacques Fath recalled   André Ostier

People one has known at different times in one's life, now long gone, come back into the memory with certain images, almost always the same. I knew Jacques Fath very well and when I bring to mind my memories of him, I recall that very gay smile, so characteristic, as he worked in his studio preparing the dresses for his coming collection with a spirit and a joy which he communicated to all his colleagues. I remember him too in his dazzling costume of the Sun King, followed by a crowd of Venetians who so relished such spectacles, arriving with his wife Geneviève at the Labia Palace for that Bal du Siècle, famous in the annals of the city of the Doges. Between these two images, so vivid in my memory, I shall try to evoke this couturier who was so suddenly struck off the list of those great designers who knew, in the aftermath of World War II, how to give such lustre to the Parisian couture.

Jacques Fath was born in 1912: his Protestant family was both Flemish and Alsatian in origin – on his mother's side he even inherited a little English blood. When he came to the age to launch himself into life and

Jacques Fath and Geneviève, his wife, arriving at a ball in the Labia Palace, Venice, in the costume of the Sun King, Louis XIV.

Fath with the mannequin, Bettina.

think about earning a living, his family made him spend some time in a business school. 'Perhaps he could become interested in accounting. Mon petit Jacques, one must know how to count!' It was enough for his parents to make such pronouncements for figures to become anathema to him, and as soon as Jacques went to work on the Stock Exchange with a firm of brokers, it became clear that it was not at all to his taste. Among his family, one recalls a certain great-grandmother, with whom Jacques used to love to spend time in conversation. Had she not, in the great days of the Second Empire, created huge crinoline dresses, working the *failles*, the lace and the silks, to adorn those beautiful women, as we see them again in portraits by Winterhalter, gathered like a bouquet of flowers, around the Empress Eugènie?

Among the memories of childhood and youth, there are always striking impressions; a fan, a necklace, suggesting the valses of those balls, where the rustling of the silks mingled with that of the music would have sufficed for the young Jacques to become nostalgic, and to develop a taste for such things. His father was a painter – he had even shown in the USA at the end of the previous century, so that there was a tradition of art in the Fath family. No wonder that amongst the hubbub of the Bourse, Jacques grew bored. He languished in front of his account books. He was also attracted by the theatre and firmly decided that after his military service, he would launch himself into this as a new career. So, he is next to be found taking a speech course at the school of a famous actress, Eve Francis, who was the favourite interpreter of Paul Claudel's plays. Jacques now mingled with the world of the cinema, and made a film under the direction of Leonide Moguy. He felt, however, that he was destined to do something completely different. As for his gifts as an actor, we shall discover them again later in the course of certain of his own celebrations where he loved to give himself roles to play.

How brilliant was the Paris of 1937! How wonderful to be a young man of twenty-five! Ideas flow like champagne froth, and one creates enthusiastically for a society which has a taste for luxury and refinement. Jacques Fath took some small premises in the rue de la Boetie: he began by showing about twenty dresses. Little by little, people began to mention his name, and he had already become an established designer on the eve of World War II. His name is mentioned among the 70 important couturiers in the American statistics of the time. Among them, there is certainly a number who lead the field and Jacques Fath was easily listed among the top twenty.

This was the period when he created with especial delight dresses for a

André Ostier's first fashion shot – a model by Molyneux, 1940.

168

blonde young woman, called Geneviève Boucher de la Bruyere, who was to become Madame Jacques Fath. We find them, after a short period when Jacques was taken prisoner in 1940, in the rooms of an apartment on the rue Francois I. The Paris of the occupation was one of platform-soled shoes and swept-up hairstyles. For cycling, Parisiennes carried nothing short of bags as big as suitcases. Fabrics did not have the softness of pre-war days, but since they were well cut they did not crumple. Now, Jacques battled against the sadness of the time with colour: he was already preparing his palette. From their huge handbags in crocodile leather, the new customers, the B.O.F. ladies, as they were known (in French, *beurre, oeufs, fromages*, or butter, eggs and cheese – the new rich) would pull out huge wads of notes, and pile expensive furs on their backs, over their plain little dresses. Besides such women, who merely wanted an outward symbol of style, Jacques built up a clientèle of faithful women, a clientèle which was to be that 'very Parisian' core which always followed him.

The years after the war take us to a classic two-storey house, extremely elegant in style, situated on the avenue Pierre I de Serbie. Even the floor with the servants' rooms was turned into workrooms, as well as the rest of the house. The whole building looked out at the back over greenness, one of those secret gardens of which so many exist in Paris. This one, though tiny, is still to be found today; it is hidden by a huge building constructed on the same site as number 39. Blue ceramics with the flying bird motif of United Aircraft International decorate the arched doorway, and lead out to that shaded lawn where on so many occasions in the past, at the time of the collections (in summer for the winter season), rows of seats, one above the other, would be set up for the presentation. One was less hot there than in the salons, where in February (for the summer collections), one was packed together right up to the staircase. Besides, in that garden, a collection immediately took on the air of a 'fête'.

Jacques Fath lived in a very beautiful ground-floor apartment at the corner of the Cours Albert and the Place de l'Alma, looking onto a garden and the Eiffel Tower – Paris was always present. Jacques loved the country, the sun, travelling; for they were additional sources of inspiration: He rented a mill, shaded by silver birches, in Touraine near Saché. He went there often. He also loved the Midi: he belonged to that race of young men whose faces must always be bronzed by the sun at all times of the year. At the foot of Notre Dame des Anges, at Le Cannet, (which a recently-built motorway had made utterly charmless) he was to buy an old 18th-century mill in the depths of the valley, where bamboos and yew trees protected it from the Mistral. There one could sleep late far from all sounds within rough white-washed walls. In the evenings, Jacques gave huge dinner parties on the patio, illuminated with spotlights, and the days were spent on the beach at Cannes. He was the best customer of 'Madeleine', to which he attracted the best clientèle because of his own presence. Madeleine, launched by Jacques, achieved a fame which has not changed with the passing of time. Along with living life to the full – for Jacques Fath exemplified the phrase 'burning the candle at both ends' – he thought of what the future held for fashion, and how it should evolve.

If he planned a costume for some party, the detail which he chose to recapture a bygone age always took its place with totally modern accessories. The velvet cap of Charles IX, which he wore at the last ball of the Comte Etienne de Beaumont, stimulated his imagination just as much as Marie Antoinette's dress, when she was playing the dairy-maid at the hamlet of the Trianon, at Versailles. He always attached great importance to the variety of his own wardrobe. He went frequently to the USA, to New York, and brought back ideas which, reviewed and modified in his own style, looked completely original. On the beach at Cannes, in Vichy France, he was the first to wear shorts. At galas and premières, it was said that Jacques Fath was eccentric, for he was the first to sport a tartan dinner jacket, and he had several in green plaid. He also wore vivid red

Jacques Fath discussing and planning his collection, 1950.

blazers with gilt buttons. He influenced men's fashions by being one of the first to wear roll-necked sweaters, especially for going to work, and he was often to be seen in frilled shirts. He recognised the potential in materials usually reserved for women's suits, such as one rather lightweight fabric from the house of Lesur, from which he had made a supremely elegant and simple suit. He often draped himself with the bolts of cloth brought in by the manufacturers, unrolling them with a swift gesture of his hands. He would change the sketches for which he had produced ideas at the outset, and would often take a detail in one and add it or adapt it into a suggested silhouette for another design. (Alain Raynaud, now a successful couturier in Milan learnt his craft in this school.) This inimitable detail was only to be found in Paris, because there it was manu-

170

Two examples of his own sketches, from the notebooks for summer 1943.

factured by craftsmen whose buttons, embroideries and ribbons were unequalled in beauty and quality.

The imagination of the couturier turns him into a poet at times! One day the Vicomtesse de Noailles – Marie Laure to her friends – came to visit Jacques and brought him a huge bag of nuts from the country. They were quite dry, wrapped up in a rough material like potato sacking – made of jute. Why not let the fibres of this Indian plant provide the basis for another creation? 'Quickly, draw me a skirt with a bolero for the Vicomtesse', Jacques cried to Alain his designer, and Catherine, his première. The jute skirt took shape, held by a wide belt, and the whole thing was studded with half shells of nuts, stitched on with gold thread.

Jacques Fath was one of the first couturiers to launch younger colours, which he knew how to use with a great subtlety. He mixed blue and green at a time when it was considered that black and brown were the only colours an elegant woman could wear. Young women loved to be dressed by him: he knew how to transform them and managed to give older women too the same youthful silhouette. Modelled by Bettina, his collections always led up to the most ravishing wedding gowns. One would see them in pale yellow, then in pale pink, or pale blue; which of course does not surprise us now in an age when a whole wedding with a bride in blue jeans is advertised on a huge street billboard. The brides of Jacques Fath, perhaps without knowing it, prepared the way for our new life style.

In each couturier, and it is here that his artistic soul is expressed, there lies a dormant Pygmalion. Jacques Fath started by pleasing the rather fanciful tastes of his wife, Geneviève. When one saw her, so impeccably dressed, on the day of the collection in her place of honour in the salon, with their son Philippe beside her, a little prince in his black velvet costume, one was in no doubt about all the remarks and observations which must have preceded this fateful day, and which could have easily degenerated into tedious domestic squabbles. 'Geneviève, do smooth your hair a little'; 'Geneviève, let's choose another dress'; 'I assure you this colour doesn't look good on you at all'; 'Geneviève, take off those jewels'. What was the result? A perfect, consummate elegance which triumphed over the most critical gaze. The immediate consequence was that all the clients wanted to place orders, begging for rapid delivery. With his mannequins, Jacques Fath was equally demanding. He formed a stable of star models, just like Christian Dior. Bettina, whose image was so popularised by the magazine world, and who influenced a certain type of woman, owed her success to our couturier. It was due to Jacques Fath that she was to be found in the midst of this café society, which moved between Paris and Acapulco, between Rome and Sardinia. Bettina came from her native Brittany and presented herself at the house of Fath. He liked her. To her chagrin, however, Jacques picked up her hair and looped it into large plaited mounds on either side of her face. Bettina protested: 'I don't want to look like all the others!' In effect, she looked as if she was wearing headphones. But she inspired Jacques Fath, happily, a great deal.

On a cold morning in 1949 I remember taking Bettina and Sophie in my car to photograph them. I stopped my car on the viaduc de Passy, near the Eiffel Tower. Despite the cold, the girls changed in the car – a real striptease. To get an interesting background, I was photographing Bettina underneath the arcades, which one could have imagined like those of a Roman arena. A starched white collar encircled her neck, contrasting in its whiteness with a bolero embroidered with seed pearls and bright sequins. It was matched with a long black skirt, buttoned at the side, and on which was draped a big black tassel of velvet. A sort of toreador's hat was placed on her hair, cut almost in a Joan of Arc look which framed her face. A certain boyish influence was to be seen in this model; a new

The famous Bettina fashion photograph of one of Jacques Fath's most popular designs.

Sketches from Fath's 1949 summer collection, by Francis Marshall.

eroticism had come out of the nightclubs of St Germain des Près and heralded a new conception of femininity. This picture was reproduced in all the newspapers and magazines in the world, and was one of the most successful numbers of that spring collection.

Another model, called Lucky, wanted to work in the maison Fath. 'My girl,' Jacques told her, 'perhaps. But first, you must change.' First of all she had a facelift. She came back. It was not enough. So she had her face peeled. She came back. She still did not please Jacques Fath. So she had a third operation: her nose was turned up. She came back. She always lacked something which gives a face character. Fourth operation: she had her eyes re-shaped. 'Come back', again, said Jacques, after all these operations, which still did not please him. On the fifth visit, she announced that her husband had asked for a divorce, and she had changed the colour of her hair. Fath said: 'I'm like your husband. You definitely don't please me anymore. You're not for me.' Happily for Lucky, she had a very brilliant career with Dior, where she had a very sophisticated way of entering like a plumed horse in a circus, pirouetting on her heels. In this prestigious *cabine* at Fath there was Doudou from Martinique, for whom Jacques made really swishy numbers. To make Doudou's beauty more classic, he had also asked her to have plastic surgery on her nose. By his charm, Jacques got all he wanted from men and women alike.

The house was working flat out, at full capacity: eight workrooms, and approximately 400 employees. From 1948, Jacques visited New York twice a year, and took with him Charlotte, his secretary, and, above all, a designer, some toiles, and a workroom *première*. In a few weeks, not even a month, he would put on a collection of dresses, coats, and tailored suits, for Joseph Halpert, one of his important buyers. He would start with twenty models, and add up to forty for the ready-to-wear manufacturers. He was criticised a lot at the time for selling himself outside his house. His example was taken up and other couturiers were soon delighted to be approached by other American 'off-the-peg' manufacturers. Equally he was one of the first to open a boutique, in 1950, where one found those little trifles which women cannot resist: scarves, costume jewellery, bags, and sunhats and unusual sun spectacles. To get to the salons the customers passed through the boutique; even if they came for a couture dress-fitting they would enjoy lingering there for a moment, and would allow themselves to be persuaded into buying a simpler, less daunting model from the ready-to-wear range.

Among its clients, the house of Fath had its ostentatious characters. One of the most famous was a Mrs Biddle, who would arrive with her jewellery casket, and order her dresses to match the colour of her necklaces and set off her gems. She often ordered the same model in different shades, as well as fur coats and hats to complete the outfit. In 1947 one Mme Anchorena ordered 28 million francs worth of dresses. She was a petite woman, who adopted a strange style of make-up so that the only features one saw were her lips and her eyes, dilated by the effect of false eyelashes.

At this time, the Anchorenas (who were soon to disappear almost without a penny), received the fashionable world and the artists of Paris in their apartment on the avenue Foch. Here, the doors were renowned because they were all decorated by a different well-known painter. For her fittings, Mme Anchorena was always trailed after by her husband.

Equally famous for her extravagant orders was the Princess de Faucigny Lucinge; to the list of faithfuls one can also add the Princess de Rethy, who was always very elegantly dressed. The collection of the house of Fath was considered a 'must' by both North and South Americans . . . they all placed orders, be it Paulette Goddard, or Maria Felix, or the Madrazzos, or that famous Mme Rubio, who could not wear a glove on her right hand because her diamond displayed so many carats. There were clients who were personal friends; but really, all his clients became so.

I can remember Jacques Fath one July, when on the eve of a collection, a strike suddenly developed in the couture and threatened to do irremediable damage to all the plans for the showing of new models. No more seamstresses: the workrooms were deserted. During this July strike, Jacques Fath in a way defied the Chambre Syndicale; he called on his friends, and the Princess Troubetzkoy and Marie Helène de Ganay were co-opted as his assistants. The Vicomtesse de Noailles came to boost morale and all the *beau monde* did its utmost whilst Jacques was huddled over his sewing machine. Everybody laughed and worked with the greatest good humour. Jacques kept up his spirits with peaches in wine and steak tartare. Thanks to this make-shift teamwork, a collection of about one hundred models was shown, in which originality prevailed over perfection!

At the time of his death, Jacques Fath employed 600 people. An excellent businessman, he added to the parent company a number of licensed outlets. Of the total revenue of his house, 36% was made up by the boutique, hat and perfume sales. The last was established in a shop almost opposite the maison de couture. Then, there were stockings, scarves, and ties. Shortly before his death, he accepted financial backing from Jean Prouvost, a big press and textile magnate, to set up mass production of ready-to-wear clothes, in the 'Fath Université' range, inspired by the methods which he had seen tried and tested in the USA. He made the same model, with different measurements for the back, the skirt, and twelve different sizes for the hips and waist. These models were distributed to licensees in France as well as abroad. At the time, this gave couture a revolutionary direction. Today, we can see how right he was, in wanting to please and reach the anonymous mass market. The ties, the Jacques Fath scarves, were always on sale in the big stores and at thousands of stockists. It was a well-known trademark, and a great one.

Between 1944 and 1949, a period of increasing prosperity was ushered in for Jacques. Thanks to the clients and the buyers, thanks to the USA and its dollars, Jacques Fath realised a long-standing ambition: he acquired a country house not far from Paris. With his extravagant tastes, he poured his profits into the Château de Corbeville, 45 kilometres from the capital. It was a beautiful 17th-century structure, with an impressive approach, a drawbridge over a moat, a roof of slate tiles, and walls covered with ivy. It had a central building with wings on either side, nobly proportioned, and faced a park with ancient trees.

Touraine had been abandoned: the mill near Saché was only rented. In the outbuildings, he started to make alterations, and had an enormously luxurious swimming pool built, where he often went from Paris during the lunch-hour, even if there was only a glimmer of sunshine. He presided over the alterations at the château which were carried out as quickly as could be done. He brought all the contemporary tastes which he loved to these old walls, without removing their period charm. He had numerous

Mme Schiaparelli at Jacques Fath's 1925 Hollywood party.

175

guest rooms and bathrooms built, and for the large reception rooms he scoured the antique shops and chose exquisite period furniture, such as 18th-century chairs inscribed with the name of the maker. One day, Corbeville opened its doors to a great invasion of guests, curious to see whether this couturier, who for years had been entertained by others, knew how to give parties himself. It was a revelation. I recall with great fondness those July days, when the conversation spread as quickly as the gossip on the length of hems: after the presentation of his collection, Jacques Fath would invite the press, the buyers and his friends to a huge party given on a theme, which was kept a secret by him until just a week before. Then, quickly, one had to put together the suitable accessories to be in the groove. One year, it was the square dance. Another time, a 1925 Hollywood. On this occasion, Jacques Fath staged a real 'show' in which he wore himself out, oblivious to his tiredness, and recaptured his gifts as an actor. During that evening, he appeared successively sporting a Charlie Chaplin moustache, a Maurice Chevalier boater, or with his face unrecognisably painted in black to mimic Al Jolson. He swept Paulette Goddard after him into the dance, with her ostrich feathers afloat. All Paris had dreamed of being invited that night to Corbeville.

In 1952, there was also a Brazilian ball, for which he had specially-charted plane-loads of singers, and orchestras flown in. Leather *vaquero* costumes were considered not authentic without horses, so they too were ordered at the last moment. Mme Vargas, wife of the Brazilian president, was there. Just as in Brazil, they danced till dawn. Hundreds of invitations would be sent out for these balls, and in the park, buffets or tables managed to satisfy everyone. No expense was spared. What publicity!

Jacques Fath's extravaganza, with himself as Maurice Chevalier.

A Francis Marshall sketch from the summer 1955 collection. After Jacques Fath's death, his wife Geneviève continued to run the house, until 1957.

176

Illness, meanwhile, was beginning to undermine him. Often, Jacques Fath would set out for Cannes, to rest at the mill Joko, which he had bought in 1952. He would return fit and suntanned, a fact which he would underline by wearing white suits and bright-coloured scarves. This way, one forgot his disguised pallor. He managed to lead an unremitting, intense existence, to which he had become accustomed, he never broke with a tempo that was now slowly killing him. Jacques Fath wanted to remain on stage until the end, even although he knew that he was incurably ill.

Like playwrights, like writers, like many artists, Jacques Fath considered himself the best, although that did not prevent him from checking up and keeping an eye on the creative work of his contemporaries. In his opinion, Balenciaga emphasised too strongly the strict and the severe. He admired Christian Dior, but his irony sometimes made him tease Christian about his '*bourgeois serieux*' manner; he used to say he was like 'a little notary from the provinces'.

Stricken with leukaemia, Jacques Fath died in November 1954. He had created a style which was utterly individual. It was on the basis of this world fame, that his wife Geneviève was to continue running the house, keeping close to her all those who had the taste and the Fath spirit.

A PARIS MODEL

8

The World of the Mannequins

Penelope Portrait

Penelope modelling a 'fifties Lanvin design, which epitomises the 'jeune fille' look for which that house was famous.

Soft and easy, that's how my life and times were, as a Paris high fashion model in the early 'fifties. Or is it just that one always looks back through rose-coloured glasses? Certainly, in retrospect, nothing about those years seems anything but fun. Not the endless, boring pre-collection sessions, sitting around waiting for fittings. Nor the exhausting hours of standing for the fittings themselves, while the clothes were pinned on to, or more often, in to one. Nor even the fact that I was almost constantly broke and never ate anything but croissants and café-au-lait unless I was invited out. What, after all, were the occasional pangs of hunger compared to the glamour of modelling, the Haut-ness of Couture and the triumph of wearing the most beautiful clothes in the world and actually getting paid for it?

I'd stepped boldly into it with neither experience nor training, but so, I was to learn, had all the other girls. In spite of all the model-school claims, I've yet to meet a Paris fashion model who's actually been trained to do her stuff. Either you can wear clothes or you can't and that's about it.

Each house has, at the outset, a preferred physical type and its own style of showing but I've seen small, curvy brunettes engaged on the spot, by houses reputed to like only tall, skinny blondes, and Pierre Cardin once took a little sewing girl out of his own workrooms because he was short of a mannequin on Press day. She not only looked nothing like the sort of girl he normally used but as far as walking, turning or getting on and off the cat-walk was concerned, she hardly knew her left foot from her right. That didn't stop her doing several Cardin collections, then going on to other glories in other houses.

As for showing-style, unless you're doing something the house actively dislikes, you make up your own, vaguely following the pattern set by the other girls. Here, you smile, twist, twirl and whizz through each presentation as if you were competing for the one-minute mile. There, you assume a disdainful look, drift langorously along gazing lovingly at yourself in every mirror, and snub the admiring customers with all the scorn you can summon up. Some girls can actually muster a sort of elegant sneer, but, though it was one of my burning ambitions, I never quite managed that.

Since no one ever *told* me how to do anything, I invented my tricks as I went along. For an outfit which included gloves, and they nearly all did then, I found it useful to be wearing one as I appeared, pulling on the other as I walked. It's a graceful gesture and helped me out of the dread 'What shall I do with my hands' feeling I had at the beginning of my modelling career. If it was a 'dash-and-smile' house, where one was twirling about every few seconds, I used to put the back of my left wrist behind me as I turned, letting it swing up naturally in front as I came into the straight again, it somehow made the turns look more natural. In a haughty 'How-dare-you' house, where it was customary to stare coldly at the people in the front row, I'd pick out some woman I didn't like the look of, stand thoughtfully in front of her for several seconds, adjusting whatever I'd got at my neckline, then, just before sweeping off, switch my gaze to her feet. She would then, invariably and infallibly, look down and change their position! I used to have bets with myself about this, win them all and have a lovely little giggle when I got back to the *cabine* to change my clothes.

Armed then with nothing more than youth, red hair and confidence I'd presented myself at Carven. I tried there, because they had a reputation for liking frilly, jeune-fille sort of girls, with small waists. I was the former and had the latter, though, until very recently, my waist was to be of little or no fashion use to me again. It went modestly unseen beneath the 'trapeze', the 'sac', the tunic and trousers, and the smock.

Some years later I was watching a show at Dior, this time in the capacity of fashion correspondent for a national daily newspaper, and I said to the young man sitting next to me 'Isn't it lovely waists are back in again?' He looked totally blank and replied 'Waists? I've never thought about waists really. I'm very attracted to nice hip bones though'. Still, he *was* young.

Meanwhile, back at Carven, I was trying for and getting, my first haute couture job. I was the only English girl there. The others were French except for one tall, ravishing, Swede, who spoke nothing but Swedish, poor soul, and was for ever getting up when she should have been sitting down, putting on this when she should have been taking off that, and generally having a very muddled time of it. Everyone was pleasant and helpful to me, except 'C', the star model. She was, at the time, not only the *mannequin vedette* at Carven, but one of the top girls in Paris, sharing her honours only with Bettina and Sophie from Jacques Fath. At Carven she did exactly as she pleased and was catered and curtsied to, by everyone, including me. She looked like a queen, spoke like a fish-wife and frightened me to death. She really was quite the most difficult girl I've ever encountered. Perhaps I'd have been the same with her face. In those days of frizz and chignons, her short, black, centre-parted hair, hung like a straight silky curtain, the ends falling inwards towards her mouth with its naturally curved bow and curly corners. She had large, brown-pansy eyes, brush-stroke brows and a creamy, perfect skin.

'C' always had the prettiest clothes made on her, as a matter of course. What's more, if on Press day she fancied one of *your* dresses, she just took it off the rack without so much as a by-your-leave. I had a memorable fight with her, over a primrose printed, organdie, garden-party dress, which was to be worn with a wide brimmed, floppy, primrose-trimmed hat. It was my first Press showing, and I was far too excited and nervous to realise the extent of the *lèse-majesté* involved. Furthermore I was actually being buttoned into the dress when 'C' took a shine to it, so she'd have had to literally rip it off me to get it, which she immediately prepared to do. The atmosphere, though, had quite gone to my head, and I struggled, vanquished, jammed on my hat, its primroses quivering, and appeared on the platform with a large tear in the back of my skirt (the invention of floating panels?) but victory sweetening my smile. Strangely

Changing in the dressing room.

enough, there was no sequel to this incident. 'C' wanted what she wanted, when she wanted it, but had a short memory and was not in the least vengeful.

Traditionally, a haute couture collection closes with the appearance of the wedding dress. For my first few seasons at Carven, I was the 'bride'. We did it in a big way in those days. Sometimes with a bridegroom, always with the other girls following behind as bridesmaids. All except 'C' that is. Beautiful she was, but bride-like she most certainly was not. *Femme-fatale* was her style, so, since she couldn't lead the finale, she never appeared in it at all. White velvet and ermine in winter, voile or lace in summer, I drifted along looking as saintly as possible, hands piously folded, eyes downcast, vaguely trying to work out whether it would be better to have yet another sub on my ever diminishing pay packet or pawn my gold bracelet with the heart on it, once again.

The *première* is a very important person in a fashion house. She runs her workroom and sewing girls and supervises the making up of garments assigned to her. There are the specialists in *flou*, that is anything soft, un-structured and limp, whether it's dresses or suits, and specialists in tailored clothes. These are often men. A certain rivalry exists between the work-rooms and the *premières* like to have some say in which girl actually wears her clothes, feeling, rightly perhaps, that to some extent the success and sale of the dress depends on the model. The models all feel that the entire success or failure of the dress depends on them, but that's another tale. At Carven, the clothes were made up from sketches, so we got our first glimpse of them in recognisable, if rudimentary, state.

We'd all be sitting around in our undies and pink smocks (everyone wore wired bras and girdles, no matter how non-existent their bosoms or hips) while Mademoiselle Carven (all women couturiers are called

Mademoiselle, by tradition; Chanel was known as La Grande Mademoiselle), the *premières*, assistants, tailors, and sometimes the chief saleswomen, reviewed these pinned and tacked garments, discussing in very candid terms who should wear what, and why.

'That's a marvellous colour for Geneviève, try it on her, but the back'll have to come up higher – she's got those awful shoulder blades.' 'I'd thought of Penny for this, because of the low neck and the smocking at the bust.' This from Madame Valérie who was my special chum, but . . . 'Vous êtes folle! Think of her bottom! Give that to Nicolette and give Penny the mauve with the flared skirt, that'll hide it.' *This* from Carven, who was no-one's special chum at collection time, though a great charmer otherwise.

There was no room for complexes at fitting sessions. We were treated and talked about like objects. Heaven knows what the Women's Lib. ladies would have thought of it, but they didn't exist then and I loved every minute of it. I learned all sorts of odd things that were really nothing to do with fashion at all, but which have stayed with me, and, I think, served me well since. One day, for instance, after hours of standing and being stuck with pins, I flopped down into a chair beside the man who designed the extravagant, beaded embroidery used on the evening dresses. He was a charming old man, sympathetic and invariably good tempered. 'Oh Lord, my feet are absolutely killing me', I moaned, rubbing them. 'My dear', he replied, 'never, ever say "My feet hurt", it's squalid. If you're tired and want to stop, say "My *foot* hurts". It gets the same results and makes a man think of a delicate, flower-like little foot, too fragile to take another step'.

182

Of course, sometimes one delicate flower-like little foot, hurts as much as the other delicate flower-like little foot, but, as in love affairs, the phrasing is at least as important as the feeling. In love affairs in fact, the phrasing can be more important, for it may crystallise an emotion, till then too nebulous to be conveyed.

The subject of this discourse, however, is fashion, so let's not stray. House models were, and probably still are, very badly paid. I hadn't yet begun to do pictures for magazines or outside fashion shows and was constantly in debt, so I decided, simply enough one might think, to ask for a rise. I made out a neat little list divided in two columns. One column was essential outgoings, like rent, Mètro tickets, and croissants, one of incomings, namely, my very modest salary. My earnings were between 30 and 35 thousand old francs a month; my modest hotel rooms about 300 or 350 old francs a day, not including breakfast, service, or baths! Foreign girls were still rare in those days, and the fact that the French girls lived at home while we had hotel bills to pay, was not taken into consideration. No matter how I figured it, I couldn't make those two columns balance out.

I asked the girls if they thought I should see Carven about it. They said it was useless seeing any one at all, as I certainly wouldn't get a rise, but in no case Mademoiselle herself, as she had nothing to do with vulgar stuff like money. Perhaps Madame L who actually dished it out at the end of each month? Off I went then and explained it all to Madame L. 'So you see, madame', I finished earnestly, 'I just can't manage on this money'. 'Mais ma chère, Penelope', replied Madame L kindly, 'no one expects you to. Surely a pretty girl like you has some one to help her?' Déscartes would certainly have approved this neat Gallic solution to an international problem, but unfortunately I couldn't put it into operation. Not that it was purity, indignation or moral fibre that stopped me. I just hadn't had any offers. My gentlemen friends all seemed to be young and broke like me and when the rich and willing (and incidentally, extremely attractive) chap did turn up, I was already doing magazine pictures so didn't really need him. . . .

We did a lot of travelling at Carven. Deauville, Cannes, Switzerland, Belgium for week-ends, and further afield for longer periods. Africa, Sweden, or South America. We'd leave Paris in impressive style, eight or ten models, dozens of trunks and hat-boxes, dressers, people from the public relations department, people from the perfumes department, and often Carven herself. We were photographed, fêted, laden with flowers and generally given the good old Hollywood star treatment wherever we went. Always travelling first class, always staying in the most luxurious hotel in town. You had to keep a level head not to get confused by the difference between these trips and normal Paris life, which was, with the exception of a few perks like free hairdressing (by Alexandre, who was then an assistant to Antoine), just like any other working girl's life.

It was on one of these expeditions to South America that a rather curious thing happened. We'd arrived in Bogota on the morning of the day we were due to show. This was unusual but we'd had engine trouble and been grounded for two days in the Azores, while waiting for spare parts to be flown in. Colombia has a rich, social, sort of 'café-society' set, so we'd brought mostly evening and 'cocktail' dresses. Satins, taffetas, laces, embroidery, all the most elaborate clothes in the collection. Sometimes in the original colours, sometimes in colours chosen specially for Colombia. I remember one of my dresses, called 'Clair Obscur'. It had a strapless bodice entirely covered in tiny black and white bugle beads, and a wide,

Penelope Portrait travelling with a collection.

black velvet midriff made to fit an eighteen-inch waist. The long skirt was velvet too, skin tight to hip level, then flaring into a corolla with a little, oval train.

This dress was really the couture version of The Iron Maiden. The boned, midriff section not only prevented me from breathing but dug so hard into me, above and below the waist, that it actually made dents. Nevertheless, I adored it, would cheerfully have worn it night and day for a week if necessary, and couldn't wait to show it. Alas, I was never to show anything at all in Bogota, for as soon as we got off the plane I began to swell. And swell and swell and swell. I thought I'd burst and be spattered in a million pieces all over the walls of the elegant Tequendama Hotel. My fingers, wrists and ankles had become puffy sausages and my face had turned into a smooth pink mask with neither hollows nor protuberances. The altitude, it seems, sometimes does this to people. I was the only one afflicted, though, which led to some ribald comments, totally unfounded, from my colleagues, on what little English girls were made of.

I stayed in my room consoling myself with tequila, while the balloon I'd become, gradually deflated, and someone else wore 'Clair Obscur'. It wasn't till we got to Cali, the next stop on our itinerary, that I was able to squeeze into my clothes and honour the Colombians with my presence.

After a few seasons of this amusing existence, I decided to try my luck in America. I made a lot of money, but missed Paris so much, I soon came back. I waited till a few weeks before the new collections were due, when all the houses are on the look-out for models and started off on my rounds.

I tried Pierre Cardin first. He was not by any means the international name he was to become, but he was well on the way up and it was a very chic house to have in one's résumé. He is a spare, remote, sort of man, difficult to approach, but, after being passed from vendeuse to press girl to assistant I did manage to see him.

He gave me a very cool once-over while I tried things on, then said that he quite liked my face and general style, but my figure wasn't right for his collection. He said it in French and because my French was by no means what it is now, I just stood there politely waiting to know if I was in or out. Seeing my blank look, he kindly translated into English: 'Very nice, but too beeg 'eeps'. There was no reply to that. I had and have a neat 34-inch bosom, a 22-inch waist, but 35-inch hips, and in the modelling world, those are *hips*. When bottoms were being handed out, I received one and not all the bouncing along the floor on it, banging it against the wall and cramming it into rigid girdles had been able to reduce one inch of it.

I didn't try Patou because I knew they liked girls with no bosom and had heard dark tales of special bosom flatteners that even the girls they did engage had to wear! I'd yearned for years to wear one of those draped, silk jersey, Grecian-style dresses for which Grès was famous, so that was where I went next.

Madame Grès is an unusual woman, tranquil and reserved. The atmosphere that reigned in her house was unusual too, with none of the gay hustle and bustle of Carven. Grès is small, neat, delicate looking and never seen without a turban which hides every strand of the hair I presume to be beneath. But *never*. Twenty years after I'd left her, under rather delicate conditions about which more later, I saw her at Smiths English Tea Shop on the Rue de Rivoli. Her face and figure hadn't changed a scrap and her turban was still bound and tucked about her head in the same nun-like way. She was eating poached eggs on toast with lemon tea.

On the day that I applied for a job, she and her assistant watched as I tried clothes on. 'She's not very tall', said the assistant doubtfully. 'That's true, she isn't', Madame Grès replied, '*mais elle a du charme et une jolie ligne de postérieure*'. Oh the balm of soothed pride. Cardin's 'beeg 'eeps' were Grè's pretty posterior, so one need never despair. The following week my charm, my posterior and I went to work at Grès.

Madame Grès had a bizarre, withdrawn, aura about her. She spoke in a

gentle, elegant voice, behind which, one soon discovered, was a steely, elegant mind. Velvety power emanated from her and an air of mystery. This impressed everyone at Grès, including the models who were always very quiet and submissive in her presence. I was, in fact, not at all the type for the house, either mentally or physically, which only goes to prove what I wrote earlier. Except for one delicate, little Chinese girl who had a contemporary look about her, the models were very much in the traditional couture style. Tall, thin, their hair dressed in chignons, they were not so much girls, as efficient props for the clothes they showed. This used to be the ideal model in many haute couture houses.

Fitting sessions here were referred to as *la pose*. We were summoned one or two at a time to the 'studio' where Mademoiselle draped us in various lengths of fabric, to see which would suit each girl best. The procedure was quite different from anything I'd known, for Grès folded, pinned, and held the cloth against one, almost making the dress then and

A portrait study of Penelope 1971.

186

there. She had, or affected to have, a great scorn for worldly things and would keep girls standing for hours while she meditated. If a model had the temerity to suggest that she was tired or hungry or that it was late, she was released at once and icily informed by Mademoiselle that love of art and creation appeared to have gone and that models before the war were much more interested and involved in their work!

In 1934 Grès had been called Madame Alix and known for her apparent timidity, sudden tantrums and the mystery which surrounded her private life. Very little was known. She had an Italian grandmother, a German grandfather and was married to a Russian painter called Serge Czerefkov, who signed his paintings *Grès*. She has a daughter. One journalist who, after inordinate effort, had finally succeeded in obtaining an interview, was told by Grès, that after only three months fashion-cutting study, she had felt herself ready to launch out alone. 'It's the fabric that matters', she said, 'I sense it, feel it, am inspired by that and what I see about me.' Needless to say, Grès found mini skirts in bad taste, especially in the Mètro where she was more or less forced to look at them! Not surprising, for her creations closely reflect her secretive personality. The name of the Grès perfume is *Cabochard*, which should surprise no one who knows her. It is the French word for stubborn. *Very* stubborn.

I loved the clothes at the house. They were not *jeune-fille* in the least, but womanly and romantic. Miraculously draped dresses, intricately cut capes, wraps and coats. Grès has a tremendous feeling for the dramatic. What appeared to be a simple greyish chiffon dress on the hanger, turned, when actually worn, into a moving, grey, pink and white cloud, the yards of diaphanous fabric in the bat-wing sleeves and layered skirts, swaying and floating with every step.

It was at Grès that I saw and spoke to the fabulous Cécile Sorel. Sorel died in 1966 at an age somewhere between 89 and 93, according to which report you read. She'd started her stage career in variety and then become a classical actress. Perhaps it would be more accurate to say that she played the great classical roles at the Comédie Française and l'Odéon. The reviews of her performances were always very mixed, to say the least, one noted critic of the time remarking that 'It is impossible to be less natural with more ardour'. It was not for her acting ability though, that she became a legend in France, but for two quite different things. One was her varied, active and imaginative love life. She married the Comte de Segur when she was well over fifty. The other was a short phrase.

She was the leading lady at the Casino de Paris and had to descend the steep, centre-stage stairway that has defeated many an entertainer before and since. It's a difficult, even dangerous, feat but Sorel sailed down, ablaze with confidence and charm. Her heavy plumed head-dress and high-heeled sandals might have belonged to someone else, for all the attention she paid them. When she reached the bottom, she walked to the footlights and, her smile full of triumph and mischief, called out '*L'ai je bien descendu?*', which translates, in spirit if not in words, into 'Now didn't I do that splendidly?' The entranced audience burst into rapturous applause and the words have been cited a million times since.

In the 'fifties, feeling perhaps that it was time for something new, Sorel joined a lay-order called the '*Tiers Ordre de St. François d'Assise*'. The habit for this order was made of rough white sackcloth with a corded rope at the waist and a *scapulaire*, a sort of religious image, worn as a pendant. Sorel's outfit was not quite the same as that worn by the other women of the order. It had a flattering cowl neck, a face-framing head-dress, and was sometimes completed by a blue satin cape. It was rumoured that the costume had been re-designed for her by Dior but she always denied this. It was a little different, she admitted, but that was from a desire for frugality. She was simply wearing the costume she'd worn when playing Queen Christina at the Edouard Sept Theatre in 1934, which greatly resembled the habit of the order. She was often photographed in it, usually in her garden with her two large dogs and a hundred white doves. She almost got drummed out of the order for this, as the cord at the waist and the *scapulaire* are considered sacred and not to be photographed. She, not surprisingly, got herself out of this little spot of bother somehow and went on to be received by the Pope. Her semi-religious activities didn't put a complete stop to her theatrical career and she adorned her sumptuous hotel rooms with a crucifix and always had a small altar in one corner.

It was in this much discussed habit that she appeared one morning at Grès. We'd been summoned to put on a show for her and she sat with her companion in a corner of the show room. We paraded in front of her, turning and twirling in the usual way. She said nothing. When we got to the evening clothes her attention sharpened and her eyes shone. Sometimes we showed in twos, and in one of these duets, another girl and I came out wearing the same silk georgette dress. Mine was navy with tiny white polka dots, my colleague's, brown with cream dots. These dresses had a vaguely 1900 air about them. Floor length, low necked, backless, with long, boned torsos, the folds that draped across the skirt in the front, turned into a sort of bustle at the back. There were large, lovely sprays of silk flowers down one, shoe-string shoulder strap.

My friend swept off and I was following when Sorel made a gesture towards me. It was a very explicit gesture. It said 'Stay, I want to look at you'. She did, lengthily and unblinkingly. I stood fascinated in front of her. Sorel . . . all the things one had read, heard, half believed. Difficult to say which of us was more transfixed by the other. Her voice came rumbling up from her pointed little boots: 'Ah', she cried 'c'est ravissant. If only one were forty again!' Cécile Sorel! An ex-Belle if ever there was one. A woman who'd had La Du Barry's bed, a title, jewels, furs, countless admirers and professional success, yet, when faced with the sort of dress she'd never wear again, it was neither twenty nor thirty she longed to be, but forty. A time when, presumably, she'd considered herself at the summit of her beauty and power.

It's quite the most encouraging statement I've ever heard and explains the difference between French women and all others. Not that beautiful eighteen-year-olds don't get their share of adulation in Paris as elsewhere, simply that they are not the only ones. This, I believe is largely due to French men. They are at least as interested in charm, warmth, intelligence and wit, as youth. At many a French dinner party, ladies are to be found, holding court for an admiring male group, at an age when English women have long since given up men and taken to gardening and good works . . .

Modelling in Paris was becoming more professional. Agencies were started, though for years they were illegal and the people who ran them were accused of living off the earnings of women, which indeed they were, but not in the way the law interpreted it. Dorian Leigh, an ex-model of outstanding success, and sister of Suzy Parker, one of the most beautiful girls ever to model in Paris, had a great deal of trouble with the police about her agency. It did get sorted out in the end. I think it was the composites that upset the French, those leaflets every model girl must have,

A typical fashion shot on location in Paris, in the 'fifties.

and in which are her measurements and pictures in various get-ups, plus the phone number of the agency. French men are not nearly as one-track-minded as the rest of the world seems to think them, but nevertheless women do take up a lot of thought and time in their lives and the fact that, with one of these leaflets, you could actually ring up and find out how much an hour a girl cost, upset them a great deal. It was years before photographic modelling, from an agency was considered a respectable activity.

There was money to be made in the newly born ready-to-wear market. They put on shows in department stores, went on tour in the provinces and generally opened up new vistas. The atmosphere at Grès was beginning to depress me, and I was looking for fresh fields. I did do ready-to-wear shows in the mornings, but couldn't leave town because I had to be at the house every afternoon, even if there were only five or six women to see the collection. I was working for the McCall's pattern people at the Porte de Versailles exhibition hall when, quite out of the blue, they told me that when the Paris stint was over, they were taking the group to Barcelona for a month. Would I like to go? Would I! Would I like a cottage in Ireland? Would I like some eighteenth-century emerald earrings? Would I like 33-inch matador hips? But what about Grès?

My conscience had a brief and unsuccessful skirmish with my baser instincts, I made up some absurd story and took off for Spain, where I had a marvellous time and didn't regret my disgraceful behaviour for a minute. Naturally, when I came home there was a very nasty, official looking summons to see Madame Grès. I had a thoroughly unpleasant and deserved interview with her, what the French call a '*mauvais quart d'heure*', and very *mauvais* it was too. It all calmed down though, and from then on, I left the prestige of couture for the fun and money of ready-to-wear. In those days, it impressed the ready-to-wear people if you had worked in haute couture, and the money, was, of course, very attractive. Everything was staged in a luxurious way – a model could earn anywhere between 5 and 10 thousand old francs for each show. Still, today, house models earn far less than the girls in ready-to-wear – the average salary is only about 1000 new francs a month.

Then, of course, there was photographic modelling, and for once all those characteristics which had made it so difficult for me in haute couture – my size, my curves, my curly hair, suddenly became an asset. To look 'different' was an asset, and as there were still so few of us foreigners living and working in Paris, we had the best of it. Besides, I liked the relaxed atmosphere, everyone calling each other 'tu', and no black-clad, pearl-entwined sales-ladies rushing in to tell me my bra straps were showing with the mustard dress or my stocking seams were crooked, and no awe.

The 'seventies girls earn a great deal more than we did, but they have much shorter working lives. Fifteen-year-olds nudge their elders very smartly off their thrones and a wise girl has her, sometimes huge, earnings, stashed discreetly away in boutiques or laundrettes before she's twenty, knowing that is about as long as she can hope to remain in the big time. I don't suppose the present bunch get taken to Maxims quite as often either, but then, they wouldn't want to go, would they?

As I write, Paris haute couture is in a state of total confusion. Firm statements made by the great houses on Tuesday, are qualified by complicated explanations on Thursday, and withdrawn by Friday. French ready-to-wear gets better and better. Its designers are young, full of talent and in touch with what is always referred to in the fashion Press as 'the street'. This simply means that, unlike their haute couture colleagues, the ready-to-wear creators go where their prospective customers go. To the same discos, sidewalk cafés, restaurants and avant-garde theatres. Each inspires the other and together they produce on the one hand, and wear, on the

One of the other tasks of the Parisienne model!

other, those chameleon outfits that make each woman an individual.

You need imagination and flair to bring it off and you have to be nippy about doing it too, otherwise, by the time you've got it all together just right, something new has come in and your perfect outfit looks as quaint as the crinoline. Quainter perhaps, for it may be the crinoline that's somehow beginning to look right again! So, if 'king couture' is dead (and nothing is less certain), long live the King. Don't believe the people who tell you we're heading towards a unisex, jump suit type uniform. Nor those who say nudity in climate-controlled streets is the ultimate end. As long as there are women, and men to look at them, there will be new fashions.

Since new fashions are by their very nature ephemeral, I'd like to make a bet that, a hundred years from now, some woman will be gazing dolefully at a cupboard full of clothes and saying, 'I haven't a thing to wear!'

9 SPACE AGE FASHION

Courrèges & Ungaro   Cardin

Ann Ryan   Serena Sinclair

It was a brilliantly sunny July day and the Parisians were out in force, enjoying the weather, shopping, strolling, gossiping in the sidewalk cafés. Little did they know, or care, that two floors up in a large house on the rue François Premier, yet another comedy in the Theatre of Fashion was playing to a capacity house. Courrèges was showing his collection.

In a stark, all-white room, as clinical and unadorned as an operating theatre, a dozen or so tall, athletic mannequins with healthy freckles painted on their tanned faces were bounding energetically on and off a white stage, in time to background beat music. They sweated – yet they smiled and smiled, as though their hectic gyrations were the greatest pleasure, performed in air-conditioned luxury. I very nearly fainted. We, the audience, were perched uncomfortably in rows before them, jammed thigh to thigh, our bottoms resting on square cubes of white vinyl. It was a Press show, and the international fashion writers were there in force, their pens racing across their notebooks although their eyes never left the stage. For if you look away for a moment during a Courrèges showing, the

Courrèges with some of his space-age models in his rue François Premier showroom.

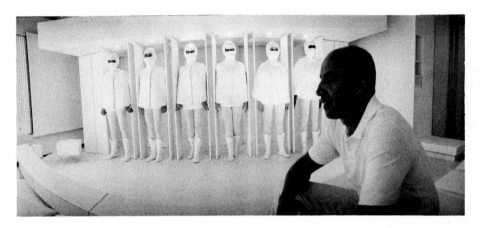

chances are you will miss the *bonne bouche* of the collection – a totally top-less girl, maybe, or a model with a bare behind. So swiftly do those laughing, bouncing mannequins whizz in and out of the openings on to the stage that you dare not even blink for fear they will be gone before you have taken in every detail of every piece of clothing they are wearing.

The stools of penance on which the audience were forced to sit that day were just one of this designer's quirkish attempts at a total and uncondi-tional departure from the old world of haute couture. In nearly every other salon in Paris, one was at least given a little gilt chair to sit on. Hard and uncomfortable though they were, they did have a back against which one could lean one's shoulders, often aching from days of clothes-watching, but this might have led to lounging, which Courrèges abhorred and found unaesthetic. Neither did he believe in air-conditioning and, as the ceiling of his small showroom was low, the oxygen, when several hundred journalists were wedged into it, was soon used up. It occurred to me, as I wiped the chilly sweat from my face and willed myself not to pass out, that if I had lost consciousness, no first-aid could have been administered, owing to the sheer crush of bodies around me.

From the beginning of his career as a couturier, Courrèges has despised the trappings of traditional haute couture and worked untiringly at creating his own ultra-modern atmosphere and image. In the clothes he designs, in the décor of his premises, in the showing of his collections – a cross between a leg-show and a striptease – there is a flat rejection of the chandeliered salons of the old-established maisons de couture and all they stand for. The adjective coined early on to describe the clothes and the mood he created was, naturally, 'space-age'. He has never looked back to any period in history for his inspiration. He designs for now, and for the future. Through the cut, the fabric and the detail, a Courrèges garment can be identified easily in any corner of the world. It has borrowed nothing from the 'twenties, the 'thirties, the 'forties, nor from 'Bonnie and Clyde', 'Death in Venice' or any other fashion-setting film. It is more likely to jerk your imagination into outer space, towards the moon-walkers' uniforms.

André Courrèges.

When he opened his own house and showed his first collection in 1961, the rest of the Paris couture was living in a world of smug security. Rich clients were bowed up the sweeping staircase of great houses like Dior, Lanvin, and Balmain, and settled in comfort on plushy seats in the magnificent showrooms, where silent, unsmiling mannequins showed the clothes, hand on hip, pelvis thrust forward in the traditional toe-first mannequins' gait. Madame's every whim was cared for attentively by a sombrely-dressed, elaborately-coiffed vendeuse and her assistants.

Courrèges, at the age of thirty-six, set about creating the reverse of that scene when, in 1961, he opened his doors to his first clients in a small flat reached by a tiny lift in an apartment house on the avenue Kléber, far from the other couturiers. His first showroom, a narrow room into which only about fifty buyers or journalists could be crammed, was more cottagey than space-age. Yet it could have been on the moon, so far was it removed from the gilt and plush of rival houses.

The walls, carpets and curtains were white; so were the cushions on the small, rustic chairs. When asked by an English journalist why, in his salon, he had only plain old oak furniture and not modern things, he replied: 'There is no poetry in modern furniture. Only Scandinavian furniture is modern and it is so cold. And I haven't the money to design my own. I could find an aeroplane to match my clothes, but not furniture. I want nature in everything. We must translate things to our new way of life. But like my clothes they must keep femininity, sexiness and poetry. Nature isn't just functional, it is gay. Grass, for instance, grass is so gay, is it not? When people buy my clothes, they buy a way of life, a philosophy.' His interviewer, Quentin Crewe, ventured to say that £230 for a coat was not cheap. Particularly as if one bought a coat, only a Courrèges dress would go with it. 'Yes', said the designer apologetically, 'it would be more up to date to have a low price. I will try and find a way.'

That dream, to bring his designs within reach of many modern young women and not only of the pampered, chauffeured rich couture clients, kept nagging at the back of his mind during those early years in the avenue Kléber.

André Courrèges was born on 9 March 1923, at Pau in the Basque district of France. Before the war his father became major-domo in the household there of a M. Olivier and his English-born wife. 'It was there', Courrèges said, 'that as a young man I first observed and became fascinated by elegance and fashion. There were many English house parties – and there is nothing so elegant as the perfectly groomed English gentleman and his wife.'

The young André's parents persuaded him to study civil engineering. This he did for a while, but realised that he could never become an engineer. 'I believe', he once remarked, 'that I wanted especially to be an architect. But I preferred to be able to create and finish things myself without interference. Luxury in clothes to me has no meaning. It belongs to the past. My problem is to resolve functional problems harmoniously – just like the engineer who designs a plane.

'If the clothes are well designed one cannot put the waist round the knees or under the chin. One has to follow the line of the body. The woman who interests me doesn't belong to any physical type. She lives a certain life, however. She is active, moves fast, works, is usually young and modern enough to wear modern intelligent clothes.'

All his life, André Courrèges has kept a close contact with Pau, his birthplace in the Pyrenees, forty kilometres from the Spanish border. 'I am French, but I feel Spanish too', he says today. 'My parents are the same. They are both eighty-seven now and still living there. My sister lives there too. She is married, with three sons. My mother didn't actually influence my early ideas about fashion. She taught me to dream. She loved nature and she taught me to try to understand nature.' Preoccupation with nature has always been a vital factor in Courrège's approach to life and to design. 'This need to create', he expounds, 'the word is too strong, because it is only God and nature who create.... Concerning creativity ... this outburst of enthusiasm and of love which is in us, this need to become saturated in everything one touches, the extraordinary happenings which are life, joy, dreams of beauty ... it is born every morning with each dawning day ... with the sun and the rain ... with the clouds in the sky and the stars in the night.' To make a collection, he continues, 'it is all that ... it is to let our imagination wander according to the whim of our desire, of our love of life ... of this being that is part of us'.

This poetic side of Courrèges is hard to equate with the stark modernity of the physical environment in which he works and the tough *chic* of the clothes that have become his signature. Yet it is as strong as ever today, and he told me recently, when he was elaborating on future plans to add

yet more dimensions to his designing activities, that he is also '. . . going
to plant flowers. Perhaps in Morocco. To say *bonjour* to nature, to the sun
and to the rain. To get away from grey skies, to work and design there.'

When he realised that neither engineering nor architecture were for
him, Courrèges turned seriously to the study of textiles and fashion design
at a college in Pau and later in Paris. In 1950, his studies completed, he set
about looking for a job in a couture house. 'I made a tour of all the
houses', he said, 'but I had already chosen Balenciaga because he corres-
ponded most to my style. He didn't need anyone and I had to wait six
months to be admitted. But I forced the door open by my determination
and my tenacity.'

Cristobal Balenciaga, one of the few great couturiers of this century,
was a legendary figure. Basque-Spanish, he was born in the same corner of
the world as Courrèges. Brooding, withdrawn, he presided like a mystical
deity over his imposing couture house in the avenue George Cinq and was
revered by customers and staff alike. The impression he made on the young
Courrèges was profound. He engaged him as a cutter and, in the ten years
Courrèges remained with him, Balenciaga taught him everything, not
only about couture but about life. Those ten years of hard work, amount-
ing almost to slavery, were, I believe, the clue to his success in later years.
He learnt, under the tuition of the master, to sew, to fit and to draw. This
apprenticeship put him in a class above the designers who work only from
sketches and cannot take up a pair of scissors and experiment themselves
with a new cut, or who have not had the personal experience of stitching
a collar to a jacket so that it rolls perfectly away from the neck. Of his
years with Balenciaga, Courrèges says: 'They were hard, but that didn't
worry me. Difficulties interest me. Balenciaga was very exacting, very
hard to please. Everything had to be done for him very quickly and very
well. I am the same now, to the detriment of my collaborators. I demand
the best.'

When the child-pupil finally decided that the time had come for him to
leave the parent-master and to strike out alone, the break was painful. 'He
didn't want me to go. It took three years to leave him. I said that when I
left I would put somebody in my place. I felt very grateful and responsible
to Balenciaga. I knew a young man called Ungaro who made the same
sort of clothes as I did and I put him in my place. After ten years I still
admired Balenciaga's work very much. But at thirty-five I had done
hardly anything by myself, taken no risks. I wanted to prove myself.
Certainly my first few seasons on my own were influenced by Balenciaga.
But in 1963 [two years after his first solo collection] his influence was
already waning. 1964 and 1965 were my strong statements.'

After the influence of Balenciaga, another strong personality came into
Courrèges' life, that of Coqueline Barrière, who is now his wife and
mother of their two-year-old child, Marie-Clafoutie-Ustoa (the last name
meaning 'little leaf' in Basque), on whom he dotes and whom he calls
Fou Fou.

Some of his tailored classic models
which reveal his debt to Balenciaga; from his first independent
collections.

A coat from the 1961 collection.

A suit from the spring 1963 collection.

Coqueline also spent three years under the tutelage of the master, Balenciaga, and from 1955 onwards she and Courrèges were inseparable. They married in 1967, 'just an official act', he says, for their lives had been spent together for many years before that. Little is known, written, or spoken, of Coqueline. She rarely appears in public, shuns interviews and prefers the world to think that Courrèges alone is boss, designer and creator of the business which bears his name. But that is not the truth. From the outset she has been as much the boss as he. A close associate told me recently: 'She's a terrific influence. She designs most of the clothes, chooses the model girls, stages the shows.'

Courrèges agrees it is his wife who is responsible for the elaborate shows they have been putting on each season for several years, and he says she is his assistant in fifty per cent of his creativity. Together they designed, cut, sewed and presented their first collection of thirty models in 1961 in that little apartment in the Avenue Kléber.

Courrèges is primarily a tailor. Even his rivals admit he is the best tailor in the business, and the tweeds and soft woollens he showed in 1961 were beautifully worked and designed, in the manner of Balenciaga. The fashion writer of *The Times* wrote of that collection: 'This must be regarded as a house of promise.'

Overseas buyers found it more than promising. They sniffed commercial success as well, and visitors to that tiny apartment during the week following Courrèges' Monday morning opening were greeted by the unusual sight of some of the more important American buyers sitting patiently on the winding stairs, waiting to be admitted. There followed two years of gruelling work for Coqueline and Courrèges, building up their clientèle, taking on more staff, establishing the signature of their design talent and at the same time gradually breaking loose from the spell of Balenciaga.

Concurrently, the New Wave was beginning in Britain. Mary Quant, her business equally small and little known, was designing revolutionary clothes which went straight to the hearts of the deprived teenagers. Until then, the junior league in Britain had had to be content with watered-down versions of the sort of clothes their mothers wore, or some hideous teenage ranges which, a few years later, would have disgusted any self-respecting Kings Road teenager.

Mary Quant was leading a revolt and, like all revolutionaries, she was extreme in her views. The battle cry was – shorten your skirts. Now this, after the mid-calf skirts of the 'fifties, was indeed a revolution. But Britain's youth grabbed the new line joyfully and bared their knees.

Across the Channel, Courrèges alone was shortening his skirts, and to the uninitiated French and Americans this was sensational. It was acceptable perhaps to the poor benighted British teenagers, but from a Paris couturier? It was shocking, it was exciting and it was giving grown women a whole new slant on life. Courrèges slowly perfected his look, from which he has never entirely departed. Mostly in gaberdine, his clothes have

197

always had an architectural base, a definite shape. His skilled cutting gave his suits and coats a triangular flare which disguised any protuberances underneath. He loved white and pale pastel colours and banded practically everything with white. There were no 'little black' cocktail dresses in Courrèges' collections, and nothing bore any resemblance, in the traditional sense, to a ball dress.

What women loved most about his clothes was an exultant feeling of youth. One could run and jump and show off one's legs in them. They made one feel young and carefree. The strapping mannequins he hired epitomised the look with their bronzed, athletic legs, their stride which had in it more of the hockey field than the couture salon. The flat-heeled white boots and little flat shoes they wore offset their short A-line dresses. Week by week the Courrèges look was gaining more followers. The clothes were becoming more widely copied, which led to the short skirts and triangular shapes cropping up in High Streets from San Francisco to Hatch End. Most of them were perhaps horrible travesties of the originals, but the girls who bought and wore them were not concerned. They were buying a little bit of Courrèges and the look he was establishing made them feel marvellous.

Over the years, arguments have raged as to which designer, Courrèges or Mary Quant, actually invented the miniskirt, the symbol of youth in the 'sixties. Courrèges has been quoted as saying: 'I was the man who invented the mini. Mary Quant only commercialised the idea.' To which Mary replied: 'That's how the French are. . . . I don't mind, but it's just not as I remember it. Fashion, as I see it, is inevitable. It wasn't me or Courrèges who invented the miniskirt anyway – it was the girls in the street who did it. Designers simply anticipate what the public wants. I really don't believe in designers squabbling like a lot of kids. Maybe Courrèges did do miniskirts first, but if he did no-one wore them.'

By miniskirts, both were meaning, of course, the miniscule skirts which reached their dizziest heights towards the end of the 'sixties and have survived subsequently, in spite of the appearance of midis, maxis, on-the-knee demis and trousers. The rise of skirts in the first half of the decade was fairly gradual, joyfully adopted by the youngsters, and with their elders regaining their youth by raising their hems a few inches each summer.

The most unforgettable collection I have ever covered was the spring collection shown by Courrèges in 1964. To the fashion Press and buyers it was a revelation, a shuddering jolt into the present and the future. Held in that tiny white showroom in the avenue Kléber, to a background throb of erotic, tom-tom music which set one's senses tingling in anticipation, the show was truly an occasion. The tall, bronzed model girls came out one by one in their perfectly cut coats and dresses, their immaculate pants outfits. But it was the extreme sexiness of the clothes which had us almost holding our breath with excitement. One had never seen anything quite like it before.

Courrèges check coat, spring 1965.

A typical suit, from the controversial collection in autumn 1964.

A pinafore dress, spring 1965.

Courrèges looks on bras as ridiculous Victorian relics, but at that time to go bra-less was daring indeed. Not only was there not a bra in the whole show, but the clothes were designed so that bra-wearing was obsolete anyway. The natural curve of the breast was accentuated by the cut of the bodices. Midriffs were bared, bare backs were on display, trousers were cut to dip low in the waist at the back to reveal an erotic curve of firm young flesh which had never before been exposed. This collection was a fashion turning-point. Not only did it establish Courrèges as the most space-age couturier, but it marked his break away from old-style couture and the hovering presence of Balenciaga in his work.

Along with the miniskirt revolution, Courrèges was having an impact with the superbly tailored trousers he was showing for all hours of the day. At that time, trousers on women were accepted only in the country or for casual holiday wear. Courrèges started introducing them for all occasions, including gala evening functions. His trouser outfits were, of course, masterpieces of cutting and workmanship, the legs cigarette-slim, the porportions perfect.

Felicity Green wrote in the *Daily Mirror* of that spring '64 collection of the buyers' and journalists' 'admiration at the sight of his piqué two-piece

The bonneted, silver trouser ensemble which startled the fashion world with a new talent in autumn 1964.

A trouser suit, spring 1965.

for morning wear, his jersey two-piece for an afternoon's stroll round the park, his ribbed cotton two-piece for holiday wear and his glamorous lace two-piece for grand evenings.

'The surprising thing about all these stunning outfits is that where most two-pieces have a skirt, these have pants.

'They are mostly in white, they are worn with flat, white boots and, where appropriate, the ensemble is topped off with a huge flowered pot hat.'

When Felicity Green asked Courrèges whether he was serious about the pants-with-everything idea, he replied: 'Something has to happen to women's clothes. They are no longer designed for the life you lead. You run. Can you run in high heels? You drive. You need a special pair of flat shoes in your car. All women want to look young, and short skirts help you to do so, but skirts cannot get any shorter and still be decent.

'As for trousers, they are comfortable and practical for living today and, if they are beautifully cut, can flatter a woman's figure and be every bit as feminine as anything else she wears.'

His trouser outfits, like everything he has ever designed, bore the unmistakable stamp of their designer. *Women's Wear Daily* said of them: 'His message is strong – pants for women for all hours of the day. His clothes are perfection. They have the pride of a Spaniard. His Look . . . bold, heavy, almost square blocks . . . severe, almost architectural . . . which come at you in a clinically white salon . . . and the proportion is perfection.

'Courrèges clothes have a hardness, toughness, an anti-femininity that is against what's coming, but . . .

'Courrèges is the Le Corbusier of the Paris couture.'

The reference to Courrèges being 'against what was coming' was based on what the other couturiers were doing. Courrèges, after all, was a comparative newcomer, and the established houses such as Dior and Chanel were equally important arbiters of fashion. Saint Laurent, darling of the Press, was designing in a totally different way from Courrèges. He was discarding the tough, 'beatnik' clothes he had created in previous seasons, for a refined, feminine, soft and fluid look. Marc Bohan at Dior was also preoccupied by a softer style and crêpe was his favourite fabric that season for fluid clothes and for Oxford bags in white, topped by a navy blazer and red silk scarf; which were very reminiscent of Mrs Simpson in the 'thirties. Coco Chanel was giving her devoted clientèle some trouser outfits, but her trousers were the full slacks of the 'thirties, worn with a typical Chanel cardigan jacket and the two-toned high-heeled sling shoes which she showed with everything.

No one was thinking like Courrèges where trousers were concerned. Yet he was proved right subsequently and, although women accepted the pants-with-everything idea timidly at first, their teenage daughters grabbed the idea and wore pants on every conceivable occasion. Several years later, a twenty-one-year-old friend confessed to me that she did not possess a single skirt.

Having made his point, Courrèges softened his trouser look the following season, Autumn 1964, with more flattering tops, less bulky shoulders, much smaller hats and soft, swinging hair pieces added for evening. His clients went overboard for the collection launched at the beginning of August, and so overwhelming was the success that he had to close his order books for part of September and put clients' names down on a long waiting-list. Among the fortunate ones who ordered early were the Begum Aga Khan, Princess Lee Radziwill and the blonde American grand-daughters of Henry Ford. Those two seasons, and the one which followed in January 1965 piled triumph on triumph for Courrèges. The Press wrote ecstatically about him. His clientèle expended dramatically. The little apartment in the avenue Kléber was besieged.

Courrèges was forever being interviewed and asked his philosophy. His replies were consistently characteristic: 'The woman of 1964 still dresses as in 1925. A modern woman wants to work, travel, even run. She can't do these things properly in a skirt. We are experimenting with trousers to find a new way of dressing which fits the age. . . .'

Even the Duchess of Windsor succumbed and was ordering his clothes; not the pants outfits, but the perfectly-cut, fitted and flared coats and dresses with their high-shaped bodices, high-set sleeves and flawless proportions. Courrèges was as tough with her as he was with his lowlier clients. In 1965 he went on record in an interview with *Life* magazine as saying that what he asked for and what he had always got was cash on delivery. Not only from socialites and entertainers, but from the Duchess herself. Although he admitted that very special privileges and long-term credits were a way of life in certain high places, it was not so with the House of Courrèges.

He is quoted as saying: 'Our directrice told the Duchess's secretary that the coat would not be delivered unless the right hand that would take the coat would at the same time hand us the Duchess's cheque.' No cheque, no coat – to a 'best dresser' for whose patronage some lesser-known designers might have given their right hand! Such tough talking and tough tactics astonished the other couturiers. His rivals, at that time, were gazing on Courrèges with a mixture of envy, fury and respect. For he was the star, in spite of having only sixty employees, as opposed to the one thousand at Dior and the six hundred at Balmain.

The attitude of the house was a proud separatism towards the rest of Paris, and the atmosphere was totally different from that in any other house. Brisk, bizarre young women with short hair, blinking through white spectacles, little white boots at the end of their athletic legs and stark white triangles of dresses skimming their skinny hips would flash with arrogance through his showrooms. He was charging the highest prices in Paris, yet business was so good that he could not promise delivery for at least six weeks.

One would have thought that all this success would bring only happiness and a sense of achievement to the man who had set out four years previously to 'do something of his own'. But Courrèges was far from contented. The rag-trade manufacturers had grabbed his short, flared silhouette and were making it their own through millions of cheap copies which were mostly travesties of his pure technique, his immaculately placed details and his flawless proportions. Ugly designs were appearing in fashion departments all over the world, labelled 'Courrèges-style'.

Coco Chanel, as Chapter 5 reveals, found the copying of her famous suits the sincerest form of flattery. But to Courrèges, the sensitive perfectionist, it was unbearable. The first sign of his opting-out came when the Chambre Syndicale de la Couture Parisienne published the calendar of their Winter 1965 openings, and his name was not on the list. There was consternation in the Paris fashion world. What was Courrèges up to? He was about to start realising the dream which he had had from the beginning – to create in the authentic Courrèges manner for girls who could not afford his couture prices, and to earn for himself a good share of the harvest that the copyists had so successfully reaped from his work.

It took him two years to establish himself in larger, more spacious premises on the rue François Premier, and to raise the cash to finance his dream. 'I perfectly well realise how utterly immoral my prices are', he said in 1965. 'My public is far too limited. Soon I shall have the possibility and the means to dress the woman who cannot afford to dress in original Courrèges.' Between 1965 and 1967 he continued to make clothes for his private clientèle, but he gave no Press shows, and buyers were kept out too. His main activity at that time was raising money, and when finally in 1967 newspaper headlines announced joyfully 'He's back!' he had amassed a solid £850,000. It was the State-run bank, the National Bank of Commerce and Industry, through a subsidiary firm created to finance French export ventures, which put up half the amount. The rest came from Courrèges himself, from Coqueline, and from a group of his admirers. The terms were simple. Courrèges maintained complete control of the operation. The rest took a percentage of the profits. What he succeeded in doing was to establish workshops in Paris which could produce Courrèges clothes at boutique prices for direct marketing. In an atmosphere of the greater excitement, the Press gathered in his new salon (still totally white, but bigger and even more modern than his last in the avenue Kléber) for his come-back collection that February in 1967. But the collection was disappointing. It contained the same mixture as before. It was as though there had been no two-year pause. The skirts which had once looked so deliciously brief were now normal length – four or five inches above the knee. Almost the whole collection was in the fabrics Courrèges had always liked so much, flat, smooth-surfaced wools and whipcords. There were jumpsuits, trousers, shorts, and again, a lot of bareness. 'The Courrèges girl is not the red hot revolutionary she used to be', one journalist wrote rather sadly.

Neither has she ever been since. Courrèges has established his basic look, and he is too clever to make drastic changes each season. In ensuing years he has built it up, consolidated it, changed a detail here and there to meet the changing whims of fashion – a dropped hemline, a season of see-through and nudity, or a scissor-happy spree with cut-outs. But his ever-growing public loves him as he is, and he has only to add to his ranges, without pandering to the grumbling Press, who still flock to his shows, but can find little news in them. Every season Coqueline is inspired with a new way of presenting the clothes – always in the noisy, jazzy, cabaret way that was so revolutionary at first.

Courrèges used his favourite details for this black wool poplin dress: side buttoning and leather seam binding. (Autumn 1970.)

The Courrèges model girls, such as English-born Tania Machenand, (now married to a Frenchman) who has worked for him for six years, are essentially his type and, of course, totally different from the rest of the girls in the Paris couture. Tania told me: 'I walked into his salon and asked for a job. I'd never modelled before. I was very sunburnt, with long blonde hair and no make-up. I have very square shoulders so everything hangs on me as if on a coat-hanger. He liked by broad shoulders and he took me on.

'It was his first season in his new premises and I did everything, modelling, selling, answering the phone. It was great fun. It's still fun now, but it's grown a lot. Now I only model.'

The business has, in fact, grown enormously. Courrèges employs five hundred and fifty people inside the house and six hundred and fifty outside. He believes passionately in haute couture and produces it each season as a line called 'Prototypes', which accounts for only 10% of his turnover. 'But', says Courrèges, 'it remains the prototype, the indispensable experiment on which I try out my fabrics, feel my clients' reactions and base my other lines.'

The other lines are 'Couture Future', a range of clothes designed for and bought by thirty- and forty-year-olds which sell at about one-third of the couture prices; the 'Hyperbole' group, aimed at the twenty-year-olds and selling at about one-fifth of the couture clothes, and a recently-introduced knitwear line called 'Maille', which reaches the juniors and accounts for 25% of the turnover. The house has no licensing contracts, but the turnover increased by 100% in 1971 and its upward trend shows no sign of levelling off. Courrèges and his wife Coqueline are constantly in demand to present their wares in other countries, which they often do.

There are also the Courrèges accessories, the Courrèges luggage and a newly-launched Courrèges perfume called *Empreinte* which has had a big success. It is sold in handsome gold bottles which are as space-age as the rest of his products.

He plans to launch a range of menswear designs, which will also be as ultra-modern and far removed from anything else on the market as possible. 'They'll be like this', he told me, indicating the pale blue shiny synthetic two-piece he was wearing. It consisted of a battle-jacket zipped to the neck, and matching trousers. The pale blue surface fabric was bonded on the reverse side to white towelling. 'Very practical', was his comment.

Courrèges' business empire is centred in a small, unpretentious room on the first floor of his house in the rue François Premier. White and un-cluttered, as are all the rooms in the building, it contained a white wooden table, some upright chairs, the fabric swatches and trappings of his trade pinned to the white walls along with a big coloured photograph of his little girl, Fou Fou, a chubby two-year-old with straight brown hair, sitting in a field of grass and flowers.

He lives with Coqueline and Fou Fou in an apartment in Neuilly which is actually two apartments turned into one. It is very modern, but also very simple. There are no rich furnishings, hardly any paintings, 'because I don't like distractions when I go home from work'. They have another house at Pau in the Pyrenees, his birthplace, where they spend a consider-able amount of time, as two of their factories are situated there.

The pressure of work, its surprises and successes, does not seem to have abated in recent years. The January 1972 show presented by Coqueline was the most lavish. Realising, finally, how unendurable it was for the Press to be squeezed into their salon in the rue François Premier, Coqueline took over a photographer's huge white studio in another part of Paris and staged the spring showing there, with the audience seated on tiers of stone benches, cushioned with white polystyrene and with the performance played out against a white backdrop. This time it heralded the Olympic Games, with Courrèges himself bounding on to the stage wearing a silver synthetic tracksuit to fire the starting gun, a mannequin roaring about on a real motor-bike, and two others, wearing boxing gloves, pretending to fight.

Nearly all of the clothes were vintage Courrèges: the fit-and-flare, the knitted shorts and jumpsuits topped off with little sleeveless battlejackets in orange or black vinyl, the flat 'little girls' shoes, the vinyl belts with purses slotted on to them. ('Let's be free of the clutter of handbags', he seemed to be saying.) The hefty girls leapt and bounded about the stage in their clingy knitted outfits. But the shock came at the end of the perform-ance. Mood and music changed to dreamy romanticism and on to the white setting drifted the first crinoline evening dress. Followed by about twenty more.

The audience sat intent and amazed. *Crinolines* from Courrèges! Full skirts in white and ice-cream coloured organdie, swaying as the models moved dreamily around the stage. The dresses were very pretty and young and *ingénue*, the full, floor-length skirts, often scattered with appliquéd flowers, springing from little tight, high-waisted bodices. 'I wanted to bring a little poetry into women's lives after dark', the designer explained. The need for poetry, for communion with nature, for appreciation of love, joy, grass, flowers, clouds, stars is as strong as ever in Courrèges' spirit. In the mood and the atmosphere of his house in the rue François Premier, it is to be found there too. In spite of the unrelieved white of the ceilings, walls, alcoves and shelves where the clothes are hanging, there is warmth. The colours of the clothes themselves are the clear, true colours of nature. There are no formidable vendeuses in dark dresses to intimidate the customers. Instead, there are beautiful young girls with shapely figures who flit about wearing white rib-knitted catsuits which cling to every curve and turn their wearers into other-world beings who bear no relation to the dark, cold, winter scene outside, or to the people trudging past weighed down by dark winter overcoats. Inside the house of Courrèges it is always spring. Truly, he has created something unique.

The second Paris couturier to be labelled 'space-age' was Emanuel Ungaro. It is impossible not to draw comparisons between him and Courrèges, however odious this may be to the pair of them. In many ways, their lives have been similar, and at one stage their designing talents were bracketed.

Let us begin with the similarities: both men worked under, and were influenced by, Balenciaga. Both then worked together, when the outer-space outrageousness of miniskirts and pantsuits was at its height. Both started their businesses in a small way in tiny apartments far from the fashionable *quartier* of the other couturiers. Both expanded subsequently into impressive premises in that fashionable district. Each is supported by a woman whose role is closer than that of mere collaborator. Both these women abhor the limelight, are rarely publicised, yet are as much responsible for the design, production and presentation of the collections as their male partners. One cannot help speculating how different might their lives be today if Courrèges had not found his Coqueline and Ungaro his Sonja. Professional rivalry apart, one might imagine that the four would be good friends. But this is not so. For reasons best known to themselves they have no especially close relationship.

Ungaro was born of Italian parents in Aix-en-Provence on 13 February 1933, and describes himself as 'altogether Provençal'. His father was a tailor, and when Emanuel had completed his schooling, he joined the family business and worked with his father until he was twenty-two years old, learning to cut, sew and fit.

Then, as with all ambitious youngsters in the provinces, the charms of the big city became impossible to resist, and he travelled to Paris. His ambition was to join the house of Balenciaga, but this was out of the question for the time being, and he had to content himself with a job in the atelier of a small tailoring business. He did, though, make friends with a man ten years his senior – André Courrèges – who was in the coveted position of working for the master.

When Courrèges was struggling to free himself from the cocoon of safe anonymity at Balenciaga and to strike out on his own, the great man was resisting his efforts. During the three years of slowly withdrawing, out of gratitude and a feeling of responsibility to the master, Courrèges introduced Ungaro to Balenciaga, and in 1958 the latter took Emanuel on to

A beautifully-tailored coat with matching dress, in typical Ungaro colours of mint-green with white stripes, from the spring 1967 collection.

A classic coat in wool worsted gabardine, from Ungaro's spring 1971 collection.

his staff. When Courrèges left two years later, Ungaro was able to step into his place.

Years afterwards, Ungaro said: 'When I saw Balenciaga for the first time it was a discovery . . . something so important for my life and my mind. Balenciaga is an extraordinary person. He has a very strong dimension. He is generous and so clever and so human. I worked very very hard there, but I was so happy to work with him.' In an interview with the Paris journalist, Thelma Sweetinburgh, writing in January 1972 for *Réalités* magazine, he reiterated his great respect for Balenciaga, the teacher, saying: 'I learned that ideas follow opportunities. I try to adapt my style to the moment in life. In this manner it has progressed gradually, and I have kept it from taking perilous leaps.' To *Women's Wear Daily* he once said of his years with Balenciaga: 'Monsieur Balenciaga bears you . . . carries you shoulder high . . . he urges you to express yourself . . . contact with him is of a mystical quality.' Balenciaga taught him that: 'We are artisans, not philosophers. . . . '

One of the things that impressed him at Balenciaga was the quality of the women who dressed there: 'When a woman has looked at herself in a mirror for twenty-five or thirty years, she knows a good deal about herself.' Balenciaga must indeed have been an extraordinary person to have kept those two young men in willing bondage for so long; Courrèges for ten years, Ungaro for six.

When Ungaro finally left, it was because Courrèges had asked him to join him in his venture in the Avenue Kléber. The younger man felt deeply indebted to Courrèges for having negotiated his admission to the house of Balenciaga. 'I had to pay my debt to Courrèges. It was for this reason that I went to him', he explained.

The year Ungaro joined Courrèges was 1964 and he remained with him for the ensuing twelve months throughout the period which Courrèges himself recalls as his 'strongest statement'. The 'Swinging' Sixties' were in full sway and at Courrèges, miniskirts and trouser-suits were bringing a delicious new space-age (and permissive age) eroticism into women's lives.

For Ungaro, the change of environment must have been staggering. He left the cloistered portals of the stateliest maison de couture, steeped in the highest, old-established traditions of the trade, to step into the noisy, cramped, yet elatedly successful atmosphere of the Courrèges apartment in the avenue Kléber. He survived, and possibly even enjoyed it. After two seasons there, he said: 'Courrèges clothes convey a moral cleanness as well as a material one. The white, clean cut not only dresses the body but reacts on a woman's mind. The balance, the proportions are modern. What sort of life are women made to lead today? A man's life . . . so why not wear pants in town as anywhere else?'

Those two seasons were the extent of his collaboration with Courrèges,

Ungaro with his fabric designer, Sonia Knapp, 1970.

One of Miss Knapp's fabrics, used for a raincoat in the 'Paralèlle' range, 1967.

207

for they marked the high-spot of the latter's career in fashion, and also the moment when he decided to extinguish the flame he had lit until he had raised the funds to light it again in a more profitable way. In 1965, Ungaro decided to leave the Courrèges space-ship and move on alone. Three years previously, he had met a dark-haired German-Swiss girl called Sonja Knapp. She was studying art at a school in Zurich, and he was living in Montparnasse. Their ideas and talents harmonised and they formed a team of two. She moved to Paris, and together they faced the formidable prospect of opening a couture house without financial backing. They took a small apartment on the second floor of a recently built house in the Avenue MacMahon, near the Etoile. Its interior was modern and cool, with walls and toile curtains of white, and sapphire blue carpets, but it was only half the size of the Courrèges premises in the Avenue Kléber. With six helpers they went to work on their first collection, to be shown during the winter openings that July.

Ungaro fitting a model garment for Princess Ira de Furstenburg, one of his regular clients.

Until then, Ungaro was completely unknown, as he had remained in the background at Courrèges, but the fashion Press, which was in a state of consternation over the Garbo inclinations of their favourite, learnt of his enterprise, and was soon knocking on his door for interviews. One of the stories which appeared about him was headlined 'Mystery Man', and the question uppermost in fashion circles at that time was: Will thirty-two-year-old Ungaro be the new Courrèges? He received the journalists charmingly, for he is at all times a most considerate and, above all, sincere man. 'They all expect me to be another Balenciaga, another Courrèges', he said uncomplainingly. 'Well, Balenciaga is Balenciaga, and everything at Courrèges was Courrèges. I just want to work and find my own niche.' On another occasion he added: 'A pupil of Botticelli cannot paint a Picasso the next day.'

The first collection of twenty models – 'you can't call it a collection', he said modestly – was cut, sewn and fitted by Ungaro, almost single-handedly. 'I don't want to be called an haute couturier', he told one interviewer. 'It is old-fashioned. I am a plain couturier', meaning it the French way – a dressmaker. 'I am a man of this age, and I will design clothes for the women of this age. I won't be showing any evening dresses. This place isn't big enough for evening dresses, but even if I had three million francs I wouldn't do them. They are not my style. I don't want any fuss, and I hope people will not be disappointed. I am not a believer in producing theatrical shocks. It would be easy to stun everyone by sending on the girls in transparent plastic, but that's not the point. Clothes should evolve from season to season as everything else in life evolves.'

A fashion writer who attended his first Press show in his tiny white cubicle of a salon described how, 'In silence, white, hot and tense, shattered by the rip of Velcro fastenings, the tread of thin-soled, flat-heeled boots . . . and finally the short, sharp burst of applause – fashion took another leap into space.'

right
A typical Pierre Cardin evening dress, from the mid-'sixties. The couturier sometimes includes such an uncharacteristic romantic style among his space-age creations.

208

Separates from Ungaro's couture collection, spring 1971, showing his subtle mixing of striking print patterns.

left
Revolutionary concepts in women's clothing came from Cardin in the late 'sixties.

The little group of daytime clothes was well received by Press and buyers, and also by private clients who followed swiftly after his opening, although he did nothing himself about publicising his business. They all liked his short-skirted, sharp-edged silhouette that was still very much following Courrèges' lead and was to remain so for a few more seasons. Just as Courrèges had taken time to shake off the shadow of Balenciaga, so Ungaro needed time to establish his own signature.

For those first few seasons, Ungaro did most of the work himself, the cutting and the fitting (even today he does not neglect this side of the business) and sometimes even seeing to the deliveries. Sonja Knapp was working on the fabrics, which made a sharp impact in his second collection of forty models shown in January 1966. This was the dawning of a rare fusion of two talents, which has since developed, until the fabrics she designs today for the Ungaro collections are hailed as masterpieces of modernity, and by far the best in Paris.

For that January collection, his first group of spring clothes, short and triangular in silhouette, with narrow tops, widening to flared hems, showing a glimpse of tight shorts, proved his sure handling of vivid, clashing colours. Awning stripes in sharp blue and red on green, or turquoise and purple on citron, alternated with equally vivid triangles and broken checks. They were combined with plain fabrics which picked up one of the colours and appeared as a top, a skirt, a yoke, a hem or a border. Brief boleros took the place of jackets and several outfits were shown as a striptease, the outer garments peeling off to reveal shorts and briefest-ever bra tops. Ungaro the man was certainly soft-spoken and modest, but with his clothes, Ungaro the designer made a loud and definite statement. Ernestine Carter wrote in the *Sunday Times* of that collection: 'This is impact fashion. It must kill the boys who have to turn out two hundred and fourteen models to have Ungaro make it with forty.'

Others have hailed 'Ungaro's girl' as the female version of Superman. She was tall, athletic, muscular, sun-bronzed, and slightly terrifying. For that second collection she wore a slanted Vidal Sassoon haircut. I once asked Ungaro what he looked for particularly when he was choosing his mannequins. His answer: 'To be very careful to choose girls who do not look like mannequins.' A favourite in those days was a girl called Maulis, who had graduated from the Sorbonne and was modelling to make money and pass the time before landing a more permanent job. Her description of life in the maison Ungaro was: 'It's like working with friends, not bosses. The atmosphere is very relaxed.'

When the time approached for him to show his third collection, Ungaro was sufficiently sure of himself to announce, in spite of the hem-line beginning to drop elsewhere. 'I want dresses short enough to seduce all the men in the world'.

The hallmark of this show was silver. It was as if his mannequins had been newly minted before they stepped in front of the audience. They glinted from the crowns of their silver-wigged heads to the soles of their silver boots. Silver details rippled over them in the form of silver buttons, silver collars, silver stripes on their mini-length coats and tunics. And they wore silver mesh stockings. As he had promised, their skirts were incredibly short. Although his designing at this stage may sound more as if it were science-fiction than reality, his public took Ungaro seriously, and each collection proved to be progressively more successful with the three vital elements, Press, buyers and private clients.

By this time he was feeling the restrictions of the tiny apartment in the Avenue MacMahon, where only about twenty-five people could be accommodated in his minute salon. For his next showing, held in January 1967, he rented a photographer's studio and seated his audience in cardboard chairs, rather like hip-baths, arranged in semi-circles around the catwalk. His Supergirls marched out from behind screens which resembled the alabaster baths in a hydropathic establishment. This time, his short, flared silhouette seemed softer, and as always, his blending of fabrics and colours, playing stripes and jacquards against plain materials, delighted his public. He showed bermuda shorts for day and bloomers for evening. His 'baby' coat, double-breasted and flared from a high waistline marked with a belt, was a huge success with the buyers. White, orange, lime and lemon were his favourite colours that spring.

The collection put Ungaro into the First League. *Women's Wear Daily* hailed it with: 'This season, Ungaro's buffeted talent finally opened up like a flower. . . . The clothes have a harmonious richness, rightness of detail and line in which nothing is gratuitous.'

His acclaim was attracting the rich and the famous; people such as actress Jean Seberg and socialite Princess Radziwill were dressing at Ungaro. He realised that the moment had arrived to expand into bigger, more impressive premises, and in the spring of 1967 he found what he needed, the ground and first floors of 2 Avenue Montaigne, a few doors away from Dior, and a five-minute walk from the all-white space-ship in the rue François Premier where Courrèges had just staged his come-back.

While he prepared his next collection, to be shown that July, the carpenters and decorators moved in to transform his new surroundings. A charming little garden was planted at the entrance. The interior, which has remained much the same, began with a foyer, which is now the boutique. From it, white tiled screens (which critics have likened to a public lavatory) lead into the showroom, where the mannequins come out from behind a tiled screen to stand nonchalantly on a circular raised white stage in front of the audience, who are seated on little white toadstool chairs. Upstairs are offices, workrooms, and Ungaro's white-painted office, ablaze with flowers, some of them growing in a circular brick tub in the middle of the floor. The labyrinth effect of the tiled screens leading inwards gives one at first a slight shock, and then a little thrill of excitement.

To prepare the new premises and the collection in time for that July opening was a nightmare. 'Sonja Knapp and I and even the mannequins sewed throughout the last three nights to get everything done', Ungaro recalled.

He was richly rewarded, the collection was a total success, and newspaper headlines proclaimed him The New Star, praising him for the nuances of shape, the tailoring, and the brash, bright effect of the clothes. The silhouette was still high-shaped, with seams curving close to the bosom and then flaring to a wide hem. The length was very short. Ungaro's triumph was, in his own words, a journey out of hell. He had staked his career on this collection, assembled while the carpenters hammered and sawed in his new quarters, in which he had invested everything he possessed.

He has never sought outside backing for his business, preferring to let it develop slowly out of its own resources. Four years later, when Courrèges was well entrenched, with the business rolling along nicely, though still far smaller than most of the big names with which he ranks, I was to ask him whether he would not find life easier with outside financial support. Courrèges, after all, had found it vital for the realisation of his dreams. He replied: 'My house is entirely free from any financial pressure. I have no outside backing and I don't want it. I've paid too much for my freedom to lose it.'

For his first few collections, the very special fabrics designed by Sonja Knapp were made by the famous fabric house of Nattier. But when problems developed in the Nattier factory, Ungaro and Sonja switched to an Italian fabric firm called Helita, which has since made all the fabulous prints and the incredible weaves they dream up in subtle or vivid colourings, some of which look positively three-dimensional.

Since that important collection in 1967, Ungaro has continued his process of gradual evolution, each season developing naturally out of the one before. In the following year, he introduced a ready-to-wear line which he called 'Parallèle'. Four years later it accounted for 55% of his turnover, with his couture clothes bringing in the remaining 45%.

The ready-to-wear, like the fabrics, is made in Italy, in a factory in Turin. Although Ungaro was born in France, his background is, after all, Italian, and he understands the Italian mentality. 'I prefer working with the Italians to working with the French', he says, 'because at first the French found it difficult to understand what we wanted. They were afraid. But in Italy everything is easy, the people understand very quickly. Nothing is impossible.' In spite of ready-to-wear taking over the major part of his turnover, Ungaro, like Courrèges, believes passionately in the need to continue haute couture.

Ungaro says: 'It costs so much to produce a couture dress that the relation between the first cost (the cost to the house minus profit) and the price the customer pays for the dress is very very little. But – we live off the couture. It makes money. I need the couture – I need this freedom to do things.' It would be a pity indeed if he was ever to cease producing the ideas, the fabrics and the colour mixtures which make his couture collections a joy to witness each season.

I have always been a fan of Ungaro and I love the way he injects a dash of craziness into his collections: such as the metal sculptures which were shown at the end of one of his collections – aluminium necklaces-cum-bras teamed with aluminium hip-belts on see-through flower-appliquéd trousers. There was once a transparent silver-grey cape covered with tiny metal cylinders, and on another occasion a group of futuristic, metal, evening fantasies; one a gilded metal birdcage and matching metal skirt worn by a bare-breasted girl. Some fashion writers who tend to take his whimsies too seriously and to concentrate only on this side of his creativity are inclined to scold him. 'But I don't mind now,' he smiles. 'I used to get terribly upset, but now they don't bother me.'

With his small, devoted staff of sixty, his sparkling modern premises and a glittering clientèle which includes Lauren Bacall, Melina Mercouri, Catherine Deneuve, Jeanne Moreau, Bettina, Nan Kempner, Mrs Carter Burden, Princess Radziwill, Mrs Aristotle Onassis and her daughter

Ungaro's cape and separates for the 'Paralèlle' range, 1970.

'M UNGARO **FORTNUM** U
)N UNGARO **& MASON** U

left and above right
Styles made by Ungaro for Fortnum and Mason, the London store and sold exclusively through this outlet: a flowered blazer and trousers (summer 1972), and a beautiful short pinafore dress with toning jumper (1972).

far left
A perfect blending of geometric patterns which is characteristic of Ungaro's work: autumn 1971 collection.

Caroline Kennedy, Madame Valéry Giscard d'Estaing, the Duchess of Windsor, Princess Pahlévi, Baronne Guy de Rothschild, Jane Birkin and Mrs Yul Brynner, he has indeed found success. 'I enjoy dressing women who lead an international sort of life, because by wearing my clothes all over the world they help me spread my work everywhere', he acknowledged. Of his designing, he says: 'I am obsessed by the same woman, always the same image in my mind. It is not important, the dress or the coat. The woman inside is important. The way she walks, talks, looks, eats.'

How does he manage to keep not only contemporary but out ahead, in outer space as it were? 'If you live in a contemporary way, you don't change. I don't live with my past. Most important is to have a vision of the future.'

Ungaro the man is slim, with Latin good looks, and almost always dressed in black. With Sonja Knapp, he lives in an apartment in Montparnasse, 'with very very little furniture. Because I need the calm. I need to be free of any distractions. When I relax, I read a lot and I play chess.' He also has a house in Klosters, Switzerland, where he goes 'to rest and to think, to prepare my collections. I have lots of friends there – Irwin Shaw, Deborah Kerr . . . very interesting people live there.'

And what of his dreams? He has a new contract with Japan for the design, strangely enought, of home furnishings. 'Sheets, wallpaper, curtains, fabrics for walls, that sort of thing. I had the opportunity to introduce our designs there in this way. They are doing very very well. Maybe we will develop this idea for Europe soon.

'I hate to be shut in. I must open my mind. I'd love to have a team around me to do a lot of things. I believe in a team. A perfume and menswear will come soon to complete our image and identity. And furniture, certainly. I would love to design furniture – if I could find the time.'

Talking to Ungaro, one is left with the impression of a man well aware of his own potentialities, of a man with a strong degree of humility, who is at the same time contented, who knows where he is going. Challenge him with this, and he replies with a Latin Shrug: 'I am looking for the serenity.'

Cardin, seated at his electronically operated, colour-changing desk, directs his many operations.

Sleek transistors, khaki plastic with all edges rounded; chocolates in plastic containers, hexagon shaped; tissues in silver-foil boxes; belts, shoes, jumpers, cuff-links, shoes, bags . . . all with the stamp of Pierre Cardin. Even a theatre designed and owned by him called L'Espace. There is something of an Orwell quality in the ever-widening influence of this strange couturier; especially in his penchant for publishing his philosophies ·wherever and whenever he can. Certainly, Cardin is everywhere.

Cardin, more than any other couturier in Paris or anywhere else, is the merchant extraordinary. He symbolises the modern approach to couture, and he personifies all that recluses like Madame Grès or Balenciaga have shunned. He will survive when dozens of others have fallen to the scythe of the increasingly hard commercial world, for Pierre Cardin has a sharp nose for a new deal round every corner.

His newest venture takes the breath away – the problems that it posed

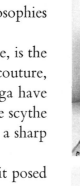

and that will surely continue are dazzlingly numerous. He makes clothes in India, of local materials designed by himself, and then has them shipped to the USSR. This makes him yet once more unique, for no other couturier has succeeded in selling to this vast untouched and hungry market. The 20 dresses, all in printed Indian cotton, will sell in Russia in the summer of 1973, say Cardin's associates. Although the deal was worked out by the Indian and Russian governments, using the Handwork Export Company of India, from which Cardin had already bought many fabrics in the past, he had to go to Moscow in late 1971 to finalise the details for himself.

Yet will these dresses be typical Cardins? Think of Cardin clothes and you think of jersey: supple, softly gliding over the body, everything with that typical nonchalant chic. In 1957 and 1958, it is startling to recall that in complete contrast to his now characteristic look, he was cinching in the waists of stiff little organdies, happy and skilfully at ease, in the crispest fabrics available. He has always been an expert with materials, as you can see from his extraordinary collars; he pioneered those huge cape

shapes, often fluted or cartridge-pleated, on the slender coats of the late 'fifties. A Cardin collar was often double-layered; a technique with collars that was swiftly seized upon by the manufacturers, and many a woman who had never heard of the designer before came to realise that she was wearing a Cardin invention.

These 'signatures' of the couturiers are fascinating to recognise, for like the motifs on the ruins or the artefacts of an ancient civilisation, they are the instant mark of their taste. Cardin will be known to future archaeologists by his giant collars and the geometric detail of his dresses. He has always had a passion for architectural shapes, and expresses them in various ways. In 1960, he took the diamond, and made cut-out patterns at the breastbone of his models. Or he made beaded diamond-shapes, anchoring strapless tube dresses to their dog-collars. Another year, he took the circle and used it in the same way, or again, the rectangle, which

right
A classic Cardin collar.

The manufacture of chocolate wrappings; menswear, 1971; 'unisex' designs (which were sent for a special collection at the Victoria and Albert Museum, London, as typical examples of his style); his famous cut-out dresses, which have been successful for several seasons; coffee machines; alarm clocks; and paper tissues, all designed by Pierre Cardin.

appeared as 'letter-box' pockets, especially on coats, where they were emphatically welted and stitched. These decorative motifs mean that jewellery is completely unnecessary for wear with a Cardin model. Almost without fail his own appliqués replace it, and the effect is ruined if you wear anything but earrings.

Cardin has been architectural where everyone around him turned madly to Art Nouveau for inspiration. This is not surprising, as he has always been a solitary figure. Never a man to move, as does Saint Laurent, in a posse of devoted chums, Cardin prefers to be alone. He gives this appearance even when he is in a crowd, at one of those *tout Paris* receptions his associates insist he attend. He will often take his old friend, the actress Jeanne Moreau, to these. In 1962 when their friendship first burst into print, she was quoted as saying, 'When we do marry, M. Cardin and I, we shall make no secret of it . . . but in the meantime our love is special and quite private.'

Private it may have been – they holidayed in the South Pacific to get away from it all – but at his shows during this era she was the brightest spark there. I once sat right behind her, she sun-tanned in white linen, alert, amused, laughing as the photographers snapped her every reaction to every dress. Many people were sorry that a marriage did not take place. It has been suggested that their relationship was as much a business arrangement as anything personal, and that Jeanne Moreau's fortune helped Pierre Cardin to finance his operation for a time, but no one has ever confirmed the rumour.

Like any creator with more ideas than time, Pierre Cardin is always a little breathless, a little behind his deadline. He designs his collections at the last possible moment. One fabric manufacturer, Nattier, was interested to discover that by mid-June Cardin still had not unpacked the rolls of cloth to be used for the mid-July show. He designed the interiors of the Simca 1100 and a new Chrysler, but cannot be bothered to own a new car himself. He drives a six-year-old one, walks, or takes the Metro. People who do business with him report that he often does not seem to hear what is said to him, and when he talks he gazes moodily at a point over one's head, discoursing poetically on space and the stars.

A business run by such a man could be chaotic. Mme Herve Alphand makes it less so. Nicole Alphand is everyone's dream picture of the soignée Frenchwoman, crackling with sophistication, and with unrivalled social experience. She was the wife of France's ambassador to Washington during the Kennedy era, in which time the two couples became good friends. She joined the house of Cardin in 1966 under a flurry of protest from the French establishment. Was it indeed quite suitable for a wife of a head (as he then was) of France's Foreign Office to be working for a dress house? Nicole Alphand stuck to her guns, and worked hard to bring hundreds of clients from both the diplomatic and the social world into the Cardin fold. She arranged for shows, tours, and galas, made sure Pierre was dragged from his comfortable Left Bank riverside flat to the soirées at which he had to be seen. She has pleased and astonished many would-be critics by taking her job very seriously indeed, clocking in at the salon as a regular worker, and instilling a discipline among the staff which was until then lacking. Cardin enjoyed designing for Mme Pompidou's trips to the USSR and Africa, and one feels that Nicole Alphand had no small part in these commissions.

But how does it all start – the career of one of the most successful contemporary couturiers? Pierre Cardin was born and brought up in Italy, although his parents were French. After a childhood spent in Venice, he

Cardin dress styles, showing his unerring eye for sculptured shapes and neatly-tailored edges. The scallops on the white wool crêpe suit (spring 1971) are his particular signature. Trapeze dress, 1967.

216

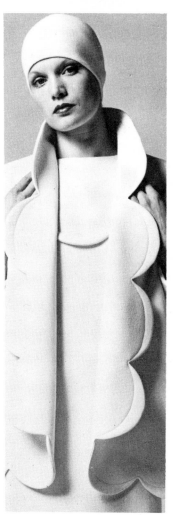

emigrated with his family to France, and his first job was as a book-keeper. But in Paris, he became interested in clothes and the couture, and he soon found work at the house of Paquin, where he learnt a great deal. It gave him surprising opportunities, like designing the embroidered velvet costume for the Beast, Jean Marais, to wear in Jean Cocteau's great 1945 film *La Belle et La Bête*. His next move was for a spell at the house of Schiaparelli. When he heard, during his time there, of a vacancy at the house of Dior, he was on the doorstep at eight in the morning. Dior liked him, and taught him 'everything I know' Cardin says, 'except how to make a Cardin'. But he did have the excitement of participating in the birth of the New Look. He might well have been chosen for the Dior succession – much of Paris thought he would be, although he had left the house in 1949 to set up on his own. Instead, Yves Saint Laurent was appointed. The two men have remained, as their statures have grown, rivals – both appealing to the lighthearted young of the world in a unique way. When Saint Laurent left and Marc Bohan took over at Dior, Cardin determined even more to make his own house a brilliant success. He moved from rue Richepanse to the Faubourg St Honoré in 1953, and set up, in 1962, his complete menswear line in a separate building nearby, in the Place Beauvau.

He longs, says *Elle* magazine, to be regarded as the number one figure in haute couture. He runs neck and neck, some seasons, in critics' estimation, with Jules Crayhay, now at Lanvin. Ask a French journalist and she will respond, 'He's the only one who understands modern elegance'. But unanimity in saluting him as the king of couture, as Balenciaga was once known, still eludes him. Perhaps this is because he is always looking to the future, not to the present. 'The clothes I prefer, I invent them for a life that doesn't exist yet – the world of tomorrow. They demand of me costumes with three buttons, yet I show dresses of the cosmocorps. *Après moi le désert . . .*'

Twice a year he holds captive the press of the world. Sitting through a Cardin collection used to be a pyrotechnic of delight – a dizzying sequence of idea upon idea. They go on forever. He shows far and away the most clothes of anyone in Paris. He has his audience clamber up the concrete steps of his beloved new Espace theatre and wedge onto tiny white plastic chairs.

Why does he do it? Is it a sort of megalomania? We long to know, for everyone's story (even a couturier's) is better by being kept brief. Perhaps the secret lies in Cardin's immense wealth of creativity. He acts as an ideas factory for all Paris, but in his own work, he cannot be ruthlessly disciplined, and is reluctant to edit out any of his innovations.

Cardin's relations with the press have often been on a see-saw. As far back as January 1958 a highly senior critic was writing, 'I was lost in admiration . . .' Throughout the next few years his shows were hailed as avant-garde, and he was the darling of the press. The rapture fell off for a while, then climbed high again with his soft, understated little wool crêpe coats, shown in L'Espace in the spring collection of 1971. He evidently thinks his press relations are fine, for he stated in an interview in *Environment*, 'When I travel I see many journalists – sometimes for four or five hours a day. We grapple with many things – archaeology, paintings, technology, people . . . it's the press that has made me.' Part of the unevenness of his press coverage comes from the impatience writers feel with the length of the Cardin show. They often fail to photograph Cardin copies made by ready-to-wear manufacturers because they are downright weary of Cardin.

Another part is the déjà-vu his critics feel with Cardin's space phobia. It is significant that he called his theatre (formerly Les Ambassadeurs) L'Espace. For years he showed casual yet aggressive clothes for weekend and student wear inspired by astronauts. In another life probably he would have adored being Neil Armstrong. James Brady, describing Pierre Cardin for *Harper's Bazaar*, said: 'Head cocked to one side, speaking without the slightest regard for the microphone, Cardin goes on interminably expounding his fashion philosophy while restive Italian editors shout, "basta, basta". Nothing perturbs Cardin. He goes on talking through the roar of the crowd and when he is good and ready, the first model steps onto the runway.' A third possible reason for press exasperation might be the topsy-turviness of the man. Pioneering the way on an April showing coinciding with the prêt-à-porter season, and the first to abandon, loudly, the traditional January and July dates, he then reneged and sneaked out a show in early February 1972 of one hundred garments to which the press were not invited.

Known from the very first as a designer of the avant-garde Cardin has paid the penalty that pioneers pay. His timing has been terrible. Although he has been first with many a look, the times were not as swift or as subtle as he. This is the history of the success or failure of all the couturiers – timing. Later designers have often received all the credit for his ideas. It is revealing to leaf back through his career, to see that he was in 1966 showing the tweed pinafores with polo-necked sweaters that so many girls adopted in the 'seventies. Then he showed a fabric waistcoat often patterned, back buttoning, with skirt and polo-necked sweater, also as early as 1966. (Richard and Patricia Nixon were present at that show and they loved it.) He also fought the midi (how the USA must have loved him!), much preferring to startle his audience with what proved later a smash-hit combination – the maxi-coat over the mini-dress. His intuition has often been right, if mistimed.

Cardin has always experimented more with the products of technology than have his colleagues. His love of vinyl was almost wearisome, as he used it year upon year in sports garments, and to decorate, with characteristic circles or diamond patterns, the necklines and waists of plain wool jersey dresses. His moulded dresses in 1966 caused general dismay but everybody had to admit that they were consistent with his ever-thrusting curiosity. Coloured stockings to match or dramatise the day dresses were

Two of Pierre Cardin's designs which are to be manufactured in Indian cloth, for sale in the USSR.

seen at Cardin long before they became part of everyday life. His boots were immensely exciting, sometimes thigh-high in silver kid. Giant industrial zips were in evidence in his collections from the start of their popularity.

A perfectionist with pleats, Cardin has mastered every possible variation, using them as no one else does. Anyone can pleat a skirt, but he often pleated an entire coat, swirling it into a cone from a high ring neckband. His sun-ray pleated suit jacket, although not intentionally designed for the purpose, remains the prettiest maternity-wear in the world. He uses tweed in fits and starts but his lines always show themselves to best advantage in wool crêpe or wool jersey. All that fluid pleating and draping, those sinewy body lines, require a subtle fabric to show them well.

Cardin's colour sense is a controversial point. Some praise it, but I have always found it either shrieking or muddy. For me it is a blind spot in a designer with an otherwise incredible eye.

It is interesting to consider some of the high points in Cardin's career, which seems to grow so logically, with complete assurance. His first major success was a variation on the sack dress, in 1957, with looped back, and marvellous draping. The following year, he took his spring collection to London for the Berkeley Debutante Dress Show, and his models that autumn won ceaseless applause. This led to his suits being copied under licence in the UK by the firm of Berg (the first of many such links); to selling patterns to the London *Daily Telegraph*, and to a commission to design the wedding dress for the bride of the Crown Prince of Japan. This last was an appropriate liaison, as Cardin has always favoured oriental looks, and has Asian mannequins for each season's showings.

Cardin was now sufficiently well established to launch into new fields, and his first menswear boutique opened in that same year. His comment, 'It's more lasting than haute couture', shows his basic business sense rather than any flagging romanticism about the world of high fashion. Unlike other women's couture designers who dabble in menswear on the side, Cardin dedicated himself to this with real passion, and became a world leader. His menswear now nets him five times as much income as his clothes for women. He has been responsible for many looks, including the collarless jacket, curly-brimmed tweed hat, skinny double-breasted suit for young men, at prices young men can afford. (These were copied for Neville Reed and John Temple in the UK. By spring 1965, the tie-up with the UK was complete and a Cardin copy could be bought at any of 20 shops for £15.34. You could, in those days, buy a tie at Cardin's men's boutique for under a pound, or three dollars. In the USA, his success was as rapid as it was in France and the UK. His turnover in the early 'sixties was second only to Dior's. He established separate studios for men's and women's clothes, and declared that he still cut all the toiles himself. If anyone could do it, Cardin could. He once said, in a conversation with Marc Bohan of Dior, that design schools did not matter – hard work did. In March 1967, he signed a deal with the Intercontinental Men's Apparel

Corporation of the USA to produce his suits, on which he acquired an 8% royalty. They expected first-year sales of $10 million. Menswear licensees followed thick and fast: now, Pierre Cardin has contracts with such prestigious firms in the USA as Fieldcrest Mills, Host Pajamas, Lark Luggage, Lucien Piccard watches, Commonwealth Shoe and Leather, Swank, and Jacqueline Cochran.

The Cardin menswear division, bringing in 60% of his annual profits, has as its core a creative laboratory with eight designers, all of whom carry out Cardin's ideas after frequent conferences. He gives his indications, and his redoubtable aide, André Oliver, sees that they are carried out. Cardin has a rare provision among the commercial men who manufacture his menswear: he has the right to insist they do a certain style even though it is not among the 100 commercially viable models they have themselves selected.

But menswear is only one of his many diversities. His scents, 'Suite Seize' and 'Amadis' were selling well by 1964, and every elegant man visiting Paris bought one of his pork-pie hats or puffy caps. He launched out with a children's range, and this in turn led to another development: cut-out clothes for children by Cardin which you stitch together yourself. In 1966, he signed one of his most widely known contracts with Selfridges, the major London store. All these activities brought about the inevitable withdrawal from the lofty ranks of haute couture, and in that same year he resigned from the Chambre Syndicale de la Couture Parisienne because his activities were much too diverse and up-to-the-minute, and Cardin wanted an immediate reaction to his work. There seems to be no end to his enterprise. He has shocked South Africans with his preference for rough, unpolished diamonds, on the silver medallion discs and rings he designed, and brought his mind to bear on such an unlikely subject as household plumbing.

Two of Pierre Cardin's designs which are to be manufactured in Indian cloth, for sale in the USSR.

Probably no designer works harder, and holidays less. People who work with him love his keen sense of family among the team but they find his changeable temperament disheartening. His moodiness has grown, in recent years, in emphatic fashion. The man with whom I once lunched at London's French embassy, who chatted so enthusiastically and charmingly about Romanesque churches in the French countryside, can suddenly forbid anyone in his firm to talk to a journalist.

His very diversity is a godsend and a curse. It may well be that his designs for industry, packaging, and above all, menswear, will supersede in lasting value his designs in women's clothing. Certainly, all these other activities fascinate and lure him, like a hypnotic piper's changing tune. He finds it desperately hard to delegate, and even straightens the shelves in his boutique in Paris personally. The staff smile on this: they know it calms his nerves. If he did not have these fiddly little outlets, if he lacked the taste and discipline for solitude, Pierre Cardin might snap. He extends himself more than any designer I know, and he must live with a thousand niggling anxieties on so many levels of design. One can never isolate him

Material handled as only a French couturier knows how: Pierre Cardin, 1968.

niggling anxieties on so many levels of design. One can never isolate him from all these multifarious outlets and consider him solely as a designer of women's clothes. Each reflects the other to a marvellous degree and his actual stamp is as clear on whatever he touches as was Balenciaga's, as is now Saint Laurent's.

Is all this moodiness, irritability and isolation the price of greatness in couture? Is it necessary to be remote to be a great creator? It is an ageless question. For all his faults, Pierre Cardin more than any of his rivals, is in his field the real Renaissance man.

LEFT BANK COUTURE

10 Yves Saint Laurent   Felicity Green

Classic Saint Laurent: a midi-coat, 1969.

right

Designs by Karl Lagerfeld and Jean Louis Scherrer at Chloé, spring 1972. A fine example of how close ready-to-wear and couture clothes are becoming in styling and finish.

At the beginning of the 1970s it was generally considered by all but the most myopically optimistic that haute couture was at a serious turning-point, a moment of crisis in its history. If any one person could be said to have effected the revolution in style which came at this period, then the honour must undoubtedly go to Yves Saint Laurent, the young French designer who, despite a deceptive mildness of manner, re-directed the course of fashion history. Where he led, others followed, some protesting as they went, others insisting they were going to opt out anyway.

His path had been fairly clearly ordained ever since the mid-'sixties, at which time Saint Laurent began gradually to shift his loyalties away from the exclusive world of haute couture and move over to the popular front of ready-to-wear. The most significant decision of his career came in January 1972, when Yves Saint Laurent finally announced that he would withdraw from the twice-yearly Paris collections. It was the combined efforts over the post-war years of the member houses of the Chambre Syndicale which helped to bring into France an average annual income of £100 million – plus the inestimable amount of prestige that is only now, some believe, dwindling away.

The collections, as such, came into their own in the late 'forties, when creative fashion was considered to be suffering from a depression. It was then that the collections became the life blood of the French fashion industry and guaranteed Paris a place among the big, black newspaper headlines all over the western world. 'Paris puts women in the sack!' 'Paris abolishes the waist!' 'Paris banishes the bust!' The top designers were dictators and their word was law. In those days haute couture was an irresistible force sweeping round a receptive world, and copying Paris, adapting Paris, or being inspired by Paris, were the main aims of the fashion world. Those women who could not afford to dress in Paris wanted to look as if they did.

In recent years, however, tastes and attitudes have changed completely. The days when the length of her skirt was the problem uppermost in a woman's mind have passed. Public reaction is reflected in the industry, itself: like a disenchanted audience leaving an over-long recital of a recherché concert, the trade buyers have been drifting away from the haute couture showings. It cost them a great deal of money to sit in the front row of those hot uncomfortable salons, and an increasing number of them began to feel the expense was no longer justified. At Dior the 'caution' (explained in Chapter 1) in 1972 is $2000 for two people, at Patou it is $1000, at Ungaro $1800 per person. At Lanvin a buyer gets two models for $1500, at Ricci, $1100 for one. Unless the pickings are plentiful, say the buyers, the price becomes too high.

As a result, in recent years, the buyers have been increasingly directing their attention to the French ready-to-wear market where many haute couturiers are already trying to establish a foothold for themselves among the fast-growing numbers of the mass-market manufacturers. However, the adjustment in many cases has been too radical to be achieved with any

left
Yves Saint Laurent demonstrates that couture is as vital as ever; from his spring 1968 collection.

great degree of success, since this is a world where couture is an anachronism, a world that has nothing to do with riches and elegance, or the romantic world that, quite simply, no longer exists.

One designer who quickly recognised this changing world, and responded with a totally contemporary attitude to fashion-designing is Yves Saint Laurent. An early believer in the wind of change, Saint Laurent predicted the demise of the so-called fashion 'edict' as early as 1966.

'Now that women have liberated themselves from our dictatorship and the corset of other people's ideas', he said, 'they themselves become infinitely more important than the clothes they wear.

'Women should be terrified of mere elegance as of the grave, for it is the death of fashion.'

Acknowledging the influence of the outside world on Paris fashion, rather than the reverse, is a state of mind that does not come easily to those designers who still regard *la mode* as a kind of religion. To Saint Laurent this shift of emphasis has never been a problem, despite the fact that his original entrée to the Paris fashion scene could hardly have been through a more conservative door, for his first job was with none other than Dior himself. Saint Laurent had arrived in Paris from Algeria when he was 17. His family – his father was in insurance and his grandfather had been a lawyer – sped their talented lad on his way. He arrived in the city where his ambitions lay, armed with a portfolio of fashion drawings and theatre designs.

Yves Saint Laurent's talent was first publicly recognised· in· 1953 when he won First Prize in a competition organised by the International Wool Secretariat. The model of his winning sketch (shown in the background) was made up by Givenchy.

To those aspiring unfortunates who spend uncounted hours knocking on unwelcoming doors, Saint Laurent's path to recognition was enviably brief. He showed his work to Michel de Brunhoff, then editor of French *Vogue*, who in turn took them to his friend, designer Christian Dior. Dior immediately hired Yves and, spotting the potential, was often heard to refer to him as 'My Dauphin'.

'I have been thinking about the future of our House', said Dior, having signed up Yves to a long and binding contract, 'and I have never come across a boy with so much talent.' It is still not generally known that during his three years as Dior's assistant Saint Laurent used to submit as many as 400 sketches for each collection. Dior, of course, did many more, but the result was often a combination of ideas. In the Dior collections as presented to the press and to customers, there were many pure Saint Laurents – sometimes, he says, as many as 50 out of about 180. In 1958, when Dior died in the south of France from a heart attack Saint Laurent was already established as the master's successor. Whatever doubts existed in the hearts and minds of the hierarchy in this most successful of Paris couture establishments, the leader had spoken and the deed was done. Thus· Saint Laurent found himself, at the age of 21, perching like an acrobat, on the top of an edifice that represented a multi-million franc empire the size and like of which had not been seen in Paris before or since.

Saint Laurent's first solo collection in January 1958 – his Trapeze line –

was a complete success. 'Amazing scene', read the headline in one of Britain's most conservative newspapers, whose report recorded the scene of hysteria in the Avenue Montaigne. 'A gesture even Dior himself never received', it admitted, referring to Saint Laurent's 'royal' appearance on the balcony waving to the crowd outside the house which was chanting his name. Those inside shouted 'Bravo!' and jumped on and over the little gold chairs in order to kiss or embrace their new national hero. It took an hour for the rioting emotions to cool down and the *eminences grises* behind the Dior scenes breathed for the first time in months and said 'But, of course . . .' In a city where fashion is as important to the natives as is whisky to the Scots, Saint Laurent had overnight become nothing short of a patron saint. Despite his youth, his sureness of taste was impressive.

Christine Tidmarsh, an English girl now herself a successful designer in Milan, Italy, was one of the models who worked for Saint Laurent from the time of his very first collection. 'He was wonderful to work for', she told me. 'Although he was so young he always knew exactly what he wanted, but he'd always ask what *you* felt about a particular dress or colour. And he'd listen! Very rare. He was always sweet to everyone.

'He had perfect taste, and this was reflected in everything about him – his home, his pictures, everything. And he was fun, too. He knew everyone by name and the atmosphere in the house was marvellous. I remember when one of the boys who used to run round getting fabric samples was leaving, Yves gave a party for him at his home.'

'We always seemed to be having parties', she recalled. 'I don't know if this is very usual among the other couturiers but I doubt it.'

Among the clothes Christine Tidmarsh collected during her stint with Saint Laurent is a black taffeta dress that was originally shown in a 1958 collection. 'It's all swathed and sexy with a low neckline and thin shoulder straps and it was called "Marilyn Monroe". I could wear it now', she said 'and it would look absolutely fabulous.' It is an intriguing thought that in 1959 Saint Laurent was harking back to the 'fifties, anticipating the taste for nostalgia that took over the fashion world so strongly in the late 'sixties. But fashion never has and, I suspect, never will, pursue a straightforward path, and hot on the heels of praise all too often comes the blame. From being fashion's darling in the late 'fifties, Yves soon fell heavily from favour.

First came the rough tongue of criticism. In his second post-Dior collection in the autumn of 1958 the 'boy wonder' became a 'monster' overnight. He had the temerity to lower the hemline four inches, and women, it appeared, would have none of it. In those days the length of a skirt was a matter of national importance and no young upstart was going to cover a million knees on a personal whim. Who did he think he was? Dior? Describing the stony reception that replaced the cheers and the kisses of the previous season, one British fashion editor commented that after looking for half-an-hour at these new long skirts the gloomy audience resembled 'drug addicts done out of their dope'. Then, 12 months later, in the autumn of 1959, Yves went into reverse and shortened the skirts to knee level, whereupon all hell broke loose.

'Dior's man can do what he likes', exploded one headline, 'We won't show our knees!' Matching the hemlines, feelings ran very high indeed and one doughty British woman Member of Parliament announced: 'I think it is ridiculous for a youth of 23 to try to dictate to sensible women. British women have not taken any notice of this nonsense for the past few years and are to be congratulated on their common sense.' The British Housewives League joined in. 'I don't think knee-showing skirts would be successful in this country', said their spokeswoman. 'I don't think many women would show their knees.' Newspapers, television and radio joined in the debate and women everywhere were quizzed about their attitude to the knees-or-not issue.

At the moment when his popularity barometer was beginning to drop to alarming depths Yves received the most crushing blow of all. After three deferments he was finally drafted into the French Army. However, his stay with the military was brief and unhappy. Never was a draftee less suited to army life, and the chances of his adapting to circumstances where, for the first two weeks he could not even take a bath, were non-existent. Hardier recruits might withstand this deprivation along with other far worse hazards, but to Saint Laurent it was too much to bear. He suffered a total nervous and physical collapse and the newspapers of that time showed pictures of him lying prostrate, en route to a psychiatric clinic near Paris. After two months he was medically discharged from the army as being 'unadaptable on military grounds'. He flew off to Majorca to recuperate, before, as he thought, returning to take up his designing duties at the house of Dior.

However, there were further hazards ahead. During Saint Laurent's enforced absence, the 35-year-old Marc Bohan – originally recruited as Saint Laurent's assistant to concentrate solely on the ready-to-wear for London and New York – had been elevated to chief designer. Saint Laurent, who was formulating plans to open his own house, went to law and sued his former employers for £48,000 damages. It was a time of highly charged emotions and divided loyalties among the Dior staff. Because of Yves' personal popularity, a large number of Dior workpeople chose to follow the young 'breakaway', and it was estimated that those who went with him in his new venture included seamstresses, salesgirls, van drivers, and a senior vendeuse who booked £100,000 worth of orders a season – and, unkindest cut of all, one of Dior's most famous model girls, the attractive and bosomy brunette, Victoire.

The press took up the cause of the young rebel, the David who planned to take on the fashion Goliath. The House of Dior promptly counter-sued for 'enticement of staff'.

However, once the litigation was over, business went back to normal and the new launching of Saint Laurent was achieved with a degree of success which has proved less ephemeral than the first. His first independent

The three-quarter length coat, 1963.

Yves Saint Laurent has developed an increasingly casual look in the *tailleur,* as shown with these two from the autumn 1962, and autumn 1963 collections.

collections proved that Dior's loss was the fashion world's gain. The opening in January 1962 at 30 bis Rue Spontini was an unqualified success. To repeated questions about the source of the capital required to mount such a mammoth operation Saint Laurent refused to comment. It was not until a year later in March 1963 that he confirmed that he had received backing from various outside sources including Swiss and French businessmen but that the principal investor was an American named J. Mack Robinson from Atlanta, Georgia. However, these backers left the designer alone as far as his creative talents were concerned. Untrammelled by the overwhelming big business interests, combined with the committee-style organisation that exists in the Dior conglomerate – the world's largest fashion empire of which the haute couture side is merely the cherry on the chocolate sundae – Saint Laurent could work at his own pace. As his reputation gathered strength he began to develop a highly individual style that had less and less to do with the rich world of elegant women who wanted mostly to continue to dress in the present as they had in the past. Very soon, as his ideas crystallised and his philosophy strengthened, Saint Laurent began to break the unwritten rules of haute coutiure.

He produced the first 'fun' clothes in Paris, and the ladies who were used to wearing sensible suits by day and formal frocks by night looked on more in sorrow than in anger at his first solo flights of fantasy. There was the cowboy look in 1962, soon followed by a sailor-look pea-jacket, stylised 'beatnik' clothes, the British 'mods and rockers' look, the gipsy and the rich hippie. There was the 'Robin Hood' look when a goodly proportion of his rapidly increasing clientèle took to wearing clothes hitherto seen only on that female phenomenon of the English theatre, the principal boy in the pantomime.

However, if any one season could be pinpointed as the moment when the seriousness and the dedication finally went out of Paris, then it was 1966. This was the season when Yves Saint Laurent introduced Pop Art to Paris and never again would haute couture be quite so sacrosanct. Buyers and press, raised on a diet of good taste and elegance, knew not whether to laugh or cry at the sight of dresses that were a cross between a strip cartoon and a poster destined for walls rather than for women's figures. A black dress with a nude pink torso splashed down the front. Another with a boldly outlined profile. Another with a huge pair of lips where a bra ought to be. Saint Laurent was having his little joke – again. Of course, he was not the first joker on the Paris scene. Elsa Schiaparelli had been doing roughly the same thing back in the 'thirties, but at that time Paris was a vast and exclusive stage-setting producing exotic clothes only for the people who actually wore them. The audience at a Schiaparelli show was not likely to be filled with hard-headed businessmen and women looking for commercially sound ideas on which to gamble a considerable amount of capital. What they wanted were good, copy-able ideas to take home, ideas that could be incorporated into clothes that were recognisably of Paris origin. Some of them were visibly worried. Others had faith – and

These two evening dresses reflect Saint Laurent's enjoyment of 'fancy-dress' clothes, from his spring 1972 showing.

Yves Saint Laurent's 'Pop Art' dresses were inspired by the American artist, Andy Warhol, and figured in his autumn 1966 collection.

hoped for better things next time. But the rot had set in and although Saint Laurent could hardly be accused of undermining the structure, all by himself, he certainly recognised the cracks in the walls and knew what was causing them.

Social barriers were breaking down, the duchess wanted to look like her daughter rather than the contrary. The rich look was out of fashion, even for the rich. If one word had to be found to describe the look of Saint Laurent's contribution to fashion at this time, it is undoubtedly casual. He brought leather into the drawing-room, made brass studs smarter than rubies, made boots a fashion accessory rather than an outdoor necessity, and in general produced clothes so relaxed that, unlike many Paris outfits, they looked as though they would not stand up all on their own. Deceptively stark in cut, his day clothes were almost provocative in their simplicity. It took some time for the buyers to warm to the Saint Laurent jackets cut as softly and simply as a man's shirt. Was it not too simple? No built-in, rigid shaping, no tricky, over-elaborate cutting. Throughout all the years of his development he has remained faithful to a simplicity of line that sets him apart from the other couturiers.

Jane Fonda and Elsa Martinelli, watching a collection at Yves Saint Laurent in 1965. Miss Martinelli is wearing one of the couturier's Mondrian-inspired models.

His critics look at a typical Saint Laurent collection of clothes of almost throwaway simplicity and fail to understand that clutter and complication have little place in today's life. Perfection of line is a better substitute.

In this philosophy, one can trace a similarity with the ideas of the only other designer who, as the chapter devoted to her describes, has been a great influence on Saint Laurent – Coco Chanel, who once said of Saint Laurent, with typical acerbity: 'The poor boy might turn out all right if he simply copied me and cut his hair.'

However, it was in 1965 that Saint Laurent's own influence reached such immense and measurable proportions, when he introduced his Mondrian Look. Mondrian, the French painter who saw everything in square blocks of colour, inspired Saint Laurent, who in turn 'inspired' a million copies of those well-known checkerboard dresses. In rag-trade back rooms, machinists were running up batches of budget-priced Saint Laurent–Mondrians that were in the shops before the Paris originals were even finished round the hem. It was at some unknown point in time that Saint Laurent radically changed fashion direction, and this mass and uncontrollable 'pirating' of one of his ideas might well have been the decisive factor. If the world was going to wear Saint Laurent copies, why did he not copy

231

them himself? The move that encouraged the erstwhile refugee from the massively commercial Dior enterprise to become commercial himself was undoubtedly master-minded by his business manager and constant companion, Pierre Bergé.

Bergé's path to Saint Laurent's side was via what might be called a varied career. He arrived in Paris to indulge in some short-lived enthusiasms – paintings, journalism, and an association with Gary Davis, an American who believed in the apparently non-viable idea of world citizenship. His first important and successful job was promoting the French artist Bernard Buffet whose paintings, under Bergé's aegis soared to unprecedented heights of price, prominence and popularity. However, shortly after a protracted disagreement with Buffet, Bergé met the young Saint Laurent at a Paris dinner party given by the then Paris editor of *Harper's Bazaar,* Marie Louis Bousquet, and since that time the two men have been close friends, as well as business associates.

It was due to an introduction by Bergé that the house of Saint Laurent was sold in 1963 to Mr J. Mack Robinson, a self-made American businessman who started with a finance firm in Atlanta, Georgia, and built it up to the point where he had cash to spare for profitable investment. 'No', he said when asked the obvious question. 'I'm not fashion-minded. I'm just out to make a profit.' This he did, and since that time the holding company which keeps the Saint Laurent balance-scales in their profit-orientated hands has changed twice.

In 1965, J. Mack Robinson passed his share over for a round million dollars to Lanvin-Charles of the Ritz set-up. Their urbane chairman, Richard Salomon, has always been much in evidence among the front row fashion élite at the Saint Laurent showings.

Lanvin-Charles of the Ritz organisation has itself been taken over by the pharmaceutical giant, E. R. Squibb & Sons, who produce, to name but an unglamorous few, tea bags, aspirin, baby foods and chewing gum. Sensibly enough, neither of these commercially-minded firms have tried to reorientate the Saint Laurent endeavours, which continue to flourish along the somewhat unorthodox paths chosen by fashion's freethinker.

It is generally acknowledged that in all his most successful post-Dior business ventures, Saint Laurent has been both projected and protected by Bergé, whose circle of friends and acquaintances, then as now, came from the world of the arts – writers, actors, celebrities from the theatre and films. From the start, Saint Laurent had fitted into this atmosphere and had found it more to his liking than the hot-house world of haute couture which had previously been his environment. The influence of this group has, of course, had a profound influence on him as a designer. He has always been intensely receptive to the trends and crazes in the world of the arts and their effect on his designs are strongly visible. Perhaps he is a little too impressionable? Too vulnerable? Certainly, those around him try to shield him from over-exposure to the world at large. To approach Saint Laurent, as his business associates need to do, is to approach Pierre Bergé,

Yves Saint Laurent sitting at his desk, with sketches, and choosing feathers.

232

and this, as those nursing their wounds can confirm, can sometimes be a hazardous thing to attempt.

A smiler with his lips but not his eyes, the 'stocky', cocky, tough and cultured' Bergé emerges as a cross between a father-figure and a body-guard to the extremely gentle Saint Laurent whose talent, say his friends, is equalled only by his shyness. A Parisian journalist who has interviewed him several times for her newspaper had always been addressed by him most politely and formally as 'Madame'. At the ninth meeting, Saint Laurent enquired diffidently if he might call her by her first name. 'Mais, oui, M'sieur', she said, enchanted, feeling as though a milestone had been passed. The next time they met he greeted her with 'Bonjour, Madame...'

But when it comes to deeds rather than words, his shyness disappears and he is a determined man who goes his own way, and it is often into uncharted territory. Although a product of the couture world, from the

Designs by Yves Saint Laurent for the ballet.

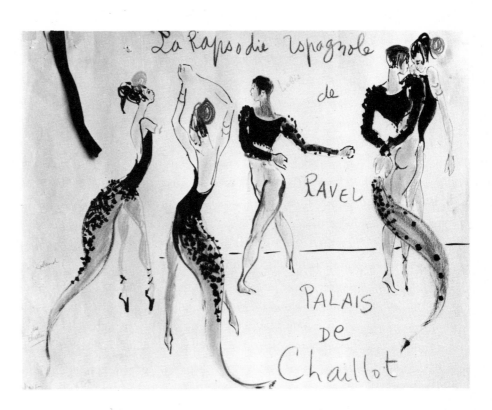

moment he became a designer in his own right he began gradually to turn away from the idea that Paris must remain only a Mecca for the faithful few who were prepared to pay as much for a dress as most would pay for a car. He began to issue statements guaranteed to offend the traditional Paris clientèle. While his house grew in stature and strength and his repu-tation soared to match, his designing philosophy began to be affected more and more by the aspiring masses rather than the privileged few.

The youth revolution, the upsurge of technology, the importance of the mass media, the struggle for class equality, for sexual equality, were all influences that changed Saint Laurent's ideas about fashion and its relative

233

place in the world. For him it has long since ceased to be a thing apart. When the world is in turmoil, when there is a revulsion against opulence, it shows up in the sombreness of a Saint Laurent collection. Perhaps one of the greatest assets he has as a designer today is his ability to relate to the contemporary scene and to absorb outside vibrations which then manifest themselves in his work. This preoccupation shows up in designs which are clearly influenced by the world of theatre, films and the 'pop' age generally. His first attempt at film designing came in 1967, when he created the

These two evening dresses reflect Saint Laurent's enjoyment of 'fancy-dress' clothes, from his spring 1972 showing.

clothes for one of his favourite clients, Catherine Deneuve, to wear in *Belle de Jour*, the Luis Buñuel film about sexual fantasies. 'Didn't like the film', said one critic, 'but I came out humming the clothes.'

Over the years Saint Laurent's contribution to theatre designing has been considerable, due to a large extent to his friendship with dancer Zizi Jeanmaire and her husband, choreographer Roland Petit. When he dresses Zizi in black tights, silver sequins and pink ostrich plumes for one of her 'spectaculars' Saint Laurent can indulge himself in his love for the exotic that he feels has little place in the cold hard light of everyday life, but for which he has a permanent affection.

Even in his most commercially successful collections there is always room for a few fantasies to demonstrate his belief that women may be practical creatures by day, needing clothes to match their mood 'but they must always dream a little at night'. Saint Laurent's preoccupation with fancy dress for after-dark is well known and certainly his 'gag' dresses would be sadly missed from a scene that all too often totally lacks humour. They have all caused giggles in their time – the Carmen Miranda look, the

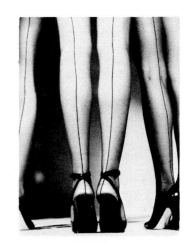

The 1971 'tarty' look epitomised by Yves Saint Laurent's stockings.

Hooker look, the African Primitive look, the famous 'Golden Falsie' look when a model girl appeared in a skirt and a couple of moulded golden metal breasts. It was rumoured that the famous six-foot photographic model Verushka had posed for the originals, but Saint Laurent gallantly refused to confirm or deny. 'They were sculptured by Claud Lalanne', he said, 'who is a friend. Together we decided it would be interesting to make some dresses with them.' They were, he insisted, more like jewellery than mere gimmicks.

'I feel in sympathy with the young people of today', he says. 'I feel they are right. They are really changing the world. Fashion has ceased to be the prerogative of the rich. The office girl, the girl in the factory, can now follow fashion movements almost with the same ease and often with more conviction than the duchess.'

'I merely translate what youth wants', he says, pointing out that although he was responsible for making the trouser-suit into a respectable, universally acceptable fashion, it was the young girls in the streets who invented it in the first place.

'Young people didn't wait for me to tell them to wear pants', he says, with refreshing honesty, and admits that he merely looks at what is happening around him before translating it into commercial designs. His cool attitude on the subject of fashion is remarkable, remembering that even in its newly changing state, haute couture still has some of the trappings of a closed religious order. 'I detest couturiers who confuse their work with art', he said. '*Couturier, haute couture, la mode* – they're all terms that are *passé*.'

It was this distaste, bordering on disgust, that turned the young man who had become one of the most powerful designers in Paris into the world's most influential shopkeeper. In 1966 he opened his first Rive Gauche at 21 Rue de Tournon, Paris, and his path altered course irretrievably from that moment. A 17th-century bakery until Yves moved in, with his chosen décor of blood-red walls, steel and glass fittings, the little shop was the forerunner of an empire that today has an annual turnover of 24 million dollars.

Until Saint Laurent made his momentous move, no couturier had given any serious thought to the revolution on his doorstep. Many of them had their own boutiques on their own premises, but these were merely extensions of the haute couture salons, where their own clients could shop for accessories, perfume and, in some cases, a few items of clothing – skirts, shirts, negligees, and so on, which could be bought without interminable fittings.

When Saint Laurent opened that first Rive Gauche shop he changed all this. He was interested, he said, in dressing the girl in the street. The girl who could not and would not, if she could, pay £500 for a coat. By mass-producing his clothes, he could sell them to the kind of customer who would be unlikely ever to set foot over the scented threshhold of the haute couture world, enclosed inside 30 bis Rue Spontini. Although the Rive

Gauche prices are hardly bargain basement level, the success of the venture has been such that today, nearly six years later, there are 47 Rive Gauche outlets all over the world, the newest, the 48th, opening in Beirut.

Apart from clothes, the Rive Gauche merchandise includes bags, belts, scarves, jewellery, knitwear and shoes. Menswear, too, is an important part of the Rive Gauche merchandise as is only to be expected from one of the first espousers of the 'unisex' fashion.

Currently, there are three Rive Gauche shops for women in Paris, plus one for men only. There are six others in France in Lille, St. Tropez, Marseilles, Toulouse, Bordeaux and Lyon. There are only four run directly by Saint Laurent – the original one in the Rue de Tournon, a second for men only, and two boutiques in New York. All the others are run on a franchise system.

Asked how profitable ready-to-wear is, compared with haute couture, Pierre Bergé points out that the Rue de Tournon boutique alone makes as much as the haute couture salon in the Rue Spontini, and the three Paris boutiques – one Saint Laurent's own and two franchises – make three million dollars a year.

Saint Laurent's long-established pessimism about the future of haute couture is constantly balanced by the expansion of his Rive Gauche activities. From 1972, and for the first time ever, there will be 20 new points of sale in the USA which are not real boutiques; they are simply Saint Laurent 'corners' in the most elegant department store in each town. Starting at Bloomingdales and at Lord and Taylor in New York, and there will soon be others throughout the country. In London, where there are already two Rive Gauche shops, one for men only, another is planned to open where the emphasis will be on accessories, menswear and shoes.

Until now, all the clothes for all Rive Gauche shops, in order to guarantee uniformity of design, cut and quality, have been made in France, 80% by the Mendes factories in Angers and Chalonnes. The other 20%, raincoats or other garments that need special treatment, are made by various specialists.

However, from 1972 the American Rive Gauche boutiques will be supplied with garments made in the USA with fabrics that have also been made there. This, it is explained, is because by the time a garment gets to the USA, with import tax, transport and so forth, the price is higher than is desirable.

All of this adds up to a bustling enterprise that has more interest for Saint Laurent than the restrained opulence of haute couture. 'The people I detest are the Jet Set', he says. 'My real public is the working woman.' It was his thinking along these lines that led Yves Saint Laurent to take his unprecedented step of opting out of what he considers to be the 'Collection Circus''. Let haute couture struggle on, he wants no part of it.

So no press and no ballyhoo attended the hushed presentation of his 25th couture collection which, he insisted, was for the eyes of a few prized clients only. Yes, despite his preoccupation with ready-to-wear, he would

The gangster-look trouser suit, 1967, and the blouson jacket, 1971.

continue to make just a few beautiful things for his beautiful people, and, of course, he would, if they insisted, show them to the handful of glossy magazines whose job it is to photograph the clothes as glamorously as possible. But it had to be without criticism, without comment. The angry ladies of the international press threatened to picket his premises, but Saint Laurent remained unperturbed.

What had caused him to take this drastic step? An over-sensitivity to criticism, perhaps? Certainly he had banned unfriendly reviewers from his shows in the past, but this time he claims he came to his decision due entirely to a shift in priorities. Ready-to-wear, he feels, is now *the* force in the fashion world with haute couture coming a bad second. The press, buyers, everyone, he says, will be welcome when he shows his ready-to-wear collection twice a year, along with the rest of the rag trade.

'What a relief', he sighs. 'I always gave birth in pain. Now the agony will be only twice a year instead of four times.' With his emphasis on ready-to-wear rather than haute couture, the finger of fashion is clearly pointing in the direction Saint Laurent believes it will go. 'Haute couture prices', he says, 'make haute couture clothes possible only for the sort of woman no one wants to look like anymore. Not even their own daughters.

'In my opinion haute couture will not get any new fans . . . no new workers and no new customers. It may last just another five years. Ten perhaps.'

It may, however, not take that long . . .

To the connoisseurs and admirers of Saint Laurent, the ready-to-wear collection he presented for autumn and winter 1972 was a portent of things to come.

Less 'rakish', less fun than previous off-the-peg offerings it showed a distinct sobriety of spirit. It was not a collection for youthful revolutionaries shouting 'down with fashion'. It was serious and sensible and obviously came from a couture stable, albeit a less expensive one. It was a collection for those of his clients who today want their Saint Laurents certainly more quickly, perhaps more cheaply, but always with the unmistakeable couture look about them. It was the first collection where ready-to-wear and couture met in the middle and indicated that soon they may be unable to exist apart.

Meantime, however, the Saint Laurent business grows and prospers. His perfume, '*Y*', brings in a profit of over two million dollars a year, and a range of male-orientated toiletries is on the way. For one whose shyness is legendary, he has gone to extraordinary lengths to promote his new cologne called '*Pour Homme*'. But shyness in one field of endeavour leads to boldness in another. What couturier, what designer in any field of international endeavour, would consent to appear in the nude in order to promote one of his products? Balenciaga? Dior? Chanel? The mere thought is enough to cause paroxysms of mirth or grief depending on one's point of view. Yves Saint Laurent is in no doubt about the suitability of such an unveiling and agreed to strip off, down to his beard and spec-

Catherine Deneuve waits for her fitting at Yves Saint Laurent.

tacles, in order to be photographed, legs chastely crossed, to promote the sale of his cologne.

Confined to the pages of the glossy magazines, the photograph has been defended by Saint Laurent, who says he knows he is not pretty but as he has a good body 'decided to go the whole hog'. A modern view from a modern man.

His Paris apartment, however, is not a monument to his modernity. It is a luxurious 'duplex' in a typically 'thirties Paris building. Decorated with wit and variety, it includes an Art Deco room, and an Oriental room panelled in smoked mirror glass with brocade cushions by the dozen in place of chairs. 'This is my late, late night spot', says Saint Laurent who likes to end his evenings 'with candlelight and a sense of intimacy'. The focal point of this room is a 16th-century Chinese Ming gilt wooden Buddha, which is typical of the exotic and precious objects from both the Far East and Africa with which the designer likes to surround himself.

Saint Laurent's friend, the sculptor Lalanne has provided a flock of mock sheep which stand around the one modern area in the apartment – an all-white living room where the designer spends most of his time and where, he says, he is most comfortable, among 'the simple, barefoot things' he loves. Washable white loose covers, sheer white curtains, books, records, green plants, an earth brown carpet – and a view of more Lalanne sheep out on the terrace and on the lawns of the beautiful rolling garden with which Saint Laurent said he fell in love at first sight when he bought the apartment in 1971. 'It represents the countryside', he said, 'and the vacations there is never time for'.

On the subject nearest his heart – the mass-production of fashion for the fashion-orientated masses – he becomes serious again. 'Yes', he admits, 'I know my ready-to-wear prices are still too high. That is the *real* problem. How to get the Rive Gauche coat that now costs 700 francs down to 300.' One analytical reporter asked what the actual difference was between a haute couture coat that sells at the Rue Spontini for around 4000 francs, and a Rive Gauche one that sells at a Rive Gauche shop for 400. 'There's no difference at all', said Saint Laurent, 'except for the fabric and the price.' In order to sell at the Rive Gauche shops, a garment must be made in a fabric costing not more than 30 francs a metre. A similar garment in the haute couture can easily be made of a fabric costing 600 francs a metre. 'When you can get such similar looking fabrics', he said, pointing at a picture of himself between two garments, identical in looks, but poles apart in price, 'no one wants the expensive one.'

This, he says, is one of the main reasons he lost his love for haute couture. His one aim and only regret so far, he says again and again, is that he has not been able to bring his prices down much more, and reach a larger public of young girls who cannot afford his clothes. But he definitely will. Perhaps it is this preoccupation with the High Streets rather than high places which should ensure him a continuity of clientèle long after haute couture as we know it has finally passed away.

238

11

CONCLUSION

Prêt à Porter v Couture   Hebe Dorsey

PARIS – Haute couture has been compared to a beautiful courtesan. 'Everybody wants to sleep with her, but nobody wants to pay for her upkeep.' A boutade, perhaps. But boutades are often anchored on solid truth. In this particular case, it can be safely said that couture and courtesans have gone out of style, forced out by economic conditions.

But money is not the whole problem. After all, people still buy multimillion dollar yachts, paintings, and diamonds. But too many things have changed in the last couple of decades for couture to remain static. Fashion has changed because women and the times have changed.

If we look back to 1950, French women at that time dressed either at the couturiers or at their little dressmakers around the corner. The couturiers were elegant, arrogant and generally difficult artists, who went around with haloes above their heads. They functioned from their ivory towers out of which they rarely emerged. Couture was a thing for the élite, a sort

240

of pyramid with the world's eyes firmly glued on Paris. Every six months, the couturiers would make their pronouncements as women all over the world held their breaths. Then the axe would fall – A Line – H Line – the Sack – that was it.

No longer. Fashion liberation has taken over from fashion determinism. Each woman is free to choose for herself, to interpret the mode according to her own style, taste and figure, to participate in creation without being reined by absolutes. To keep up with fashion these days, a woman needs wit, a quick mind and as often as not, a trip to the Flea Market. Fashion travels fast, so fast that it can safely be said that in our instant-made world, fads have taken over from fashion. Saint Laurent himself conceded defeat in no uncertain terms: 'In fashion', he said, 'we've reached complete freedom of expression. There is a spirit of total liberation and freedom. Before, women had confidence in us and followed our diktats. Now, there are no more diktats and they will never come back.'

Gradually, the very atmosphere of the fashion house has changed too. Gone is the velvety jewel box, with cherubs sticking out of the ceiling, crystal chandeliers, grand staircase and spindly gilt chairs. The new couturier now functions from a stark, lab-like set-up, all steel and plastic, with avant-garde sculptures, spotlights, and a cut-and-dried, no-nonsense, no frou-frou atmosphere.

The Maison Dior, once called a temple of elegance, installed a runway in its pearl-gray salon just as in 7th Avenue showrooms. Givenchy painted his salon solid white and put spotlights in place of the famous crystal chandeliers. Capt Molyneux, who came to Paris in 1919, and a legendary figure in pre-war designing, said when he made his come-back 'Things have changed around. The days of the rich old duchesses are gone. I could not face the idea of a terribly luxurious house with dozens of vendeuses and second vendeuses and fitters and crystal chandeliers. I think those days have gone.'

Now, let us see how women changed. Of course, quite a number of rich women still dress at the fashion houses and always will. But the number has dropped – and keeps dropping. One of the reasons is all to the credit of women. In the last two decades, they have become more mature, more intelligent and better informed. Once a pampered little thing with nothing much to do except think about dresses and tea parties, a woman today generally works, which means she has a greater respect for money. She takes a close look at what she wants to do with it: send the children to winter sports, buy a new car, or go on a cruise with her husband, as against buying a couple of couture dresses. Chances are, the dresses will come last.

Another factor to be remembered is that travel became the order of the day. During the 'fifties, rich women often became jet-setters, and that, too, cut down the interest in couture. Women found out that they no longer needed such an extensive wardrobe. The same set of dresses would do very well in New York, Paris or Rome, since they would not be seen

An Yves Saint Laurent design for spring 1972.

in the same closed circles. As women became busy, they also became impatient. They could not wait for weeks to have their dresses and many simply refused to put up with hours of fitting. Despite sky-high prices, which were all justified by rising labour and fabric costs, couture kept losing money.

In 1968, all of the problems inherent in the industry were accentuated by the French political events of May and June. An aristocratic house such as Dior reported a drop in business of 67% in the second half of May alone. When the uncompromising master Balenciaga closed his doors in 1968, it was an indication not only of financial difficulties but that there was no room left in fashion for a genius who would not make concessions to the various currents sweeping modern society.

Daniel Hechter design for a girlish pinafore, 1972.

In 1969, high fashion continued on the road to instant fashion. The venerable house of Jeanne Lanvin simply became Lanvin and the transformation was not just into a strikingly handsome modern salon, but into a basically high-priced ready-to-wear outfit which offered some 14,000 items, ranging from gold rope belts to sunglasses. At Guy Laroche, financial problems led to the sale of a large interest in the house to none other than Bernard Cornfeld, in an effort to strike out into the boutique field. After Mr Cornfeld's notorious financial problems, Laroche found another more stable angel – the powerful hair products firm, l'Oréal.

What else precipitated couture's fall from its pedestal? The youth movement, of course, changed the whole picture. Again, twenty years ago, every young girl's dream was to make her debut in a couture dress. There was a whole section devoted to doing just that at Jacques Heim, called Heim Jeunes Filles. The girls could not wait to be old enough to imitate their mothers.

In the last decade, the cult of youth was felt in fashion as well. Young girls, shopping in department stores for economic reasons, came out with unexpected, amusing and younger fashions. Women found out that, in buying couture dresses, they not only spent considerably more money, they also often ended up looking over-precise and ten years older. Now, with the new emphasis on all things young, they wanted to look like their daughters and they turned to their source of supply – the ready-to-wear market. Brigitte Bardot, whose pink and white gingham, off-the-rack wedding dress sold by the thousands, pronounced the death sentence on the whole couture. 'Couture', she said, 'is for the *mémées* (grannies). It is *da-dame* (dowdy, or worse).'

Ready-to-wear had a hard struggle for dominance. Whether she went to the couturiers or her little dressmaker around the corner, a lady expected to be properly fitted and fussed over. The term *prêt-à-porter* (ready-to-wear) came as a happier replacement for another unpopular term, *confection*, which, for many years, had a pejorative connotation for many women because of the inconsistent quality of some of the first machine-made, mass-produced garments. Nobody would be caught dead in a *confection* dress – just too cheap for words. So the French had a few sticky years dispelling that myth.

In 1950, Jacques Heim, then a prominent couturier, went to one of the few ready-to-wear manufacturers and asked him to make a few boutique dresses which Heim sold in his shop. The transaction was a deep, dark secret. Other couturiers simply could not, and would not, cope. One American velveteen manufacturer once offered Balenciaga and Dior a fortune if they would each design an exclusive dress for him. Without preconceived notions, Balenciaga went to work for three utterly disagreeable days, then rang up Dior. ''allo Christian, Ici Cristobal. Have you been able to do something with that horrible fabric?' 'Not yet', said Dior. 'Fine', answered Balenciaga. 'I understand. Alors, we refuse.'

What little there was of ready-to-wear existed initially by copying couture lines. Fashion was simple and clear-cut for everybody. There were the couture collections, then two polite months later, the ready-to-wear, which was a direct, watered-down adaptation of couture ideas. In Paris, the whole industry copied couture, but one particular shop really demonstrated that rich women could be just as happy in a boutique as at Dior's.

Marie-Martine, the brain child of two Peruvian cousins, Marcel and Frederico Salem, did such a good and quick copying job that they soon became the first ready-to-wear shop in Paris to have a clientèle in the same class as the couturiers. Their list of customers included Mrs Henry Ford II, Mrs Herve Alphand, whose husband was then ambassador in Washington, Mrs Helène Rochas and Geneviève Fath, both widows of great couturiers, and film stars such as Brigitte Bardot and Sophia Loren.

The key to Marie-Martine's success was a huge alteration room staffed by two dozen women and several superlative fitters, recruited from haute couture workrooms. But the real secret was the Salems' acute fashion sense and their talent for picking the latest trends. They presented extreme ideas taken from haute couture with a minimum of changes and brought them out as quickly as possible. They made a fortune with couture copies, until the tide changed again.

By 1963, a new species surfaced, the *stylistes*, or ready-to-wear designers, who started producing new clothes, based not on an élite's needs but on what women in the streets wanted. Their fresh and unconventional ideas began to catch the eye of foreign buyers who used to come to Paris just for the couture collections. The *stylistes*, first launched by French fashion magazines, became an instant success with foreign buyers. Some opened their own boutiques; others were hired at handsome fees to design collections for big manufacturers.

In general, the new *stylistes* have much in common. They are a bit like The Beatles, with a great appeal to the masses from whence they came. Usually, they are anti-establishment in dress, life style, and creation. They are free, unafraid – and will do vulgar things with fun and flair. They shun cocktail parties, premières and most of the *tout Paris* affairs that so many couturiers dote on. They go to *La Coupole*, a huge, brassy Left Bank café and a rendezvous for models and photographers. While many have accumulated sizable fortunes, theirs remains a mostly Bohemian life, with artist friends, kooky parties, and a gauchiste, Left Bank, cliquish existence.

Many are sincere designers who refuse to be bound to anyone. Karl Lagerfeld, for instance, works for twenty-five companies, with products ranging from buttons to shoes, so that he can drop anyone he wants on the slightest whim. Professionally, their emphasis is on mobility and flexibility. Elie Jacobson, of Dorothée bis, said: 'I've broken that seasonal rhythm and I buy all the year round.' Their credo can best be summed up by 'A dress is a dress'. They feel hemlines are unimportant and say the midi was a good influence because it broke the cast of fashion and made it possible to have all and any length in one's wardrobe.

One can trace the beginnings of French ready-to-wear to 1962. It was the first time that young fashions and fashion designers came fully into their own. Among the new trends that developed independently from the couture were: bowlers, culotte skirts, T-shirts, knickers, battle jackets, and tiny bags worn over the shoulder with a long strap.

Not only did the young people take no notice of the grown up fashion world, but they also had the adults, if not worried, at least influenced already. In 1963, for the first time, major fashion houses tried to lure away young designers with no high fashion experience. Gerard Pipart, 27, took the jump from the world of ready-to-wear to the sophisticated house of Nina Ricci. Co-worker Emmanuelle Khanh, another bright and influential designer, declined high fashion offers and preferred to stay in touch with a larger group of people.

As early as 1963, foreign buyers were coming to Paris to look at the budding ready-to-wear. In November 1963, I wrote in the New York *Herald Tribune* (European edition): 'The tide has changed in French ready-to-wear. It used to be that American store buyers came to Paris this time of year to buy simple adaptations of French couture clothes, put out by the designers themselves in their ready-to-wear collections. Now, obscure, cheaply priced and formerly neglected houses are stealing the show from Paris big names. The reason is that they have turned over the styling of their collections to a group of new, young, original designers, of whom the most famous is Emmanuelle Khanh.' A typical buyer's view was expressed by Jean Rosenberg, then vice president of Henri Bendel, a specialty shop in New York: 'I'm no longer interested in the big couturiers' ready-to-wear. I find them not fresh and lacking in original ideas . . . whereas such houses as Nale Junior, Vager, d'Alby, and Silcret, which are cheaply priced and where I did not set foot a year ago, are suddenly fascinating because of the young designers they employ.' Of this new young school of designing, which had gained considerable ground in Paris, Miss Rosenberg said: 'These young people are producing a whole new look which is as strikingly original as any couture trend. As a matter of fact, I am sure that the haute couture will be influenced by what these youngsters are doing.'

244

A sketch by Emmanuelle Khanh, showing her droopy, layered collar design, dated March 1964.

The success of young ready-to-wear came from the fact that girls all over the world suddenly got tired of the marvellously elegant Balenciaga look. This was their reaction to it. It happened in England with Mary Quant. It happened in France with Emmanuelle Khanh.

To pinpoint the talents of French ready-to-wear, Emmanuelle Khanh, who started the movement, was, and to a great extent, still is, its superstar. Significantly enough, she was a former model at Balenciaga's. She started making her own clothes because she said she was tired of those box-like dresses. Miss Khanh started a new look, 'The Droop', which was very slim, narrow, and close to the body. Favourite details included scalloped collars, funneled sleeves and curvy hemlines indented at the knee. Miss Khanh was also famous for her patchworks which she called her 'organic approach to fashion'. For instance, on a solid-coloured suit, she would outline bosom and hips with patches of highly colourful prints.

Her collections sometimes drew pessimistic remarks from French store buyers, who were apt to find them un-commercial, but the Americans were more daring. 'I know some of these clothes will not be liked by everybody', Miss Rosenberg said. 'Many people even think they are hideous. But I find them exciting. Of course, these are young fashions which look best on young people.'

Another interesting pioneer was Christiane Bailly, an exotic brunette who had especial success with dresses. She was probably the first to show bare backs. Unfortunately, Miss Bailly has not seemed able to cope quite as well as other more organised designers. She now makes several collections, both in France and Italy, but her name does not shine as bright as it did ten years ago.

Michèle Rosier was a fanatic skier, which led her to design ski clothes that truly changed the look of winter resorts. Instead of those bulky, bear-like outfits, the girls suddenly became slim, elegant, and quite colourful. Miss Rosier abandoned the fashion field a couple of years ago.

Miss Khanh's fashions and, with her, the whole new French look of designing, soon became known in the USA. *Look* magazine came out with a feature on Miss Khanh, and Bendel was the first American store to carry her clothes in their 'Limited Editions' department. Since then, Bendel has become *the* store in New York where all the chic girls go to look for French imports.

By a strange twist of fate, I too became involved in bringing French ready-to-wear to New York. In 1966, Claude Philippe, co-founder with Elsa Maxwell of the 'April in Paris', a $175-a-plate charity ball, asked me to help organise the fashion show. This was the fifteenth anniversary of the ball and the tradition had always been to invite a French couture house to participate. I felt the times had changed and that the audience might get a livelier delivery if confronted with the new, younger French look. Claude Philippe at first shunned the idea. What did I mean – ready-to-wear? It sounded downright cheap compared to glamorous couture, but he trusted me and gave me the green light.

Paco Rabanne, with his 'chain mail' models, of the mid-'sixties.

I chose Emmanuelle Khanh, Christiane Bailly, Michèle Rosier and Paco Rabanne. They planned the whole show to be as widely different from couture as possible. The performance was totally unlike anything done before. They did, however, succeed in keeping the audience more interested in the show than in their soup, which was a feat of sorts, and in a way, made certain that the show was a success. The minute Paco Rabanne's futuristic leather and plastic number came onto the stage, under a giant *trompe l'oeil* reproduction of the Arc du Carrousel, with weird futuristic music for background, the audience sat, mesmerised. One must admit that the clothes were certainly extreme, even for fashion-eyed experts. The designers, what's more, were not trying to soften the blow. If anything, to make for a more striking show, they even bent the other way with objects like a magnifying mirror over the belly button of a white quilted dress (Emmanuelle Khanh), shredded plastic hoods swishing around like waterfalls over the girls' heads (Rabanne), menacing crushed metal yokes on brown silk (Bailly), or silver from top to toe (Rosier). (Michèle Rosier's clothes were the best received, because they were the most wearable.)

Quasar Khan's sculpture-jewellery, worn by Elsa Martinelli.

One woman in the audience exclaimed at Rabanne's aluminium dress: 'That would rust in Miami'; and fashion-conscious Mrs Rose Kennedy said: 'I think it is interesting, but I don't believe my generation will follow.'

The fashion specialists, however, took due note of the event. Diana Vreeland, then editor of American *Vogue*, asked to see the collections at my hotel. She arrived with her whole staff as well as the publisher's wife, Mrs Sam Newhouse. She later sent me a thank-you note for bringing French ready-to-wear to New York, adding that she had been most impressed. Coming from a woman who was rated as fashion high priestess, it was quite an accolade.

246

French *Vogue* followed suit by opening a *Vogue* fashion counter in the Galeries Lafayette department store. Suddenly, buying a dress off the racks did not seem so gauche any more. Chic ladies even enjoyed piling up their diamonds on a $10, run-of-the-mill shift. They felt smart as well as deliciously naughty.

The ready-to-wear scene keeps changing all the time, but it is interesting to consider some recently successful designers, who express the typical philosophy of the school. The leading designer of French ready-to-wear is Karl Lagerfeld, aged 34. His approach to fashion is altogether different from the haute couture heroes and is based, in contrast, on a definite avoidance of the personality cult. German-born Lagerfeld (he came to France when he was 14) is an accomplished all-round technician who believes fashion starts from scratch, with fabrics. His 1925 apartment on the Left Bank is a wonderful mélange of Ruhlman, Le Corbusier and Lalanne chairs, Léger and Marie Laurencin rugs, paintings by Andy Warhol, and sculptures by George Segal.

His point of view: 'In the old days, ready-to-wear only copied couture. Now fashion is created by young stylists and is in the air where it is picked up again by haute couture – whose only function is as a catalyst. Haute couture picked up all the themes that were in the streets: shorts, pop, high heels. Finally, it's life that has changed. Before, one used to dress to go out in the evening. Now, one needs clothes for a variety of occasions – sports, beach, travel. The couturiers have one big defect. They always do the same thing. I do what I feel like doing. I've done the 'forties well before Saint Laurent. But I don't do anything because of others.'

Ready-to-wear by Karl Lagerfeld for Chloé: spring 1972 collection.

Lagerfeld keeps popping up with new ideas because he designs so many different things. In France, he does an expensive retail line of dresses, coats and suits for Chloé, but he is also involved in seven more collections, including shoes, furs, sweaters and fabrics.

Unlike other designers, Lagerfeld does not want to have his own boutique. 'It's demodé', he says. 'The magic label – that's demodé too. It's egocentric and ill-founded, as well as dangerous. If I had a boutique, I would depend on people in the street. If it didn't work, it would be depressing.'

Of his first metallic heels for Louis Jourdan shoes (which were copied so widely all over the globe), Lagerfeld says: 'I can't tell you how it happened. I sat down and designed them.' His 'forties look, he traced to the Andy Warhol girls who visited him in Saint Tropez three summers ago. 'I made them wear shorts and high heels and rouged cheeks. Why? Because I felt like it. Do you know that people literally spit on them in the streets because they looked so weird?

'Price plays a role and yet, it doesn't. When fashion was inaccessible because it got so expensive, women craved for the original – but not any more. That's why I wonder why couture bothered with shorts when they are so much better looking as well as cheaper in junk fabrics . . . I don't want any signature. I don't want to be circumscribed.' For Lagerfeld, fashion does not have to be functional because 'that has no bearing on the situation . . . I don't have any message. People must make clothes they feel like making. If other people don't understand, it means the clothes were bad. It's like art.'

The Lagerfeld-type *styliste* is no more a defender of boutique than he is of haute couture. 'There are too many boutiques and too many of them are just interested in the commercial side of it. But you know, clothes are not vegetables.'

Intense, red-headed Sonia Rykiel, 39, started with tiny, skinny pullovers, quickly dubbed body sweaters, eight years ago. Her remote, out-of-the-way shop attracted a following which included Audrey Hepburn, Virna Lisi and Catherine Deneuve. Recently Miss Rykiel moved over to the Left Bank where she has added a men's sweater line to her range. She has 10 European boutiques, 25 other retail outlets (including Bendel and Bloomingdales). Her sales tower over $9 million, a massive development from that first little sweater. 'When I first showed my pattern to a manufacturer', she likes to say, 'he laughed at me. "Those sweaters are for 12-year olds", he said. Now he sells 100,000 a year, at prices ranging from $30 to $40.'

'Because I couldn't find anything I liked, I started designing for myself. Every dress I saw was wide at the top and narrow at the hips – whereas morphologically, I and most women are narrow at the top and broader around the hips . . . My fashion philosophy is really very classic. It's always the same sweater that I sell, the same shape but with different motifs.'

Skirt lengths, a point of great controversy, have now happily reached a stage where great variety is allowed. Two designs by Vicky Tiel, spring 1972.

248

According to Miss Rykiel: 'Fashion madness will force women to become more intellectual. I think it's impossible for anyone to tell women how to dress. The important thing is to offer slipovers, pullovers, dresses – and let women do their own things.'

She claims to have no strong views about skirt lengths. 'We sell lots of long dresses. If women feel like shortening them, that's no problem. It's the mood that counts. Look at me. I don't have pretty legs. You'll never see me in hot pants. One must show what's beautiful.'

After Rykiel and Lagerfeld, Mia Vicky, a creative boutique, puts forward still another point of view. American Vicky Tiel, whose partner in the boutique is Elizabeth Taylor, said: 'There are two types of boutiques. Those who buy a lot from everybody and those like me, who handle their own designs. Most of them have a small manufacturing outlet. I'm the only one who does everything here, like a cottage industry. I have 15 to 18 women, many of whom were laid off by the couturiers. The one who makes my halter neck dresses with a pleated jersey cummerbund used to be with Grès. She's best with chiffons. She used to make dresses that sold for at least $1,000. Now, I sell that kind of dress for $100.'

Vicky, who says her clothes are based 'on a woman being a real woman', is not enthusiastic about the couturiers. 'High fashion designers made couture a big publicity gimmick. Now, that's over. They're back to being dressmakers as they were before. Look at Chanel She was no movie star. She was a dressmaker. We're all making clothes now, that's all.'

Another enterprise is Dorothée bis, which is a mixture of personal designing and outside buying, but done with a very individual and adventurous eye. It is run by Elie Jacobson, and his wife, Jacqueline, who has been designing increasingly for the shop.

Elie compares his Left Bank operation to an iceberg, with the Left Bank shop and Right Bank sister above the surface, and the merchandising for thirty boutiques, reaching from Europe to New Caledonia, below. 'That way, I can get the lowest possible prices because I order as many as 1,000 pieces in a throw.'

Next to his shop, he has a research centre where girls experiment with new colours, knits and styles on a $100,000 annual budget. If necessary, Jacobson will try out a new dye in his bathtub and then develop it industrially. Apart from his wife's designs, which account for 60% of his stock, he buys the rest outside and takes in up to 2,000 collections a year.

Kenzo, 27, whose full name is Kenzo Takada, represents perhaps the second generation of ready-to-wear *stylistes* and an injection of fresh blood at a time when haute couture seems to need an imaginative transfusion. He came to Paris six years ago and began designing. A year ago, with a French partner and business manager, he opened his own boutique, Jap, in an out-of-the-way alley to which celebrities such as Sylvie Vartan and top-flight mannequins now flock. The atelier is a two-room set-up where five girls sew away frantically in the midst of a mess of bolts of fabric scattered about and bits and pieces soiling the floor. The atmosphere is chic only in the most non-establishment way.

Kenzo, a small Japanese who dresses in jeans and sweaters, said: 'I design for young girls, but in the end I find everybody is buying my clothes.'

Clearly, he has caught the message that fashion moves fast, and shows *four* collections a year, each comprising about 80 models, of which 30 are sweaters. Not only does he show at the two ready-to-wear salons, but he also times his other collections to coincide neatly with the couture presentations.

Alongside those influential but still relatively smaller establishments, ready-to-wear also produced young tycoons, such as Daniel Hechter, 32, who claims to have sales of $25 million in his three ready-to-wear lines. Since he cannot manufacture everything himself, he has licensing contracts all over the world, including the USA and Japan. He estimates that 500,000 women all over the world wear his clothes and defines his style as 'a combination of functional and aesthetic'.

While young talents in ready-to-wear became shrewd businessmen,

Knitwear by Dorothée bis: coordinates, spring 1970, and a mannish pullover, autumn 1971.

Vicky Tiel's evening dress, 1972, shows that the effect of the styling originated by Mme Grès is still as potent as ever.

and learnt how to turn art into profits, the couturiers were not sitting still. With the regression in couture, still sharpened by the May 1968 events, all, with the exception of Chanel and Balenciaga, rallied around the mass market. In 1966, Dior announced the opening of its inexpensive boutique 'Miss Dior' – which, for an institution like the House of Dior was equal to throwing down the doors of the temple. On 27 September 1966, Saint Laurent opened his first Rive Gauche (ready-to-wear) boutique on the rue de Tournon, which he filled with dresses that would not sell in his couture line. 'Some styles are either too young or off-beat to justify couture prices', he admitted. Cardin, who was first in putting his styles in a department store, followed with two boutiques; then Ungaro, Courrèges, Laroche, Patou, Lanvin, and even Givenchy, all opened boutiques – not only in Paris but all over the world.

Moving with their times, the couturiers were only doing what American manufacturers had been doing so successfully for years. The trick was to make the move with such authority and so near to home base. 'We

Daniel Hechter's ready-to-wear collection for spring 1972 included these youthful blazers and co-ordinated skirts.

have to be realistic', said Claude de Givenchy, brother of the designer. 'Couture houses are becoming laboratories of ideas. Our clientèle is not expanding. Even our own clients like to buy a cheap dress here and there.'

Of course, the success of the stylists drew blood from the couturiers, who responded in kind with their own ready-to-wear boutiques. When Yves Saint Laurent launched his Rive Gauche line, he grossed one million dollars on rue de Tournon in the first year. By 1968, couture ready-to-wear had begun to steal the show, and many avant garde stylists, whose merchandise was almost out before it was in, were wiped off the map.

Although there is plenty of room for both the couturiers and the *stylistes* in fashion today, their relationship has been tenuous at best. On occasion, couturiers, like Cardin, have scorned the opposition. 'Those shopkeepers who pretend they're *stylistes* don't know their jobs.' Just recently, some of the ready-to-wear leaders threatened to lodge a protest with the French government against the couture designers because 'we've had enough of couture copying us'.

One of Jean Cacherel's summer 1971 models.

Now the couturiers are wisely concentrating on their boutique collections which they deliver with a distinct, authoritative look, a definite quality and that famous magic label, which, come what may, still goes. They keep their couture operation going, but at a low key. Sometimes, they only make a small collection for the handful of rich women who still insist on that kind of treatment. For a while, they were having a hard time competing with the younger, livelier market, but now, they are scoring again because they are giving that wide margin of women between 30 and 60, which the young designers ignored, an essential fashion value – security.

Let us consider a few basic facts and figures, which show the comparative growth of the two fields, haute couture and ready-to-wear, in recent years. In 1969, the sales figures for the 22 houses, of which 20 can be considered 'major' establishments, totalled 113 million francs ($20,545,454 – nearly £8 million) for the 3,000 models produced each season. But this enormous amount has to be balanced against the cost of the collections, which for the same period can be estimated at between $200,000, to $300,000 (or more than £76,000). Haute couture also employs 465,000 people, which represents a very high proportion of workers, and wages, to products and profits.

Ready-to-wear, by contrast, employed 80,000 workers in France in 1969, while its sales in that year topped 1 billion, 11 million francs. Some idea of the incredible strides made over the past decade can be gathered from the fact that in 1961, only 100 manufacturers participated in the International Prêt-à-Porter Salon at the Porte de Versailles – a twice yearly event which is the shop-window for the world's buyers. In 1971, the numbers had exploded: 780 manufacturers were there, of whom more than 500 were French, alone. The reaction among buyers was equally sharp, for whereas a mere 1000 turned up to that 1961 show, 24,000 buyers crowded in for 1971.

There is no doubt that in purely economic terms, ready-to-wear is the more powerful and expanding industry. But there is no reason why the two elements should not co-exist. Couture has suffered two world wars, the Depression, and a few other disasters over the last century, and there seems little doubt about its ability to adjust to present needs. This is very much the trend.

We should leave the final words to Raymond Barbas, who, since his brother-in-law Jean Patou died 36 years ago, has been running the house alone. Chain-smoking, distinguished, M. Barbas has accumulated an experience of 50 years in haute couture. He recalled how, back in 1930, he decided that 'a name like Patou is a big asset in every field concerning women', and set up Jean Patou perfumes. 'I realised that if I wanted to keep haute couture on a high standard, a house selling only haute couture couldn't survive. It has to be subsidised by other industries, that profit by the prestige of the name.

'Six years ago, I was against ready-to-wear. But I saw that more and more women wanted it. It was not only a question of money. But the emphasis now is on obtaining instant satisfaction. Before, five fittings and two hours to see a collection were considered a pleasure. No longer – not when you can get in nine holes of golf in that same two hours.'

Three years ago, M. Barbas went into ready-to-wear with a vengeance and built a factory in Angers, employing 150 people. Conceding that haute couture has been 'a losing proposition for the last 10 years', he says: 'The future of couture houses depends on their intelligence and their ability to develop sidelines. If Patou and others succeed, they are going to take over the anonymous ready-to-wear fellow in the high quality field.'

Haute couture *ready-to-wear* (below) from Yves Saint Laurent, compared with his haute couture pure and simple (below left), for the same season: spring 1971.

In my opinion, the worst is over. If the couturiers would stop fretting about what is more important, couture or ready-to-wear, if they realise that their whole production needs to be tightened up and edited, if they can come out frankly with their ready-to-wear and be as proud of it as they once were of their couture lines, there is no reason why they should not succeed.

There is no doubt that couture and ready-to-wear are gradually sliding together. As the techniques of mass production improve, good ready-to-wear clothes will offer the elegance and finish that only haute couture could offer in the past. But this does not mean the end of haute couture: it will simply become the most luxurious end of the ready-to-wear market. For, as manufacture and production improve, ready-to-wear will become available to more women, and there will be even *more* demand from those women who like to remain exclusive. Already, women with discrimination look upon their English 'Jean Muir' or their French 'Sonia Rykiel' as models which will have a special place in their wardrobe for years to come. The ready-to-wear field attracts the brightest young talents as designers – I cannot think of any comparable figures entering haute couture now. The more enterprising ready-to-wear people, like Mary Quant, are already internationally launching accessories to accompany their clothes, like the couturiers.

Yet more proof of the 'slide' is that couture ready-to-wear has already cut into boutique sales, for it is sure that women would rather buy Dior, Ungaro, or Patou ready-to-wear than Bonwit Teller's or Harrods'. When those names have disappeared, there will be another generation of designers to take their place. For as long as there are women who are willing to pay luxury prices for luxury clothes, there will be a future for couture.

PICTURE SOURCES

THE CLASSICAL TRADITION: page 3 Richard Dormer, 10 Kublin, 12 Kublin for *Harper's*, 13 Richard Dormer, 14 Balmain, 15, 16 Givenchy, 17, 18 Balmain, 19 André Ostier, 20, 22 Balmain, 23 Francis Marshall; André Ostier, 24, 25, 27, Balmain, 29 Givenchy; Balmain, 30 André Ostier, 32 Sir Cecil Beaton, 33 André Ostier (top four); Centre, 34, 35 Francis Marshall, 36 Centre, 37 Francis Marshall, 38, 39 Givenchy; André Ostier, 41 Chambre, 43, 44 Martin Battersby, 45, 46, 48 Chambre.

THE BIRTH OF COUTURE: 51 Chambre, 53, 54, 55, 56 V and A, 57 Centre, 59 Madge Garland, 60 V and A, 61 Centre (top) V and A, 62 V and A, 64 Centre, 65 V and A, 66, 67 Centre, 68, 69, 70 V and A, 71 Martin Battersby, 73, 74 V and A.

THE 'TWENTIES: 76 V and A (top); Patou, 77 Patou, 78 Centre (top); André Ostier, 79 V and A, 80 V and A (top); Centre, 81 Madge Garland, 82 Centre, 83 Patou, 84 V and A (top); Patou, 85 Centre, 86 Madge Garland (top); Centre, 87 Mrs Kathleen Lumley, 88, Madge Garland, 89, 90 Patou.

THE 'THIRTIES: 92 Centre, 93 *Harper's*, 95 Centre, 97 V and A (top); Centre, 98 *Harper's*, 99 Seeberger Frères, 100 *Harper's*, 101 Centre, 102 Seeberger Frères, 103 Centre, 104 *Harper's*, 105 André Ostier (top); Sir Cecil Beaton, 110 *Harper's* (top and below right); Seeberger Frères (below left), 111 Centre.

'COCO': 114 *Harper's*, 117 V and A, 118 Seeberger Frères, 120 Martin Battersby, 122 British Film Institute, 123 *Harper's*, 124 Patou, 125, 126 *Harper's*, 127 *Harper's* (top); Balmain, 130 André Ostier, 132 British Film Institute, 133 *Sunday Times*, 125 Richard Dormer, 136 IWS.

DIOR: 138 André Ostier, 143 Thelma Swetinburgh and Chevojon Frères, 145, 149, 150 André Ostier, 151 Thelma Sweetingburgh and Chevojon Frères, 152, 153 André Ostier, 154 *Harper's*, 155, 156, 157 André Ostier, 158 Diana Massie, 159 Zika Ascher (top); André Ostier, 160 Dior, 161 Mrs John French, 162, 163 IWS, *Sunday Times* (below left), 164 Christian Dior London.

FATH: 166, 167, 168, 170 André Ostier, 171 Centre, 172 André Ostier, 173 Francis Marshall, 175, 176 André Ostier, 176 Francis Marshall.

A PARIS MODEL: 179–84 Penelope Portrait, 186 Gunnar Larsen, 189, 191 Penelope Portrait.

SPACE AGE FASHION: 193 Gunnar Larsen (above and below); Ann Ryan (centre), 194 Monique Valentin and Giancarlo Botti, 196, 197 *Harper's*, 198, 199 Mrs John French, 203, 206 IWS, 207 Ungaro, 208 Monique Valentin and Giancarlo Botti, 209 IWS, 212 IWS (bottom left and top); Fortnum and Mason, 213 Cardin, 215 Gunnar Larsen (right), 217 IWS, 219 Zika Ascher (top); IWS, 220 Cardin, 221 Richard Dormer.

LEFT BANK COUTURE: 224 IWS, 226 Thelma Sweetinburgh and Halléry, 228 IWS, 229 Mrs John French, 230 IWS, 231 Monique Valentin and Giancarlo Botti, 232, 233 André Ostier, 234 Yves Saint Laurent; Gunnar Larsen (bottom right), 236 IWS, 237 Monique Valentin and Giancarlo Botti, 239 Jeanloup Sieff.

CONCLUSION: 241, 242 Gunnar Larsen, 245 Wallis, London, 246 Monique Valentin and Giancarlo Botti, 247, 248 Gunnar Larsen, 250 Gunnar Larsen (left); Dorothée bis, 251 Dorothée bis; Gunnar Larsen (right), 252 Gunnar Larsen (top); IWS, 253 IWS.

COLOUR PLATES

56–7 V and A, 80 Patou, 81 Centre, 96 *Harper's*, 97 Zika Ascher, 144 Martin Battersby, 145 *Elle*, 160 *Harper's*, 161 IWS, 208, 209 Gunnar Larsen, 224 Peter Kent for Fortnum and Mason, 225 *Sunday Times*.

Chambre	Chambre Syndicale de la Couture Parisienne
Centre	Centre d'Enseignement et de Documentation du Costume
Harper's	British *Harper's Bazaar*
IWS	International Wool Secretariat
V and A	Victoria and Albert Museum, London
Balmain, Givenchy, Patou, etc.	The House picture libraries

INDEX